D0604852

Fundamental Networking in Java

Also by Esmond Pitt:

java.rmi: The Guide to Remote Method Invocation (Addison Wesley 2001) (with Kathleen McNiff)

Esmond Pitt

Fundamental Networking in Java

 Springer

Esmond Pitt BA MIEEE FACS

This book was written and typeset by the author using Adobe FrameMaker, Acrobat, and Distiller on Macintosh and PC platforms, and supplied to the publisher and printer as an Adobe Portable Document Format (PDF) file.

The text of the book is set in 10/11 point FF Scala and Scala Sans, designed by Martin Majoor, and distributed by FSI FontShop International. Program text is set in Lucida Sans Typewriter, proportionally reduced so as to match the x-height of the text, and indented in units of ems.

British Cataloguing in Publication Data
A catalogue record for this book is available from the British Library

Library of Congress Control Number: 2005929863

ISBN-10: 1-84628-030-3
ISBN-13: 978-1846-2803-6

Printed on acid-free paper

Printed in the United States of America   (SB)

9 8 7 6 5 4 3 2 1

Springer Science+Business Media
springeronline.com

For David Buxton Pitt

Contents

Foreword

The Java platform and language were conceived with networking support as a core design principle. A measure of its success in this area is how unusual it is today to find a Java application that does not have at least some measure of network awareness or dependence. Developers today routinely build applications and services that a decade ago would have been regarded as highly complex and requiring rare expertise.

Frameworks, containers, and the high-level Java networking APIs have encapsulated this complexity, insulating developers from dealing with many traditional networking issues. However, many developers still make the funamental error of taking this relative simplicity for granted by assuming that interacting across a network is no more complex than interaction with local objects. Many of the poorly performing or scaling applications I have seen are due to naïve decisions taken without considering the ramifications of distribution across a network and without attention to fundamental elements of network programming or configuration.

I was an early reviewer of this book and I admire its economical and thorough but eminently readable style, lucidly describing complex issues without ever outstaying its welcome. This book combines academic rigour with a practical approach deeply informed by real-world experience and I have no hesitation in recommending it to developers of all experience levels. Experienced engineers building network-centric infrastructure or services should not be without this book. In fact, any Java developer building distributed applications such as J2EE, Jini, and Web Services should read this book—at least to understand the fundamental implications of networking on application design and implementation.

Michael Geisler, Sun Microsystems

Preface

THIS BOOK IS INTENDED TO FILL a long-standing gap in the documentation and literature of the Java™ programming language and platform, by providing fundamental and in-depth coverage of TCP/IP and UDP networking from the point of view of the Java API, and by discussing advanced networking programming techniques.[1] The new I/O and networking features introduced in JDK 1.4 provide further justification for the appearance of this text. Much of the information in this book is either absent from or incorrectly specified in the Java documentation and books by other hands, as I have noted throughout.

In writing this book, I have drawn on nearly twenty years' experience in network programming, over a great variety of protocols, APIs, and languages, on a number of platforms (many now extinct), and on networks ranging in size from an Ethernet a few inches in length, to a corporate WAN between cities thousands of miles apart, to the immense geographic spread of the Internet.

This book covers both 'traditional' Java stream-based I/O and so-called 'new I/O' based on buffers and channels, supporting non-blocking I/O and multiplexing, for both 'plain' and secure sockets, specfically including non-blocking TLS/SSL and GSS-API.

Server and client architectures, using both blocking and non-blocking I/O schemes, are discussed and analysed from the point of view of scalability and with a particular emphasis on performance analysis.

An extensive list of TCP/IP platform dependencies, not documented in Java, is provided, along with a handy reference to the various states a TCP/IP port can assume.

---

1. Sun, Java, and many Java-related terms and acronyms are trademarks of Sun Microsystems Incorporated, Santa Clara, California. These and all other trademarks referred to in this book remain property of their respective owners.

ABOUT THE BOOK

Audience

I have assumed a competent reader familiar with the fundamentals of the Java programming language, specifically the concepts of *class, object, interface, method, parameter, argument, result,* and *exception;* with the basic principles of object-oriented programming: *inheritance* and *polymorphism*; and with the standard Java I/O, utility, and exception classes.

I have also assumed a reader who is able to digest short passages of simple Java code without requiring every line explained, and to turn English prose into Java code without requiring a code sample at every turn. A very basic knowledge of T C P programming with clients and servers is assumed, although I have provided a brief review. Finally, I assume that the reader either knows about the Internet, hosts, and routers, or has the initiative and the resources to look them up.

I have used some of the more standardized vocabulary of design patterns, as first seen in Gamma *et al., Design Patterns: Elements of Reusable Object-Oriented Software*, Addison-Wesley, 1995, specifically the terms *adapter, delegate, facade,* and *factory,* which are now in such common use as not to require explanation. I have also used UML sequence diagrams without definition or comment, as these are fairly self-explanatory.

Scope

The book covers T C P downwards from the Java A P I, through socket options and buffers, to the T C P segment level, including the connection and termination sequences, R S T segments, and—to a small extent—windowing, but excluding sequence numbering, pacing, acknowledgements, and retries.

Similarly, it covers U D P downwards from the Java A P I, through socket options and buffers, to the U D P datagram level, including unicast, broadcast, and multicast, and including material on reliable U D P, erasure codes, and higher-level multicasting protocols.

I have paid particular attention to the neglected and widely misunderstood topic of multi-homed hosts, particularly in relation to U D P unicast, broadcast, and multicast, where multi-homing presents special difficulties.

The T C P, U D P, and T L S / S S L protocols are all covered both in blocking and non-blocking mode, via both traditional Java streams and channel- and buffer-oriented 'NIO' (new I/O). Secure sockets via S S L and T L S are covered in detail, and the J G S S - A P I is discussed as an alternative.

I have devoted an entire chapter to a reduction-to-practice of the J D K 1.5 SSLEngine, with sample code for a complete and correct SSLEngineManager, making this bizarre apparition actually useable for writing non-blocking S S L servers and clients.

The organization of the book is described in section 1.2.

Exclusions

The book excludes I P at the packet level altogether, as well as associated proto-cols such as I C M P, A R P, R A R P, D H C P, *etc.*, although I G M P does appear fleet-ingly in the discussion of multicasting. These topics are definitively covered in Stevens & Wright, *T C P / I P Illustrated*, Volumes I and II, Addison-Wesley, 1994–5, whose completeness and authoritativeness I have not attempted to duplicate.

I have deliberately omitted any mention of the defunct 7-layer O S I Reference Model,[2] into which T C P / I P cannot be shoehorned.

I have excluded all higher-level protocols such as H T T P, H T T P S, and F T P. I have also excluded J 2 E E in its entirety, as well as Java R M I (Remote Method Invocation), with the exception of R M I socket factories which present special, undocumented difficulties. Kathleen McNiff and I have described Java R M I in detail in our book *java.rmi: The Guide to Remote Method Invocation*, Addison-Wesley 2001.[3]

I have resisted without apology the recent tendency to re-present all of compu-ter science as design patterns, even in Chapter 12, 'Server and client models', for which design patterns do exist. The relevant parts of Java and the Java Class Library themselves constitute design patterns which subsume many existing pat-terns for network programming.

This book is about networking, and so is the sample code. Java program code which is not directly relevant to network programming does not appear. Not a line of A W T or Swing code is to be found in these pages, nor are screen shots, console outputs, or examples of streaming audio-visuals or 3D animations. Nor have I presented the 'complete source code' for some arbitrary application of lim-ited relevance.

ACKNOWLEDGEMENTS

I am primarily indebted to the many people who researched and developed the T C P / I P protocol suite over several decades, and whose names appear in the vari-ous I E T F formal standards and RFCs which define the suite: some of these are listed in the bibliography.

Any serious writer on T C P and U D P owes practically everything to the late W. Richard Stevens, with whom I was privileged to exchange a few e-mails. Ste-vens documented the entire protocol suite, both the specification and the B S D 4.4 implementation, in his *T C P / I P Illustrated*, 3 volumes, and described the Ber-keley Sockets API in all its gruesome details in his *Unix Network Programming*, 2 volumes. These are now fundamental references for anyone who really wants to understand I P network programming in any language.

---

2. for which see e.g. Piscitello & Chapin, *Open Systems Networking: O S I & T C P / I P*.

3. Much of the present chapter on firewalls first appeared there, and is used by permission.

This book started life in 1993 as a 25-page paper written in collaboration with my brother and colleague David Pitt: the paper was privately distributed to employees and clients, and has subsequently turned up in all sorts of surprising places.

Several anonymous reviewers contributed significantly to the final form and content of this book. All errors however remain mine.

My thanks go to Sun Microsystems Inc. for producing Java and supplying it free of charge, and to Sun Microsystems Ltd, Melbourne, Australia, for providing Solaris and Linux testing facilities.

Thanks also to my long-standing colleague Neil Belford for advice, assistance, and encouragement. Finally, thanks to Tilly Stoové and all the Pitt family for their understanding and support during the writing of this book.

Esmond Pitt, Melbourne, June 2005.

Part I

Introduction to Networking

CHAPTER 1

Introduction

AFTER READING THIS BOOK you will have a better understanding of the requirements of producing industrial-strength TCP/IP network applications. You will be shown how to achieve these ends with the Java socket classes and the new channel classes introduced in JDK 1.4. You will be presented with an array of choices for the design of servers and clients, and some quantitative techniques for evaluating these choices against your requirements. You will learn how to use secure sockets and how to get the most out of them. You will learn about data streaming with TCP as well as datagram exchange with UDP via unicast, broadcast, and multicast.

1.1 WHY JAVA?

Java and network programming have always been a good match, for a number of reasons.

(a) Java's ready portability to multiple platforms and its price of zero are economically attractive to developers.

(b) Java's lightweight threading model makes it a good platform for writing server applications where threads must be allocated to connections, clients, or tasks.

(c) The Java environment is 'safe', and so applications written in it are relatively immune to total program failure: *(i)* the lack of pointers eliminates all kinds of memory reference problems: invalid pointer values, accidental overwrites, *etc.*; *(ii)* all exceptions and errors can be caught and handled—even out-of-memory conditions can be non-fatal in carefully-written Java code; *(iii)* uncaught runtime conditions are only fatal to the thread which encounters them, not to the entire process. Contrast this with the process-wide effects of conditions like S I G S E G V on Unix platforms, or of general protection faults (GPFs) on W I N 3 2 platforms: neither of these can even occur in Java except via bugs at the J V M or J N I level.

(d) Java's extensive and well-designed class library encapsulates I P networking perhaps an order of magnitude more simply than the Berkeley Sockets A P I (the original C-language programming interface for I P), without losing anything of major significance except the ability to deal with raw sockets or I P protocols other than T C P and U D P.[1] The Java networking classes are also considerably simpler and more complete than any C++ networking class library I am aware of.

The 'new I/O' package and the other new networking features introduced in J D K 1.4 now make Java the ideal implementation language for advanced network programming as well, providing well-encapsulated access to non-blocking and multiplexed I/O.

1.2 ORGANIZATION

Part I of the book introduces network programming and outlines some of the special problems associated with it.

Part II introduces the I P protocol, namely the concepts of I P address, port, and socket, and their manifestations in Java.

Part III covers the T C P protocol. Chapter 3 describes T C P client-server programming using Java streams; Chapter 4 introduces the J D K 1.4 'new I/O' package: channels and buffers; Chapter 5 describes scalable T C P programming using 'new I/O' channels and buffers; Chapter 6 discusses firewalls; Chapter 7 discusses secure sockets—S S L and T L S; and Chapter 8 discusses scalable T L S and S S L.

Part IV covers the U D P protocol. Chapter 9 describes U D P peer-to-peer programming using Java streams and DatagramPackets; Chapter 10 describes scalable U D P programming using 'new i/O' channels and buffers; and Chapter 11 describes U D P broadcasting and multicasting concepts and their programming in Java in detail.

Part V covers practical matters. Chapter 12 discusses a range of scalable architectures for Java T C P servers and clients. Chapter 13 discusses numerous fallacies of network programming.

All sources cited are listed in the Appendices. A comprehensive glossary, a cross-index of Java classes and methods, and a general index are provided.

---

1. This in turn excludes the ability to 'ping' at the I C M P level from Java, or to discover or manipulate I P routes.

1.3 Terminology and conventions

I have followed Bjarne Stroustrup in using the unambiguous terms 'base class' and 'derived class' rather than 'superclass' and 'subclass' which lead to much confusion.

Java code words appear in the body text in the Scala Sans font, so as not to impair the readability of the text. Entire examples appear in the familiar Lucida Sans Typewriter font:

```
Lucida Sans Typewriter
```

Functions from 'C' APIs such as the Berkeley Sockets API appear in the traditional C italics, for example *socket()*. Indented paragraphs in a smaller font, such as the following, contain detailed matter or side remarks which can be skipped on a first reading.

> Indented paragraphs like this can be skipped on a first reading.

Syntax is specified in the usual meta-language, where square brackets [and] contain optional elements, and ellipses ... denote optional repetions. When introducing methods or fields of a class or interface, a short-form pseudo-Java syntax format like this is used:

```java
class ByteBuffer extends Buffer
{
  ByteBuffer compact();
  // ...
}
```

These formats are *not* complete specifications of the class or interface concerned. Only those methods or fields for immediate discussion are listed: frequently the same class appears later showing a different set of methods or fields. Interfaces implemented by the class but not germane to the immediate topic are generally omitted. As we are describing public programming interfaces, the attributes public, abstract, and final are generally omitted: methods can be assumed to be public unless specifically marked protected, and private or package-private methods are always omitted. Comments with an ellipsis (...) denote omissions or continuations.

> For example, the above class is public, as is the compact method; it exports many more methods than shown; and it implements the Comparable interface.

1.4 EXAMPLES

Every complete source code example in this book has been compiled and executed on Windows and Solaris platforms, and in many cases has been used to interoperate between both platforms. Java code is presented in various formats as dictated by space and pagination considerations.

Part II

I P —Internet Protocol

CHAPTER 2

Fundamentals of I P

THIS CHAPTER INTRODUCES the IP protocol and its realization in Java. IP stands for 'Internet protocol', and it is the fundamental protocol of the Internet—the 'glue' which holds the Internet together.

2.I IP

As RFC 791 says, 'the Internet Protocol is designed for use in interconnected systems of packet-switched computer communication networks'. The Internet is nothing more than a very large number of such systems communicating, via the IP protocol, over various kinds of packet-switched network, including Ethernets and token-rings, telephone lines, and satellite links.

IP is the most fundamental element of a family of protocols collectively known as TCP/IP, consisting of sub-protocols such as ARP —address resolution protocol, RARP —reverse address resolution protocol, ICMP —Internet control message protocol, BOOTP —bootstrap protocol, IGMP —Internet group management protocol, UDP —User datagram protocol, and TCP —Transmission control protocol. This book deals with TCP and UDP; the other protocols mentioned are there to support TCP and UDP in various ways and are not normally the concern of network programmers.

IP consists of *(i)* an addressing system for hosts, *(ii)* the IP packet format definition, and *(iii)* the protocol proper—the rules about transmitting and receiving packets.

IP presently exists in two versions of interest: IPV4, which was the first publicly available version of the protocol, and IPV6, which is in limited use at the time of writing, and which offers a massive expansion of the address space as well as a number of improvements and new features.

2.2 Network addressing

2.2.1 *Network interfaces*

An Internet host is connected to the network via one or more network interfaces: these are hardware devices, usually manifested as controller cards (network interface controllers or NICs). Each physical network interface may have one or more IP addresses, discussed in the following subsection. In this way, each Internet host has at least one IP address. This topic is discussed further in section 2.3.

2.2.2 IP *addresses*

An Internet host is identified by a fixed-width 'IP address'. This is a number consists of a 'network' or 'subnet' part, which uniquely identifies the subnetwork within the Internet, and a 'host' part, which uniquely identifies the host within the subnetwork.[1]

In IPV4 an IP address is a 32-bit number, written as a 'dotted-quad' of four 8-bit segments, *e.g.* 192.168.1.24 or 127.0.0.1.

In IPV6 an IP address is a 128-bit number, written as colon-separated quads of 8 bits each, e.g. 0:0:0:0:0:0:0:0:0:0:0:0:0:0:0:1, with the convention that two adjacent colons indicate as many quads of zero as necessary: the address just given can be abbreviated to ::1.

2.2.3 *Domain names*

The numeric IP addressing system is complemented by an alphabetic naming system known as the Domain Name System or DNS, which partions host names into 'domains' and which provides mappings between IP addresses and host-names, a process known as 'resolution'.

2.2.4 *Ports*

Each Internet host supports a large number of IP 'ports', which represent individual services within the host, and are identified by a 16-bit 'port number' in the range 1–65535. Many of these port numbers are preallocated: the 'well-known ports' in the range 1–1023, and the 'registered ports' in the range 1024–49151 (0x0400–0xbfff). Servers at the 'well-known ports' require special permission in some operating systems, *e.g.* super-user privilege in Unix-style systems.

---

1. Readers familiar with NAT—network address translation—will understand that 'uniquely' applies only within the subnet(s) controlled by any single NAT device, but I don't propose to cover NAT in this book.

A specific TCP or UDP service is addressed by the tuple {IP address, port number}. This tuple is also known as a 'socket address'.

2.2.5 Sockets

A communications endpoint in a host is represented by an abstraction called a socket. A socket is associated in its local host with an IP address and a port number. In Java, a socket is represented by an instance of one of the java.net classes Socket, ServerSocket, DatagramSocket, or MulticastSocket.

2.2.6 Network address classes

In Java, an IP address is represented by a java.net.InetAddress. An IP port is represented in Java by an integer in the range 1–65535, most usually 1024 or above. An IP socket address is represented in Java either by an {IP address, port number} tuple or by the JDK 1.4 SocketAddress class which encapsulates the tuple.

The purposes and uses of the various Java network address classes are explained in Table 2.1.

TABLE 2.1 Network address classes

Name	Description
InetAddress	Represents an IP address or a *resolved* hostname: used for remote addresses. The object cannot be constructed if hostname resolution fails.
InetSocketAddress extends SocketAddress	Represents an IP socket address, *i.e.* a pair {IP address, port} or {hostname, port}. In the latter case an attempt is made to resolve the hostname when constructing the object, but the object is still usable 'in some circumstances like connecting through a proxy' if resolution fails. Can be constructed with just a {port}, in which case the 'wildcard' local IP address is used, meaning 'all local interfaces'.
NetworkInterface	Represents a local network interface, made up of an interface name (e.g. 'leo') and a list of IP addresses associated with the interface. Used for identifying local interfaces in multicasting.

From JDK 1.4, the InetAddress class is abstract and has two derived classes: Inet4Address for IPv4 and Inet6Address for IPv6. You really don't need to be aware of the existence of these derived classes. You can't construct them: you obtain instances of them via static methods of InetAddress, and you are generally better off just assuming that they are instances of InetAddress. The only difference between the derived classes from the point of view of the programmer is the Inet6Address.isIpV4CompatibleAddress method, which returns true if 'the address is an IPV4 compatible IPV6 address; or false if address is an IPV4 address'.[2] It is a rare Java program which needs to be concerned with this.

2.2.7 Special IP addresses

In addition to the IP addresses belonging to its network interface(s), an Internet host has two extra IP addresses, which are both usable only within the host, as shown in Table 2.2.

TABLE 2.2 Special IP addresses

Name	IPV4	IPV6	Description
loopback	127.0.0.1	::1	This is used to identify services the local host in situations where the host's external DNS name or IP address are unavailable or uninteresting, *e.g.* in a system which is only intended to communicate within a single host.
wildcard	0.0.0.0	::0	This is used when creating sockets to indicate that they should be bound to 'all local IP addresses' rather than a specific one. This the normal case. In Java it can be indicated by an absent or null InetAddress.

The InetAddress class exports a number of methods which enquire about the attributes of an address. These methods are summarized in Table 2.3.

TABLE 2.3 InetAddress methods

Name	Meaning if 'true'[a]
isAnyLocalAddress	Wildcard address: see Table 2.2.
isLinkLocalAddress	Link-local unicast address. Undefined in IPV4; in IPV6 it is an address beginning with FE:80.
isLoopback	Loopback address: see Table 2.2.
isMCGlobal	Multicast address of global scope.
isMCLinkLocal	Multicast address of link-local scope.

2. JDK 1.4 online documentation.

TABLE 2.3 InetAddress methods

Name	Meaning if 'true'[a]
isMCNodeLocal	Multicast address of node-local scope.
isMCOrgLocal	Multicast address of organization-local scope.
isMCSiteLocal	Multicast address of site-local scope.
isMulticastAddress	Multicast address. In IPV4 this is an address in the range 224.0.0.0 to 239.255.255.255; in IPV6 it is an address beginning with FF.
isSiteLocal	Site-local unicast address. Undefined in IPV4; in IPV6 it is an address beginning with FE:C0.

a. The IPV6 cases refer to the specifications in RFC 2373.

The methods isMCGlobal, isMCLinkLocal, etc which return information about multicast address scopes are discussed in section 11.1.4.

2.3 MULTI-HOMING

A multi-homed host is a host which has more than one IP address. Such hosts are commonly located at gateways between IP subnets, and commonly have more than one physical network interface. It is really only in such hosts that programmers need to be concerned with specific local ip addresses and network interfaces.

Network interfaces were practically invisible in Java prior to JDK 1.4, which introduced the NetworkInterface class. From JDK 1.4, the network interfaces for a host can be obtained with the methods:

```
class NetworkInterface
{
    static Enumeration   getNetworkInterfaces()
                            throws SocketException;
    Enumeration          getInetAddresses();
}
```

where getNetworkInterfaces returns an Enumeration of NetworkInterfaces, and getInetAddresses returns an Enumeration of InetAddresses, representing all or possibly a subset of the IP addresses bound to a single network interface. If there is no security manager, the list is complete; otherwise, any InetAddress to which access is denied by the security manager's checkConnect method is omitted from the list.

The accessible IP addresses supported by a host can therefore be retrieved by the code sequence of Example 2.1.

```
// Enumerate network interfaces (JDK >= 1.4)

Enumeration    interfaces
   = NetworkInterface.getNetworkInterfaces();
while (interfaces.hasMoreElements())
{
   NetworkInterface        intf
      = (NetworkInterface)nwifs.nextElement();

   // Enumerate InetAddresses of this network interface
   Enumerationaddresses = intf.getInetAddresses();
   while (addresses.hasMoreElements())
   {
     InetAddress  address
        = (InetAddress)addresses.nextElement();
     // ...
   }
}
```

EXAMPLE 2.1 Enumerating the local network interfaces

2.4 IPV6

Java has always supported I P V 4, the original version of the I P protocol. I P V 6 is the next version of I P, which is intended to improve a number of aspects of I P V 4 including efficiency; extensibility; the 32-bit I P V 4 address space; quality-of-service support; and transport-level authentication and privacy.

From J D K 1.4, Java also supports I P V 6 where the host platform does so, and it is completely transparent to the programmer. Your existing Java networking program automatically supports both I P V 4 and I P V 6 if executed under J D K 1.4 on a platform supporting I P V 6: you can connect to both I P V 4 and I P V 6 servers, and you can be an I P V 4 and I P V 6 server, accepting connections from both I P V 4 and I P V 6 clients.

2.4.1 *Compatibility*

I P V 6 supports I P V 4 via 'I P V 4-compatible addresses'. These are 128-bit I P V 6 address whose high-order 96 bits are zero. For example, the I P V 4 address 192.168.1.24 can used in I P V 6 as the I P V 4-compatible address ::192.168.1.24.

Java's I P V 6 support can be controlled via system properties. These allow you to disable I P V 6 support, so that only I P V 4 clients and servers are supported. You cannot disable I P V 4 support via these properties, although you can achieve the same effect by specifying only I P V 6 network interfaces as local addresses when creating or binding sockets or server sockets. In future there will be a socket option to obtain I P v 6 -only behaviour on a per-socket basis.[3]

These system properties are described in Table 2.4.

TABLE 2.4 I P V 6 system properties

Name	Values	Description
java.net .preferIPv4Stack	false (default), true	By default, I P V 6 native sockets are used if available, allowing applications to communicate with both I P V 4 and IPv6 hosts.
		If this property is set to true, I P V 4 native sockets are always used. The application will not be able to communicate with I P V 6 hosts.
java.net .preferIPv6Addresses	false (default), true	By default, if I P V 6 is available, I P V 4 -mapped addresses are preferred over I P V 6 addresses, 'for backward compatibility— e.g. applications that depend on an I P V 4 -only service, or ... on the ["dotted-quad"] representation of I P V 4 addresses'.
		If this property is set to true, I P V 6 addresses are preferred over I P V 4 -style addresses, 'allowing applications to be tested and deployed in environments where the application is expected to connect to I P V 6 services'.[a]

a. Both quotations from Java 1.4 I P V 6 User Guide.

2.4.2 *Programming differences in Java*

In any situation where you need to determine dynamically whether you have an I P V 4 or an I P V 6 socket, the following technique can be used:

```
if (socket.getLocalAddress() instanceof Inet6Address)
   ; // you have an IPv6 socket
else
   ; // you have an IPv4 socket
```

3. The Java I P V 6 User Guide is distributed in the J D K *Guide to Features—Networking,* and is available online at http://java.sun.com/j2se/1.5/docs/guide/net/ipv6_guide/index.html.

Apart from the formats of actual I P addresses, the java.net.Inet6SocketAddress class described in section 2.2 and the Socket.setTrafficClass method described in section 3.19 are the only points in the entire java.net package where you need to be concerned with I P V 4 and I P V 6.

Part III

TCP —Transmission Control Protocol

CHAPTER 3

Fundamentals of

TCP

THIS CHAPTER DISCUSSES the fundamental aspects of the TCP/IP protocol and its realization in Java Socket and ServerSocket objects in blocking mode. This chapter assumes an understanding of the basic concepts of TCP/IP and Java sockets, although a brief review is provided.

TCP channel I/O and non-blocking mode are discussed in Chapter 5.

3.1 BASIC TCP SOCKETS

In this section we briefly review the basics of TCP/IP sockets and how they are programmed in Java.

3.1.1 TCP in summary

TCP provides reliable bidirectional streaming connections between pairs of end-points in a client-server architecture. A TCP endpoint is defined as the tuple {IP address, port} and is represented in the TCP programming interface as a TCP socket, as defined in section 2.2.5.

By streaming we mean that data transmitted and received is treated as a continuous stream of bytes, without message boundaries.

There are two kinds of TCP socket: 'active' and 'passive' (more usually known as 'listening'). A TCP server creates a TCP socket; 'binds' it to a port; puts it into the 'listening' state; and loops 'accepting' client connections. The client creates an active TCP socket and 'connects' it to the server port. The server 'accepts' this connection request, receiving in the process a new active socket representing its end of the connection. The server and the client are now connected, and can now reliably send each other any amount of data, in both directions simultaneously if necessary. Data sent over this connection is delivered intact and in the correct sequence, as a data stream rather than as distinct messages.

The TCP connection process is illustrated in Figure 3.1.

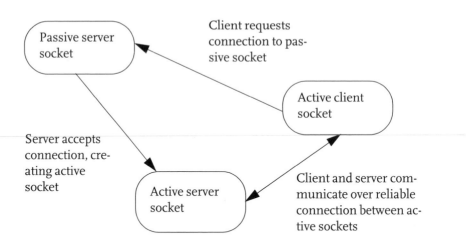

FIGURE 3.1. TCP client and server connection processing

The resulting connection is defined by the tuple {*local port, local address, remote port, remote address*}. Every TCP segment contains this tuple, which ensures that it is delivered to the correct endpoint.

The material in this section is provided to illustrate the succeeding sections on TCP options. More advanced architectures for TCP servers and clients are discussed in Chapter 12.

3.1.2 *Import statements*

The following Java import statements are assumed in the examples throughout this chapter.

```
import java.io.*;
import java.net.*;
import java.util.*;
```

3.1.3 *Simple TCP servers in Java*

In Java, a server's passive socket is represented by a java.net.ServerSocket. A TCP server constructs a java.net.ServerSocket and loops calling ServerSocket.accept. Each iteration of this loop returns a java.net.Socket representing an accepted connection.

The simplest possible TCP server processes each connection before accepting a new one, as sketched in Example 3.1.

```
class TCPServer implements Runnable
{
  private ServerSocket  serverSocket;

  // constructor
  public TCPServer(int port) throws IOException
  {
    this.serverSocket = new ServerSocket(port);
  }
  public void  run()
  {
    for (;;)
    {
      try
      {
        Socket socket = serverSocket.accept();
        new ConnectionHandler(socket).run();
      }
      catch (IOException e) { /*...*/ }
    } // end finally
  } // end run()
} // end class
```

EXAMPLE 3.1 Single-threaded TCP server

The connection-handling class for this and subsequent servers is shown in Example 3.2.

```
public class ConnectionHandler implements Runnable
{
  private Socket   socket;
  public ConnectionHandler(Socket socket)
  {
    this.socket = socket;
  }
  public void  run()
  {
    handleConversation(socket);
  }
  /** @param socket Socket: must be closed on exit */
  public void  handleConversation(Socket socket)
  {
    try
    {
```

```
      InputStream    in = socket.getInputStream();
      // read request from the input:
      // conversation not shown …
      OutputStream   out = socket.getOutputStream();
      // write reply to the output
      out.flush();
    }
    catch (IOException e) { /*…*/ }
    finally
    {
      try { socket.close(); } catch (IOException e) {}
    } // end finally
  } // end run()
} // end class
```

EXAMPLE 3.2 TCP server connection handler

The single-threaded design of Example 3.1 is rarely adequate, because it processes clients sequentially, not concurrently—a new client blocks while the previous client is being serviced. To handle clients concurrently, the server must use a
different thread per accepted connection. The simplest form of such a TCP
server, using the same connection-handling class, is sketched in Example 3.3.

```
class TCPServer implements Runnable
{
  ServerSocket    serverSocket;

  // constructor as before

  public void run()
  {
    for (;;)
    {
      try
      {
        Socket socket = serverSocket.accept();
        new Thread(new ConnectionHandler(socket)).start();
      }
      catch (IOException e) { /*…*/ }
    } // end finally
  } // end run()
} // end class
```

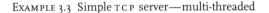

EXAMPLE 3.3 Simple TCP server—multi-threaded

A connection-handling class which simply echoes its input to its output, very useful for testing, is shown in Example 3.4.

```java
class EchoConnectionHandler extends ConnectionHandler
{
  EchoConnectionHandler(Socket socket)
  {
    super(socket);
  }

  /** @param socket Socket: must be closed on exit */
  public void handleConversation(Socket socket)
  {
    try
    {
      InputStream  in = socket.getInputStream();
      OutputStream out = socket.getOutputStream();
      // read requests from the input until EOF
      byte[]        buffer = new byte[8192];
      int count;
      while ((count = in.read(buffer)) >= 0)
      {
        // echo input to the output
        out.write(buffer,0,count);
        out.flush();
      } // loop terminates at EOF
    }
    catch (IOException e)
    {
      /*...*/
    }
    finally
    {
      try { socket.close(); } catch (IOException e) {}
    } // end finally
  } // end run()
} // end class
```

EXAMPLE 3.4 TCP server connection handler—echo

3.1.4 *Simple* TCP *clients in Java*

In Java, the client end of the connection is represented by a java.net.Socket, which is usually constructed already connected to the server port. A typical TCP client is sketched in Example 3.5.

```
class TCPClient implements Runnable
{
  Socket socket;
  public void run()
  {
    try
    {
      socket = new Socket(host,port);
      OutputStream  out = socket.getOutputStream();
      // write request, not shown …
      out.flush();
      InputStream  in = socket.getInputStream();
      // get reply …
    }
    catch (IOException e) { /*…*/ }
    finally
    // ensure socket is closed
    {
      try
      {
        if (socket != null)
          socket.close();
      }
      catch (IOException e) {}
    } // end finally
  } // end run()
} // end class
```

EXAMPLE 3.5 TCP client

3.2 FEATURES AND COSTS OF TCP

As we have seen above, TCP implements a bidirectional reliable data stream over which arbitrarily large quantities of data can be transmitted in either direction, or both directions simultaneously.

3.2.1 *Features*

In TCP, data receptions are automatically acknowledged, sequenced, and resent as necessary. The application cannot receive corrupt or out-of-sequence data, or data 'holes'.

Transmissions are automatically paced to the capacity of the intervening network, and re-transmitted as necessary if not acknowledged.

All available bandwidth is used without saturating the network or being unfair to other network users.

T C P rapidly and reliably adjusts to changing network conditions—varying loads and routes.

T C P implements a 'negotiated connect' to ensure that a server is up and running, and that the server host has accepted a client's connection request, before the client's connection request completes.

T C P implements a 'negotiated close' to ensure that all data in flight is transmitted and received before the connection is finally dropped.

3.2.2 *Costs*

All these features have associated costs. There are computational overheads, protocol overheads, and time overheads:

(a) Connection negotiation consists of a three-way exchange of packets.

The client sends a s y n ; the server responds with a s y n / a c k ; and the client responds with an a c k .[1] If the first s y n produces no response it is retried at increasing intervals a number of times. The first retry interval is implementation-dependent, typically three to six seconds, and is at least doubled on each failure. The total time spent trying to connect is also implementation-dependent, often limited to 75 seconds or three retries. Therefore, in total, a typical time for a completely unsuccessful connection attempt might be 6+12+24 = 42 seconds.

(b) Close negotiation consists of a four-way exchange of packets.

Each side sends a f i n and replies to an incoming f i n with an a c k .

(c) Data sequencing, acknowledgement, and pacing requires quite a bit of computation, which includes maintaining a statistically smoothed estimator of the current round-trip time for a packet travelling between the two endpoints.

(d) The provisions for congestion avoidance require an exponentially increasing retry timer on retransmissions ('exponential backoff') and a slow start to the transmission:[2] this implies that the first few packets are generally exchanged at a sub-optimal speed, although the speed increases exponentially to the maximum feasible.

---

1. For more information on low-level details of the T C P protocol see Stevens, W.R., T C P / I P *Illustrated Volume I.*

2. R F C 1122: Host Requirements.

3.2.3 TCP *and request-reply transactions*

TCP is designed for bulk data transfer. For a simple request-reply transaction which notionally requires sending only one IP packet in each direction, the total efficiency of the system is not very high, because at least nine TCP segments are actually exchanged, as shown in the sequence diagram of Figure 3.2.

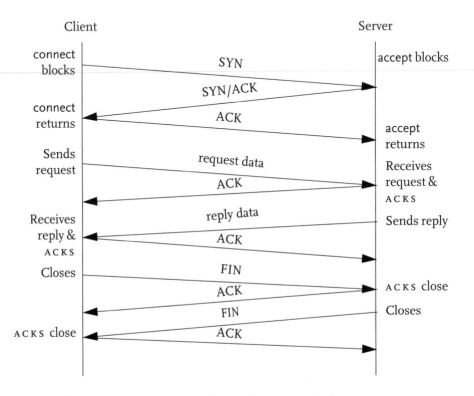

FIGURE 3.2. TCP segment exchanges for a request/reply transaction

The packets in each direction are paced and are subject to the requirement for 'slow start', with the exception of acknowledgement packets.

In mitigation of the above, the request acknowledgement can be coalesced into the reply packet if the reply is issued quickly enough, and the reply acknowledgement can be coalesced into the disconnection (FIN) packet if the disconnection is issued quickly enough.

3.3 Socket initialisation — servers

In this section we look at all the possible steps which can be taken and all possible parameter values which can be set when initializing a ServerSocket.

3.3.1 Constructors

A ServerSocket object is created with one of the following constructors:

```
class ServerSocket
{
  ServerSocket(int port)                  throws IOException;
  ServerSocket(int port, int backlog)throws IOException;
  ServerSocket(int port, int backlog,
            InetAddress localAddress)
                                    throws IOException;
  ServerSocket()                          throws IOException;
}
```

The first three of these constructors create server sockets already 'bound'. A bound socket is ready for use—ready for ServerSocket.accept to be called. The default constructor introduced in J D K 1.4 creates a server socket in the 'unbound' state. An unbound socket must be bound with the ServerSocket.bind method described in section 3.3.7 before ServerSocket.accept can be called.

First we look at the parameters for constructing already-bound sockets; we then look at the method for binding unbound sockets.

3.3.2 Port

T C P servers usually specify the local port on which they listen for connections, by supplying a non-zero port number. If the port number is zero, a system-allocated port number is used, whose value can be obtained by calling the method:

```
class ServerSocket
{
  int getLocalPort();
}
```

If this technique is used, some external means is required of communicating the actual port number to clients; otherwise clients won't know how to connect to the server. Typically this function is assumed by a naming service such as L D A P (Lightweight Directory Access Protocol). In Java R M I this function is assumed by the R M I Registry. In Sun R P C (Remote Procedure Call) it was assumed by the *portmapper* service.

The local port number used by an accepted connection, *i.e.* by a Socket result-ing from ServerSocket.accept, is returned by the method:

```
class Socket
{
  int getLocalPort();
}
```

This is always equal to the port at which the server socket is listening. That's the port the client has connected to, so there is no other possibility.[3]

Using a 'well-known' port, *i.e.* a port in the range 1–1023, in a ServerSocket may require special privileges, *e.g.* super-user permission in Unix -like systems.

3.3.3 Backlog

TCP itself can get ahead of a TCP server application in accepting connections. It maintains a 'backlog queue' of connections to a listening socket which TCP iself has completed but which have not yet been accepted by the application.[4] This queue exists between the underlying TCP implementation and the server proc-ess which created the listening socket. The purpose of pre-completing connec-tions is to speed up the connection phase, but the queue is limited in length so as not to pre-form too many connections to servers which are not accepting them at the same rate for any reason. When an incoming connection request is received and the backlog queue is not full, TCP completes the connection protocol and adds the connection to the backlog queue. At this point, the client application is fully connected, but the server application has not yet received the connection as a result value of ServerSocket.accept. When it does so, the entry is removed from the queue.[5]

The backlog parameter specifies the maximum length of the backlog queue. If backlog is omitted, negative, or zero, a system-chosen default is used, *e.g.* 50. The backlog specified may be adjusted by the underlying platform. If the backlog value is excessive for the platform it is silently adjusted to a legal value. No means exists in Java or the Berkeley Sockets API for discovering the effective backlog value.

> A very small backlog value such as 1 can be used to deliberately 'cripple' a server appli-cation, e.g. for product demonstration purposes, if the underlying implementation doesn't adjust it upwards significantly. The server still works correctly but its ability to handle concurrent clients is severely limited.

---

3. Sun's online Java Tutorial (*Custom Networking/All About Sockets/What is a Socket?*) has been mistaken on this point for many years.

4. This definition has varied over time. It used to include connections still being formed, *i.e.* those whose SYN has been received and sent but whose completing ACK has not yet been received.

3.3.4 *Local address*

The *local address* of a server socket is the I P address at which it listens for incoming connections. By default, T C P servers listen at all local I P addresses. They can be made to listen at a *single* local I P address, by supplying a non-null localAddress to the constructor. If the address is omitted or null, the socket is bound to all local I P addresses.

Specifying a local I P address only makes sense if the local host is multi-homed, i.e. has more than one I P address, usually because it has more than one physical network interface. In such a circumstance, a server may only want to make itself available via one of these I P addresses rather than all of them. See the discussion of multi-homing in section 3.14 for more detail.

The local I P address at which a server socket is listening is returned by the following methods:

```
class ServerSocket
{
    InetAddress     getInetAddress();
    SocketAddress   getLocalSocketAddress();
}
```

---

5. If an incoming connection request is received when the backlog queue is full, T C P should do nothing, rather than rejecting the request, because it is probably a transitory condition: the connecting end should enter a retry sequence after a timeout, during which room may become available in the queue. This has been the B S D behaviour since the beginning, and it is shared by all Berkeley-derived implementations including A I X, Sun Solaris, O S F /1, Linux, *etc.*

However, Microsoft W I N S O C K implementations reject backlog-exceeding connection requests with an R S T. This implementation violates R F C 793 §3.4, *Reset generation*: 'As a general rule, reset (R S T) must be sent whenever a segment arrives which apparently is not intended for the current connection. *A reset must not be sent if it is not clear that this is the case.*' [My italics.] In turn, this behaviour requires Microsoft's *connect()* implementation to loop and retry if it receives an R S T. This is poor design twice over: without the spurious R S T, the condition would have been handled automatically by the T C P stack. It also presents an interoperability problem: if the server uses a Microsoft implementation but the client does not, obviously spurious connection errors will occur at the client.

Stevens, *Unix Network Programming*, Volume I p. 98 states that 'Posix.1g allows either behaviour: ignoring the new S Y N or responding to [it] with an R S T', but I've been unable to track down any actual reference to this. Posix 1003.1 specifies that *connect()* may fail with an *errno* value of E C O N N R E S E T, but it doesn't say anything about the permitted behaviour *at the server* when the listen backlog is exceeded; in fact Posix doesn't explicitly mention S Y N or R S T at all. One of the more amazing things about the T C P / I P protocol and the Berkeley sockets A P I is that no formal document appears to exist which connects them together, i.e. which specifies which protocol elements are issued and received by which A P I s under which circumstances.

These methods return null if the socket is not yet bound, as described in section 3.3.1 and section 3.3.7.[6] This condition was not possible prior to J D K 1.4, because an unbound ServerSocket could not be constructed un til the default constructor was added in 1.4.

3.3.5 *Reusing the local address*

Before binding the server socket as described in section 3.3.7, you may wish to set the 'reuse local address' option. This really means reusing the local port.

The reuse-address methods were added in J D K 1.4:

```
class ServerSocket
{
  void      setReuseAddress(boolean reuse)
                            throws SocketException;
  boolean   getReuseAddress() throws SocketException;
}
```

This setting is useful in development where servers are stopped and started frequently. By default, T C P prevents reuse of a listening port when there is an active or, more typically, a closing connection to the port. Closing connections persist for two minutes or so, for protocol integrity reasons. In development situations, the two-minute wait can be wasteful and annoying. Setting this option stops the waste and abates the annoyance.

The behaviour when changing this setting after a server socket is bound, or constructed with a non-default constructor, is undefined.

Note that these methods set and get a boolean state, not some sort of 'reuse-address' as their names may suggest.

The default value of this setting is not defined by Java, but in MacOS/X, according to http://lists.apple.com/archives/java-dev/2004/Dec/msg00570.html, it is true. For all other systems I have ever encountered it is false.

3.3.6 *Setting the receive buffer size*

Before binding the server socket as described in section 3.3.7, you may wish to set the receive buffer size. You *must* do this before binding if you want to achieve maximum throughput by using a huge receive buffer (larger than 64KB), because a large receive buffer is useful only if the sending end knows about it, and the receiving end can only advertise buffer sizes greater than 64KB if it ena-

---

6. ServerSocket.getInetAddress was incorrectly documented in all J D K versions prior to 1.4.1 as returning 'null if the socket is not yet connected'. ServerSocket objects are never connected.

bles window scaling *during the connection sequence,* which can first occur immediately the socket is bound, i.e. before returning from ServerSocket.accept.

Therefore you must set the receive buffer size for a server socket before binding it. Sockets returned by ServerSocket.accept inherit this setting (as indeed all socket option settings).

> You *can* set a huge receive buffer size on the server socket after it is bound or constructed with a non-default constructor, but it won't have the desired effect on any connections already accepted. You can also set it on an accepted socket, but again this will be ineffective.

> Setting a huge *send* buffer size on the accepted socket *does* have the desired effect, because large send buffers are not advertised to the other end. Hence, no ServerSocket.setSendBufferSize method is required or provided.

The receive-buffer size is set and interrogated by the methods:

```
class ServerSocket
{
  void  setReceiveBufferSize(int size)
                              throws SocketException;
  int  getReceiveBufferSize() throws SocketException;
}
```

See section 3.13 for further discussion of socket buffer sizes.

3.3.7 *Bind operation*

A ServerSocket resulting from the default constructor introduced in J D K 1.4 must be 'bound' before connections can be accepted. This is done by using one of the J D K 1.4 methods:

```
class ServerSocket
{
  void    bind(SocketAddress address)  throws IOException;
  void    bind(SocketAddress address, int backlog)
                              throws IOException;
  boolean  isBound();
}
```

where address is usually an InetSocketAddress constructed with a port number as described in section 3.3.2 and a localAddress as described in section 3.3.4, and backlog is as described in section 3.3.3.

After a ServerSocket has been closed it cannot be reused, so it cannot be bound again.

The ServerSocket.bind method incorporates the functions of both *bind()* and *listen()* in the Berkeley Sockets API.

3.4 SOCKET INITIALISATION — CLIENTS

3.4.1 *Constructors*

Client sockets are created with one of the constructors:

```
class Socket
{
  Socket(InetAddress host, int port)
                                    throws IOException;
  Socket(String host, int port)     throws IOException;
  Socket(InetAddress host, int port,
      InetAddress localAddress, int localPort)
                                    throws IOException;
  Socket(String host, int port,
      InetAddress localAddress, int localPort)
                                    throws IOException;
  Socket() throws IOException;
  Socket(Proxy proxy)               throws IOException;
}
```

The first four of these create sockets which are already connected to the specified target. A connected socket is ready for use—for I/O operations.

The default constructor introduced in JDK 1.4 creates a socket in an 'unconnected' state. An unconnected socket must be connected to a target with the Socket.connect method described in section 3.4.10 before it can be used for any I/O operations.

The last constructor listed above, introduced in JDK 1.5, connects a socket to a local proxy server: after constructing such a socket you must call Socket.connect to connect it via the proxy server to the real target.

3.4.2 *Remote host*

The host parameter specifies the remote host to be connected to. It can be specified as either an InetAddress or a String.

An InetAddress can be constructed by calling either InetAddress.getByName or InetAddress.getByAddress. A host as a String may contain either a host name such as "java.sun.com", which is resolved using a naming service such as DNS, or a textual representation of its IP address. For textual representations, only the validity of the address format is checked. For IPv4 this is the well-known 'dotted-quad' format, *e.g.* "192.168.1.24". For IPv6, literal addresses are accepted in any of the the R F C 2372 literal I P V 6 address formats, *e.g.* "1080::8:800:200C:417A" or "::192.168.1.24".

The remote host can be obtained by the method:

```
class Socket
{
  InetAddress getInetAddress();
}
```

which returns null if the socket is not connected. The remote address can also be obtained via the following J D K 1.4 code sequence:

```
SocketAddress sa = socket.getRemoteSocketAddress();
if (sa != null)
  return ((InetSocketAddress)sa).getAddress();
return null;
```

3.4.3 Remote port

The *port* parameter specifies the remote port to be connected to, i.e. the port at which the server is listening, described in section 3.3.2.

The remote port can be obtained via the method:

```
class Socket
{
  int getPort():
}
```

which returns zero if the socket is not connected. The remote port can also be obtained via the following J D K 1.4 code sequence, which also returns zero if the socket is not connected:

```
SocketAddress sa = socket.getRemoteSocketAddress();
if (sa != null)
  return ((InetSocketAddress)sa).getPort();
return 0;
```

3.4.4 Local address

The localAddress parameter specifies the local I P address via which the connection is formed. If omitted or null it is chosen by the system. There is little point in specifying the local I P address for a T C P client: it is rarely done, and then only in multi-homed hosts. It might be done to force the connection to go via a network interface known to be faster than the others, or to predetermine the I P routing for some reason.

The local I P address to which a socket is bound can be obtained by the method:

```
class Socket
{
  InetAddress  getLocalAddress();
}
```

which returns null if the socket is not connected. Either way, it is of little practical use to T C P clients. The local address can also be obtained via the following J D K 1.4 code sequence:

```
SocketAddress  sa = socket.getLocalSocketAddress();
if (sa != null)
  return ((InetSocketAddress)sa).getAddress();
return null;
```

These methods also work on an accepted socket in a server. The result can be of use to T C P servers in multi-homed hosts. See the discussion of multi-homing in section 3.14.

3.4.5 *Local port*

The localPort parameter specifies the local port to which the socket is bound. If omitted or zero it is allocated by the system. There is little point in specifying the local port for a T C P client, and the operation is rarely employed.

The local port number to which a socket is bound can be obtained by the method:

```
class Socket
{
  int getLocalPort();
}
```

which returns zero if the socket is not connected. The port number can also be obtained via the following J D K 1.4 code sequence, which also returns zero if the socket is not connected:

```
SocketAddress  sa = socket.getLocalSocketAddress();
if (sa != null)
  return ((InetSocketAddress)sa).getPort();
return 0;
```

This information is of little practical use to T C P clients. These methods also work on an accepted socket in a server, although the result is always the same as the port the server is listening to, as discussed in section 3.3.2.

3.4.6 *Proxy object*

The Proxy object specifies the type (Direct, Socks, HTTP) of the proxy and its
SocketAddress.

3.4.7 *Setting the receive buffer size*

Before connecting the socket as described in section 3.4.10, you may wish to set
the receive buffer size. The receive buffer size is set and interrogated by the
methods:

```
class Socket
{
  void  setReceiveBufferSize(int size)
        throws SocketException;
  int   getReceiveBufferSize()
        throws SocketException;
}
```

You must set the receive buffer size before connecting if you want to use a huge
(≥ 64KB) receive buffer and you want maximum throughput. You can still set a
huge receive buffer size after the socket is connected, but it won't have all the
desired effects, as discussed in section 3.3.6. As also discussed in section 3.3.6,
setting a huge *send* buffer size on the connected socket *does* have the desired
effect, because large send buffers don't need to be advertised to the other end.
Hence, you can set the send-buffer size at any time before the socket is closed.

See section 3.13 for further discussion of socket buffer sizes.

3.4.8 *Bind operation*

A Socket resulting from the default constructor introduced in J D K 1.4 can be
'bound' before it is connected. This is equivalent to specifying one or both of
localAddress and localPort in the constructors described in section 3.4.1. This is
done by the J D K 1.4 method:

```
class Socket
{
  void     bind(SocketAddress address) throws IOException;
  boolean  isBound();
}
```

where address is constructed with a localAddress as described in section 3.4.4
and a port number as described in section 3.4.5.

The Socket.bind method is equivalent to *bind()* in the Berkeley Sockets API.

As discussed in section 3.4.4 and section 3.4.5, there is little point in this operation and it is rarely employed.

3.4.9 *Reusing the local address*

Before binding the socket as described in section 3.4.8, you may wish to set the 'reuse local address' option. This really means reusing the local port.

The reuse-address methods were added in J D K 1.4:

```
class Socket
{
    void      setReuseAddress(boolean reuse)
                                throws SocketException;
    boolean  getReuseAddress() throws SocketException;
}
```

Like the bind operation itself for client sockets, this operation is almost entirely pointless and is rarely if ever employed.

> Note that these methods set and get a boolean state, not some sort of 'reuse-address' as their names may suggest.

3.4.10 *Connect operation*

A Socket resulting from the default constructor introduced in J D K 1.4 or the Proxy constructor introduced in J D K 1.5 must be connected before it can be used for I/O. This is done by one of the J D K 1.4 methods:

```
class Socket
{
    void      connect(SocketAddress address)
        throws IOException;
    void      connect(SocketAddress address, int timeout)
        throws IOException;
    boolean  isConnected();
}
```

where address is usually an InetSocketAddress constructed with a remoteHost as described in section 3.4.2 and a remotePort as described in section 3.4.3, and timeout specifies the connect timeout in milliseconds: if zero or omitted, an infinite timeout is used: the operation blocks until the connection is established or an error occurs.

The connect method can wait up to timeout milliseconds before failing, but it can fail much more quickly. (If the host is there and the port isn't listening, the host can generate a T C P R S T immediately.) Normally, the timeout period will only be exhausted if the server's backlog queue (described in section 3.3.3) is full.[7]

The isConnected method tells whether the *local* socket has been connected yet. This method does *not* tell you whether the *other* end has closed the connection.

> Nobody can. Disconnection by the remote end can only be detected in T C P by attempting to read from or write to the socket. If a read incurs an E O F indication (a return value of -1) or an EOFException, the other end has definitely closed the connection. However, if the read succeeds, you still can't be sure: the other end may have been closed, but there may have been sufficient data buffered locally or in transit to satisfy the read request. Similarly, if a write throws a SocketException, the other end has definitely either closed the connection or disappeared entirely. However you may have to write quite a lot of data before getting this exception.

A Socket cannot be closed and then re-connected.

3.5 ACCEPTING CLIENT CONNECTIONS

Once a server socket is constructed and bound, client connections are accepted with the method:

```
class ServerSocket
{
  Socket accept() throws IOException;
}
```

This method returns a connected Socket ready for I/O. The connected socket inherits many of its settings from the server socket, specifically including its local port number, the size of its send and receive buffers, its blocking/non-blocking state, but specifically *excluding* its read timeout.[8]

Another setting that is not inherited is the local address. The value returned by Socket.getLocalAddress or Socket.getLocalSocketAddress is the address which the client used to connect to the server. This is important in multi-homed hosts: see section 3.14.

> To be specific, the local address of the accepted socket is not necessarily the address to which the server is listening, which is usually the wildcard address. Nor is it necessarily the address of the interface via which the connection was received. The 'weak end sys-

---

7. It appears from some reports that on Windows platforms the timeout parameter can only be used to *reduce* the default timeout.

8. This exclusion is a deliberate variation from the Berkeley Sockets A P I, where *all* the listening socket's attributes are inherited except the passive/active attribute.

tem model' described in R F C 1122 allows an I P packet to be received in a multi-homed
host via an interface other than that to which it was addressed. If this happens, the
address the client used is more useful to the server than the local interface via which the
connection was received, and the former is what is returned.

Servers need to be constructed so as to loop calling ServerSocket.accept as frequently as possible, so as not to stall connecting clients. Various architectures for
this are possible. The accepted socket is normally passed to another thread for
processing while the accepting thread loops again, as shown in the simplest usable architecture of Example 3.3. More advanced server architectures are discussed in Chapter 12.

This loop should be coded so that it cannot stall anywhere but in
ServerSocket.accept. This normally rules out doing any I/O between the accept
and the despatch to another thread, however the latter is managed. This has ramifications for the design of the application protocol: it should not be necessary to
read anything from the client before despatching the connection to its own
thread.

3.6 SOCKET I/O

3.6.1 Output

In Java, output to a socket is done via an OutputStream obtained from the socket
via Socket.getOutputStream, as shown below, or via the high-performance socket
channels discussed in Chapter 5. This section discusses output streams.

```
Socket   socket;  // initialization not shown
OutputStream   out = socket.getOutputStream();
byte[] buffer    = new byte[8192];
int offset = 0;
int count = buffer.length;
out.write(buffer,offset,count);
```

All output operations on a T C P socket are synchronous as far as the local send
buffer is concerned, and asynchronous as far as network and the remote application are concerned. All that a T C P output operation does is buffer the data locally
to be sent according to the timing and pacing rules of T C P. If the local socket
sending buffer is full, a write to a socket normally[9] stalls until space in the sending buffer is released as a result of acknowledgements received for previous
transmissions. As soon as enough local buffer space is available, control is
returned to the application. If buffer space is available for part of the data, that

---

9. *i.e.* unless you are using non-blocking I/O, discussed in Chapter 5.

part of it is buffered and the application stalls until further space appears; this continues until all the data has been written to the buffer. Obviously this means that if the amount of data to be written exceeds the send-buffer size, the initial excess will have been written to the network, and only the final non-excess part of the data will be buffered locally, when the write method returns.

This means, in the output example above, that when out.write returns, all count bytes have been written to the local sending buffer.

> This is a point of difference between Java and other socket implementations such as Berkeley Sockets or W I N S O C K. In Java stream I/O, the write method blocks until all data has been processed. Other blocking-mode socket-write implementations return a count which is at least 1 but possibly less than the sending count: the only assurance is that some data has been buffered.

After writing to a socket, there is no assurance that the data has been received by the application (or T C P) at the other end. The only way an application can be assured that a data transmission has arrived at the remote application is by receiving an acknowledgement *explicitly sent* by the remote application. Normally such an acknowledgement is built-in to the inter-application protocol and is delivered over T C P. In other words most T C P conversations follow a request-reply model.

> There isn't even much assurance that data written to a socket has been sent out to the network; nor is there any assurance that *prior* write operations have been received or sent out. You can compute how much data has definitely been sent to the network by subtracting the send-buffer size from the total number of bytes written, but this still doesn't tell you whether it's been received, so it's really pretty pointless.

It is best to attach a BufferedOutputStream to the output stream obtained from the socket. Ideally the BufferedOutputStream's buffer should be as large as the maximum request or response to be transmitted, if this is knowable in advance and not unreasonably large; otherwise it should be at least as large as the socket's send-buffer. This minimises context-switches into the kernel, and it gives T C P more data to write at once, allowing it to form larger segments and use the network more efficiently. It also minimizes switching back and forth between the J V M and J N I. You must flush the buffer at appropriate points, *i.e.* after completing the writing of a request message and before reading the reply, to ensure that any data in the BufferedOutputStream's buffer gets to the socket.

To send Java data types, use a DataOutputStream attached either directly to the socket output stream or, better, to a BufferedOutputStream as shown above:

```
DataOutput dos = new DataOutputStream(out);
// examples …
dos.writeBoolean(…);
dos.writeByte(…);
```

```
dos.writeChar(…);
dos.writeDouble(…);
dos.writeFloat(…);
dos.writeLong(…);
dos.writeShort(…);
dos.writeUTF(…);// write a String
```

To send serializable Java objects, wrap an ObjectOutputStream around your output stream:

```
ObjectOutput oos = new ObjectOutputStream(out);
// example …
Object object;// initialization not shown
oos.writeObject(object);
```

As ObjectOutputStream extends DataOutputStream, you can also use the data type methods shown above. However be aware that ObjectOutputStream adds its own protocol to the data stream, so you can only use it for output if you use an ObjectInputStream at the other end. You can't write data types with an ObjectOutputStream and read them with a DataInputStream.

As suggested above for DataOutputStream, you should use a BufferedOutputStream in conjunction with an ObjectOutputStream.

3.6.2 *Object stream deadlock*

Beware of an deadlock problem with object input and output streams. The following code fragment will always deadlock if present at both client and server:

```
ObjectInputStream in
  = new ObjectInputStream(socket.getInputStream());
ObjectOutputStream out
  = new ObjectOutputStream(socket.getOutputStream());
```

The reason is that the ObjectInputStream at one end is trying to read the object stream header written by the ObjectOutputStream at the other end, as part of their initialization, while the other end is trying to do the same thing in reverse. Always create an ObjectOutputStream *before* an ObjectInputStream for the same socket.[10]

---

10. For completeness I should mention that this strategy still has a slight theoretical risk of deadlock. This can only arise if all the relevant socket buffers are smaller than the object stream header: in practice this is never true as socket buffers are at least 8k and the object stream header is only a few bytes. To overcome this theoretical risk, construct and flush the ObjectOutputStream before the ObjectInputStream at one end and *vice versa* at the other end..

3.6.3 *Input*

Similarly, input from a socket is done via an input stream obtained from the socket via Socket.getInputStream, as shown below, or via the high-performance socket channels discussed in Chapter 5. This section discusses input streams.

```
Socket    socket;// initialization not shown
InputStream  in = socket.getInputStream();
byte[] buffer = new byte[8192];
int offset    = 0;
int size      = buffer.length;
int count     = in.read(buffer,offset,size);
```

An input operation on a TCP socket blocks until at least some data has been received.[11] However, *the length of data received may be less than the length of data requested.* If some data had *already* been received into the socket receive buffer, the input operation will probably return just that data. If the receive buffer is empty, input blocks until some data has been received, probably a single TCP segment, and will probably return just *that* data. In other words, count may be less than size in the input example above.

This behaviour is reflected in the read methods inherited from InputStream of the socket input stream itself, and of the read methods in any interposed I/O stream, *e.g.* BufferedInputStream, DataInputStream, ObjectInputStream, or PushbackInputStream.

However, the DataInput.readFully method loops internally until the data requested is completely read, or until EOF or an exception occurs, whichever occurs first. The readFully method is called internally by the read methods inherited from Reader, the data type methods of DataInputStream (readBoolean, readChar, readDouble, readFloat, readInt, readLong, readShort, and readUTF), and by ObjectInputStream.readObject, so these methods also either read the full amount of data required or throw an exception.

A count of -1 is received if and only if the other end has closed the socket or shutdown its output—see section 3.7.[12]

The InputStream.available method of a socket input stream returns the count of data currently in the socket receive buffer. This may be zero. That's all it does. It does *not* foretell the future: that is, it doesn't engage in some network protocol operation to ask the other end how much is currently in flight (*i.e.* how much it has already sent), or how much was sent in the last write method, or how big the next message is, or how much it is going to send altogether (*e.g.* how much data is in a file being sent). There isn't any such protocol in TCP so it can't.

---

11. Unless you are using non-blocking I/O, discussed in Chapter 5.

12. This is a minor trap for Berkeley Sockets and WINSOCK programmers, who are used to EOF being a return value of zero and -1 indicating an error.

It is best to attach a BufferedInputStream to the input stream obtained from the socket. This minimises context switches into the kernel, and drains the socket receive buffer more quickly, which in turn reduces stalling at the sender. It also minimizes switching back and forth between the JVM and JNI. Ideally the BufferedInputStream's buffer should be at least as large as the socket's receive buffer so that the receive buffer is drained as quickly as possible:

```
Socket        socket; // initialization not shown
InputStream  in = socket.getInputStream();
in = new BufferedInputStream
    (in, socket.getReceiveBufferSize());
```

To receive Java data types, use a DataInputStream attached either directly to the socket input stream or, better, to a BufferedInputStream (as shown above):

```
DataInputdis = new DataInputStream(in);
// examples …
booleanbl = dis.readBoolean();
byte    b  = dis.readByte();
char    c  = dis.readChar();
double d  = dis.readInt();
float  f  = dis.readInt();
long    l  = dis.readInt();
short  s  = dis.readInt();
String str = dis.readUTF();
```

To receive serializable Java objects, wrap an ObjectInputStream around your input stream:

```
ObjectInput  ois = new ObjectInputStream(in);
// example …
Object object = ois.readObject();
```

As ObjectInputStream extends DataInputStream, you can also use the data type methods shown above. However be aware that ObjectInputStream assumes that the ObjectOutputStream protocol is present in the data stream, so you can only use it for input if you use an ObjectOutputStream at the other end. You can't write data types with an DataOutputStream and read them with a ObjectInputStream.

See also the object stream deadlock problem discussed in section 3.6.2.

3.6.4 Channel I/O

Channel I/O was introduced in JDK 1.4, providing high-performance, scalable I/O via files and sockets. It is discussed in detail in Chapter 5.

3.7 Termination

The simplest way to terminate a connection is to close the socket, which terminates the connection in both directions and releases the platform's socket resources.

Before closing a socket, the T C P 'shutdown' facility provides a means of terminating socket for input and output independently, as discussed in section 3.7.1 and section 3.7.2.

Connected sockets must be closed by both parties to the conversation when the conversation is complete, as discussed in section 3.7.4.

When the service provided by the server is being terminated, the listening socket must be closed as discussed in section 3.7.4. This can be done while conversations with accepted sockets are in progress without disturbing those conversations.

3.7.1 *Output shutdown (half-close)*

Output shutdown is also known as a 'half-close'. It is accomplished with the method:

```
class Socket
{
  void      shutdownOutput() throws IOException;
  boolean   isOutputShutdown();
}
```

Output shutdown has the following effects:

(a) Locally, the local socket and its input stream behave normally for reading purposes, but for writing purposes the socket and its output stream behave as though the socket had been closed by this end: subsequent writes to the socket will throw an IOException.

(b) T C P's normal connection-termination sequence (a F I N acknowledged by an A C K) is queued to be sent after any pending data has been sent and acknowledged.

(c) Remotely, the remote socket behaves normally for writing purposes, but for reading purposes the socket behaves as though it had been closed by this end: further reads from the socket return an EOF condition, i.e. a read count of -1 or an EOFException, depending on the method being called.

(d) When the local socket is finally closed, the connection-termination sequence has already been sent, and is not repeated; if the other end has already done a half-close as well, all protocol exchanges on the socket are now complete.

This method is widely used in advanced network programming. It is extremely useful to be able to send an E O F to the other end while still being able to read the socket. Consider the case of a socket-copying program such as a proxy server, which simply copies all its input to its output in both directions; it needs to be able to transmit a received EOF from one side to the other, but it can't assume that the end to which it transmitted the EOF has finished sending data in the other direction, so it can't just transmit the EOF by closing the socket: it needs to shutdown its output.

It is also sometimes useful to initiate the connection-termination sequence early, so that the socket won't persist as long as it would otherwise after the socket is closed. For example, a client which writes a single request to a socket could shut the socket down for output immediately after writing the request, even before the reply is received, thus overlapping part of the connection-termination sequence with the computation and transmission of the reply. Similarly, a server processing single-shot transactions could shutdown its socket for output immediately after writing the reply.

> See the discussion of 'linger' in section 3.16 for an explanation of socket persistence after closing, and for other ways to control the asynchronous nature of a socket close.

Output shutdown can also be used to semi-synchronize client and server before closing, in circumstances where this is important. Before closing, both ends do an output shutdown and then a blocking read expecting an EOF.[13] When the EOF is received, that end is assured that the other end has done the output shutdown. Whichever end did the output shutdown first will block in the read for the other end to do its shutdown. This is shown in the sequence diagram of Figure 3.3.

The E O F indication from the blocking read is received more or less simultaneously at both ends, give or take a round trip, which is close enough for many purposes. By contrast, Socket.close is completely asynchronous by default.[14]

> When using this technique, the end which arrives at the shutdown/read sequence *second* will find an EOF already waiting for it and will therefore exit the sequence *first* by roughly a one-way-trip time; this can increase if network errors occur. It is not a precise science.

> The shutdown methods were introduced in J D K 1.3. Note that the close methods of socket input and output streams do *not* perform read or write shutdowns: they really close the socket, with Socket.close.

---

13. Anything else received constitutes an error in the application protocol: data sent but not received. The technique provides an opportunity to debug this as well.

14. This can be modified with the 'linger on close' option discussed in section 3.16.

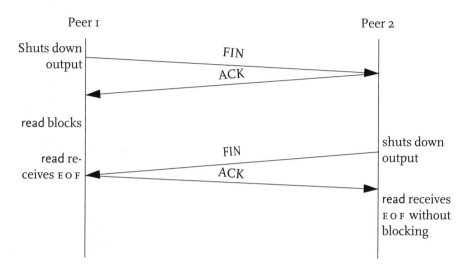

FIGURE 3.3. Synchronizing two peers with output shutdowns and reads

This technique can also be used by one end, if it is known that the other end just closes the socket when it reads an E O F: the first end does a shutdown for output and then reads until it receives an E O F itself; at this point it knows that the other end has both read all the sent data and stopped reading.

The isOutputShutdown method tells whether the *local* socket has been shutdown for output: it doesn't tell anything about what may have happened at the other end of the connection.

3.7.2 *Input shutdown*

Input shutdown is accomplished with the method:

```
class Socket
{
  void     shutdownInput() throws IOException;
  boolean  isInputShutdown();
}
```

When a socket has been shutdown for input, the behaviour at the local end is as follows: the socket and its output stream behave normally for writing purposes, but for reading purposes the socket and its input stream behave as though the socket had been closed by the other end: subsequent reads on the socket return the E O F condition—i.e. a read count of -1 or an EOFException, depending on the method being called.

Notwithstanding the current J D K documentation, the behaviour of the connection as perceived by the remote end varies depending on the platform at the local end:

(a) In B S D-based platforms, any pending or further data sent to the socket are acknowledged (at the T C P protocol level) and silently discarded. This is the behaviour described in the J D K documentation. It causes the connection to behave normally for writing at the remote end. The acknowledgement and discarding occur inside the local protocol stack. There is no outward protocol associated with a read shutdown. The input shutdown is completely undetectable by T C P at the remote end: it is only detectable in terms of the application protocol (the application does not respond to requests).

(b) In W I N S O C K platforms, any pending or further data sent to the socket cause the connection to be reset, eventually causing a SocketException with the text 'Connection reset' at the sender.

(The W I N S O C K specification is self-contradictory on this point: shutdown for input 'has no effect on the lower protocol layers', but 'for T C P sockets, if there is still data queued on the socket waiting to be received, or data arrives subsequently, the connection is reset'. The latter describes Microsoft's implementation. W I N S O C K 1.1 specifies a different behaviour again: 'the T C P window is not changed and incoming data will be accepted (but not acknowledged) until the window is exhausted', *i.e.* the local buffer and the senders' buffer will fill, and the sender will eventually stall. Neither behaviour is noted in the relevant W I N S O C K specification as a departure from the B S D semantics, and the 2.2.2 behaviour was not noted as a change from 1.1. The W I N S O C K behaviour also appears to violate R F C 793 §3.4, *Reset generation*, as cited in footnote (5) above.[15])

(c) In Linux platforms, the read shutdown is completely ignored at the protocol stack level,[16] although not at the socket level, where the socket receive buffer continues to accept data until it fills, at which point further sends to the socket ultimately stall (or return zero in non-blocking mode), because the sender perceives the lack of buffer space at the receiver. This behaviour is broken.[17]

---

15. W I N S O C K 2.2.2 specification, 7 August 1997; W I N S O C K 1.1 specification, 10 January 1993.

16. This does not affect the read behaviour at the local end, which always returns E O F after a read shutdown regardless of the underlying behaviour of the platform, because it is implemented at the Java level.

17. My tests were run on RedHat 7.2 kernel 2.4.13.

The input-shutdown technique is little used, and these major semantic varia-tions don't exactly help. Behaviour (a), if you can rely on it, can be handy: the other end can keep sending data without it piling up at the receiver, like ignoring the club bore without hurting his feelings, and while also allowing the local end to keep sending data. A server which only processes one request per connection and which doesn't need to read the entire request for any reason might do this. Behaviour (b) on the other hand allows the other end to detect the input shut-down, belatedly and fatally, by losing the connection. This seems fairly useless: you might as well just close the connection.

The isInputShutdown method tells whether the *local* socket has been shut-down for input: it doesn't tell anything about the other end of the connection.

3.7.3 *Closing a connected socket*

Once the conversation is complete, the socket must be closed. In Java this is usu-ally done via the method:

```
class Socket
{
  void      close() throws IOException;
  boolean  isClosed();
}
```

In fact there are several ways to accomplish this:

(a)   close the socket itself with socket.close();

(b)   close the output stream obtained from the socket by calling the method socket.getOutputStream().close()

(c)   close the input stream obtained from the socket by calling the method socket.getInputStream().close();

Any one of these is sufficient, and exactly one of them is necessary, to close the socket and release all its resources. You can't use more than one of these tech-niques on any given socket. As a general rule you should close the output stream rather than the input stream or the socket, as the output stream may require flushing.

Closing a socket is an output operation, and, like the output operations dis-cussed above, it normally occurs asynchronously (but see §3.13): there is no assur-ance that the other end has received the close, nor, again, that it has received the data from prior output operations. Both the server and the client must close the socket.

If Socket.close throws an IOException, it may mean that you have already closed the socket, *e.g.* in another of the above ways. It may also mean that T C P has already detected that it was unable to send previously buffered data. As discussed above, your application protocol is the only means available of detecting this problem synchronously.

> An IOException in Socket.close does *not* mean that the other end has already closed its end of the connection. The other end may have closed its end of the connection, but this is a normal condition, and the T C P protocol design explicitly caters for it. Both sides must close, and somebody has to be first. Closing a socket which the other end has already closed does *not* throw an IOException.

The isClosed method tells whether the *local* socket has been closed. It doesn't tell anything about the other end of the connection.

3.7.4 Shutting down a TCP server

The server should normally have some mechanism for being shut down. Often this is done via a protocol command sent over an accepted connection; it can also be done via a command-line or graphical user interface.

Shutting down a T C P server requires closing the listening socket. In Java this means calling the method:

```
class ServerSocket
{
  void     close() throws IOException;
  boolean  isClosed();
}
```

Any concurrent or subsequent executions of ServerSocket.accept on that socket will throw a SocketException. However any existing accepted sockets are not affected by closing the ServerSocket from which they were accepted.

> The message text of the exception thrown by ServerSocket.accept is 'Socket Closed' in J D K 1.4.1, but this may vary with both the version and the implementation of Java.

The isClosed method tells whether the *local* socket has been closed: it doesn't tell anything about the other end of the connection.

3.8 SOCKET FACTORIES

In object-oriented design, *factories* are objects (or classes) which create objects. A *socket factory* is a factory which creates sockets or server sockets, or both. Like all object factories, socket factories centralize the object-creation process; hide its implementation details from the rest of the system; and provide consistent object-creation interfaces for which different implementations can be provided.

Java supports socket factories at three levels: java.net socket factories, RMI socket factories, and s s L socket factories. These are described separately below.

3.8.1 *java.net socket factories*

java.net socket factories are used by Java to provide itself with socket implementations.

The java.net.Socket and java.net.ServerSocket classes are really facades. These facade classes define the Java sockets A P I, but delegate all their actions to socket-implementation objects which do all the real work.

Socket implementations extend the abstract java.net.SocketImpl class:

```
class SocketImpl
{
  // ...
}
```

The factory which supplies them implements the java.net.SocketImplFactory interface:

```
interface SocketImplFactory
{
  SocketImpl createSocketImpl();
}
```

A default socket factory is always installed, which delivers SocketImpl objects whose type is the package-protected class java.net.PlainSocketImpl. This class has native methods which interface with the local C-language sockets A P I, *e.g.* the Berkeley Sockets A P I or W I N S O C K.

The socket factory can be set:

```
class Socket
{
  static void setSocketFactory(SocketImplFactory factory);
}
```

The setSocketFactory method can only be called once in the lifetime of a J V M. It requires a RuntimePermission 'setFactory' to be granted, otherwise a SecurityException is thrown.

Applications have little or no use for this facility.

3.8.2 R M I *socket factories*

R M I socket factories are used by Java R M I to supply sockets and server sockets for R M I when using the J R M P protocol. Conceptually, this feature permits R M I/J R M P to be superimposed over other intermediate protocols such as S S L: instead of the protocol stack J R M P/T C P/I P you could use the stack J R M P/S S L/T C P/I P, or indeed interpose any protocol you like. You could also

replace the TCP/IP component of the stack, if you can supply Sockets and
ServerSockets which implement some other protocol, *e.g.* SNA.

In JDK 1.1 this facility consisted only of the RMISocketFactory class:

```
class RMISocketFactory
{
    abstract Socket              createSocket
                                 (String host, int port)
                                    throws IOException;
    abstract ServerSocket        createServerSocket(int port)
                                    throws IOException;

    static RMISocketFactory      getDefaultFactory();
    static void                  setDefaultFactory
                                 (RMISocketFactory factory);
}
```

Like the java.net socket factory described above, the setDefaultFactory method
can only be called once in the lifetime of a JVM, and requires the runtime permission 'setFactory' to be granted, otherwise a SecurityException is thrown.

However, as the server and client JVMs must set the RMI socket factory independently, and as RMI clients may be applets running under control of a
browser's security manager which prevents changing the socket factory, the feature as defined in JDK 1.1 was not much use.

In JDK 1.2, this feature was significantly extended by introducing the
RMIClientSocketFactory and RMIServerSocketFactory interfaces:

```
interface RMIClientSocketFactory
{
  Socket createSocket(String host, int port)
    throws IOException;
}

interface RMIServerSocketFactory
{
  ServerSocket createServerSocket(int port)
    throws IOException;
}
```

and introducing methods to associate client socket factories with remote objects
at the server end. Client socket factories must be serializable, as they are serialized
to clients when the stub for the remote object is acquired, and are used transparently by the client without its knowledge and without requiring any special runtime permissions. This design ensures that each remote object is always commu-
nicated with via sockets created by the correct socket factory, and permits use of
multiple socket factories, *e.g.* in the limit, one socket factory per remote object.

R M I socket factories can be used to supply sockets which log socket connections and disconnections, or which enforce additional security, or which interpose additional protocols as described above. The most common use of this facility is to interpose the s s l protocol as described above.

An R M I server or client socket factory *must* override the Object.equals method. The simplest such method for R M I socket factories is of the form:

```
public boolean equals(Object that)
{
  return that != null
  && that.getClass().equals(this.getClass());
}
```

3.8.3 s s l socket factories

The javax.net factory classes SocketFactory and ServerSocketFactory are discussed in Chapter 7.

3.9 PERMISSIONS IN T C P

If a Java security manager is installed, a java.net.SocketPermission is required for each socket operation.

Permissions are managed in a security policy file—a text file which by default is named 'java.policy', and is managed by the *policytool* program provided with the J D K and J R E. The Java 2 security framework is described in the J D K 'Guide to Features/Security' documentation, and I won't discuss it further here.

A SocketPermission entry in the policy file has two fields: the 'action', *i.e.* the network operation being attempted, and the 'target', *i.e.* the local or remote T C P endpoint to which the action refers, in the format:

```
host[:port]
```

where host is an exact or wildcard hostname or an i p address, and port is a port number or range. The action field and the meaning of the corresponding target field for each T C P network operation are as shown in Table 3.1.

3.10 EXCEPTIONS IN T C P

The significant Java exceptions that can arise during blocking-mode T C P socket operations, and their sources and causes, are shown in Table 3.2.

In this table, 'C' or 'U' indicates whether the exception is checked (C) or unchecked (U).

TABLE 3.1 SocketPermissions in T C P

Action	Description
accept	Required by the ServerSocket.accept method. The target *host* specifies the remote T C P endpoint being accepted.
connect	Required by the non-default constructors for Socket and by its connect method, and when obtaining InetAddress objects. The target *host* specifies the remote T C P endpoint being connected to.
listen	Required by the non-default constructors of ServerSocket, and by its bind method. The target *host* specify the *local* T C P socket, i.e. the local endpoint to which the ServerSocket is being bound. The only reasonable value for *host* is 'localhost'. The default policy file grants 'listen' permission to the target "localhost:1024-".
resolve	This is implied by any of the 'accept', 'connect', or 'listen' permissions, so there is little need to specify it explicitly.

TABLE 3.2 Exceptions in T C P

Exception	Thrown by & cause	
java.net. BindException	Thrown by constructors of Socket and ServerSocket, and their bind methods, if the requested local address or port cannot be assigned.	C
java.net. ConnectException	Thrown by constructors of Socket and its connect method on an error connecting to a remote address and port, usually because the connection is refused (nothing is listening at the specified {*address, port*}).	C
java.rmi. ConnectException	This is thrown when an R M I call fails to connect to its target. Not to be confused with java.net.ConnectException above, although it can cause this exception.	C
java.lang. IllegalArgumentException	Thrown by several methods of InetSocketAddress, Socket, and ServerSocket if an argument is null or out of range.	U
java.nio.channels. IllegalBlockingModeException	Thrown by Socket.connect, operations on Socket input and output streams, and ServerSocket.accept if the socket has an associated channel which is in non-blocking mode; from J D K 1.4.	C
java.io. InterruptedIOException	Thrown by operations on Socket input streams if a timeout has occurred; prior to J D K 1.4.	C

TABLE 3.2 Exceptions in TCP (continued)

Exception	Thrown by & cause	
java.io. IOException	Base I/O exception class. Derived exception classes relevant to TCP include BindException, ConnectException, EOFException, InterruptedIOException, NoRouteToHostException, ProtocolException, SocketException, and UnknownHostException.	C
java.net. NoRouteToHostException	Thrown by non-default constructors of Socket and its connect method, indicating that an error has occurred while connecting to a remote address and port, most usually if the remote host cannot be reached because of an intervening firewall, or if an intermediate router is down.	C
java.net. ProtocolException	Thrown by constructors and methods of Socket and ServerSocket, and operations on Socket input and output streams, indicating that an error occourred in the underlying protocol, such as a TCP error.	C
java.lang. SecurityException	Thrown by several methods of Socket and ServerSocket if a required SocketPermission is not granted as shown in Table 3.1.	U
java.net. SocketException	Thrown by many Socket methods and operations on Socket input streams indicating that an underlying TCP error has occurred, or the socket was closed by another thread other than via InterruptibleChannel.close. If the message contains the text 'Connection reset', the other end of the connection has issued a reset (RST): the Socket is useless from this point on, and it should be closed and discarded. Many exception classes are derived from this one, including BindException and ConnectException.	C

TABLE 3.2 Exceptions in TCP (continued)

Exception	Thrown by & cause	
java.net. SocketTimeoutException	Thrown by operations on Socket input streams indicating that a timeout has occurred; from JDK 1.4; extends InterruptedIOException for backwards compatibility with pre-JDK 1.4 programs.	C
java.net. UnknownHostException	Thrown by factory methods of InetAddress, and when using String hostnames which are implicitly resolved by those methods, indicating that the IP address of the named host cannot be determined from the naming service.	C

3.11 SOCKET OPTIONS

Socket options control advanced features of TCP. In Java, socket options are controlled via methods in java.net.Socket or java.net.ServerSocket.

Socket options appear below more or less in order of their relative importance.

3.12 SOCKET TIMEOUTS

It cannot be assumed that an application can wait forever for a remote service, nor that the service will always be rendered in a timely manner, nor that the service or the intervening network infrastructure will only fail in detectable ways. In fact, a TCP connection can fail in ways which cannot be detected by the server or the client. Any network program which reads with infinite timeout is sooner or later going to experience an infinite delay.

The 'keep-alive' feature described in section 3.17 provides a partial solution to this problem, if the platform supports it. Java programs can run on any platform and are not entitled to assume this. Even if the platform is known and does support keep-alive, the default delay is two hours before the dead connection is detected, and this can only be altered system-wide by an administrator, if at all. Usually this two-hour detection period is only palatable as a final fall-back.

For all these reasons, prudent network programming always uses a finite read timeout. This is managed with the methods:

```
class Socket
{
  void  setSoTimeout(int timeout)  throws SocketException:
  int   getSoTimeout()             throws SocketException;
}
```

where timeout is specified in milliseconds, and must be either positive, indicating a finite timeout, or zero, indicating an infinite timeout. By default, the read timeout is infinite.

If the timeout has been set to a positive (finite) value prior to a blocking read operation on the socket, the read will block for up to the timeout period if data is not available, and will then throw an InterruptedIOException. If the timeout is infinite, the read will block forever, or until an error occurs.[18]

For clients which have just transmitted a request and are waiting for a reply, the duration of the timeout should take account of the expected transmission times in both directions plus the latency of the request—the execution delay at the other end while the reply is being retrieved or computed. How long you should wait in relation to this total expected time is a policy question: as a starting point, the time-out might be set to twice the sum of the expected time. In general, timeouts should be set slightly too long rather than slightly too short.[19]

> Good networking programming practice requires that retries of transactions which have timed out should occur at intervals which are initially random within a reasonable interval, to avoid the 'thundering herd' problem, and which increase exponentially, to reduce the network load which may have been part of the initial problem.

For servers which are waiting for a client request, the timeout value is strictly a matter of policy: how long is the server prepared to wait for a request before abandoning the connection? The period chosen should be long enough to support heavy network loads and a reasonable amount of client processing, but not so long as to tie up precious server resources for absurd lengths of time. (The resources allocated to a server connection consist of the connected socket itself and, usually, a thread and some sort of client context.)

A timeout can also be set on a ServerSocket:

```
class ServerSocket
{
  void  setSoTimeout(int timeout)   throws SocketException;
  int   getSoTimeout()              throws SocketException;
}
```

where this timeout is also specified in milliseconds as before. This setting determines how long an application will block in ServerSocket.accept before getting an InterruptedIOException. This setting is *not* inherited by accepted connections, *i.e.* by sockets returned from ServerSocket.accept.[20] A ServerSocket timeout can

---

18. *e.g.* a keep-alive failure: see section 3.17.

19. See also Tanenbaum, *Computer Networks*, 3rd edition, Prentice Hall, 1996, §6.6.7.

20. This is a deliberate variation from the behaviour of the Berkeley Sockets API and W I N S O C K.

be used to poll a number of ServerSockets in a single thread, although the Selector class to be described in section 5.3.1 provides a better way to do this.

Setting a socket timeout has no effect on blocking socket operations already in progress.

3.13 SOCKET BUFFERS

TCP allocates a send buffer and a receive buffer to each socket. These buffers exist in the address space of the kernel or the TCP protocol stack (if different), not in the JVM or process address space. The default size of these buffers is determined by the underlying platform's implementation of TCP, not by Java. In the original TCP implementation, the send and receive buffer sizes were both 2KB by default. In some implementations they now often default to sizes more like 28KB, 32KB, or even 64KB, but you must examine your target system's characteristics for yourself.

3.13.1 Methods

The size of a socket's send and receive buffers is managed by these methods:

```
class Socket
{
  void  setReceiveBufferSize(int size)
                                     throws SocketException;
  int   getReceiveBufferSize()       throws SocketException;

  void  setSendBufferSize(int size)  throws SocketException;
  int   getSendBufferSize()          throws SocketException;
}
class ServerSocket
{
  void  setReceiveBufferSize(int size)
                                     throws SocketException;
  int   getReceiveBufferSize()       throws SocketException;
}
```

where size is specified in bytes. Values supplied to these methods only act as a hint to the underlying platform, and may be adjusted in either direction to fit into the allowable range, or rounded up or down to appropriate boundaries.

You can set the send buffer size of a socket at any time before closing it. For receive buffers, see the discussions in section 3.3.6 (servers) and section 3.4.7 (clients).

The values returned by the 'get' methods may not match the values you sent. They also may not match the actual values being used by the underlying platform.

3.13.2 *How big should a socket buffer be?*

Is 8KB, or 32KB, or 64KB, enough at today's networking speeds?

The larger the buffer, the more efficiently TCP can operate. Large buffer sizes utilize the capacity of the network more effectively: they reduce the number of physical writes to the network; amortize the 40-byte space costs of the TCP and IP packet headers over a larger packet size; allow more data to be in flight, 'filling the pipe'; and allow more data to be transmitted before stalling.

The folllowing principles should be followed.

(a) On an Ethernet, 4KB is definitely not enough: raising the buffers from 4KB to 16KB has been seen to cause a 40% improvement in throughput.[21]

(b) Socket buffer sizes should always be at least three times the size of the maximum segment size (MSS) for the connection, which is usually determined by the maximum transmission unit (MTU) of the network interface less 40 to account for the size of the TCP and IP headers. With Ethernet, whose MSS is less than 1500, this presents no issue with buffer sizes of 8KB and above, but other physical layers behave differently.[22]

(c) The send buffer size should be at least as big as the receive buffer at the other end.[23]

(d) For applications which *send* a lot of data at a time, increasing the size of the send buffer to 48KB or 64KB may be the single most effective performance improvement you can make to your application. For maximum performance in such applications, the send buffer should be at least as big as the bandwidth-delay product of the intervening network (see below).

(e) For maximum performance in applications which *receive* a lot of data at a time (*e.g.* the other end of an application which sends a lot of data), the receive buffer at the receiver needs to be large as possible within the constraints above, because TCP limits the sender according to buffer space

---

21. Stevens Vol. I §20.4; Papadopolous, C., and Parulkar, G.M., 'Experimental Evaluation of SunOS PC and TCP/IP Protocol Implementation', *IEEE/ACM Transactions on Networking*, Vol. I, no. 2, 1993.

22. Comer, D.E., and Lin, J.C., TCP *Buffering and Performance over an* ATM *Network*, Purdue Technical Report CSD-TR 94-026, Purdue University, West Lafayette, Indiana, ftp://gwen.cs.purdue.edu/pub/lin/TCP.atm.ps.Z.

23. See Moldeklev & Gunningberg, *How a Large* ATM MTU *Causes Deadlocks in* TCP *Data Transfers*, IEEE/ACM Transactions on Networking, Vol. 3, No. 4, August 1995.

available at the receiver—a sender may not send data unless it knows there is room at the receiver. If the receiving application is slow in reading data from the buffer, its receive buffer size needs to be even larger, so as not to stall the sender.

(f) For applications which send *and* receive a lot of data, increase both buffer sizes.

(g) Defaults in most implementations are nowadays at least 8KB (w i n s o c k), 28KB (OS/2), 52KB (Solaris). Early t c p implementations allowed a maximum buffer size of around 52,000 bytes. Some current implementations support maximum sizes of 256,000,000 bytes or more.

(h) To use a receive buffer over 64K in a server, you must set the receive buffer of the *listening* socket, which will be inherited by the accepted socket, as described in section 3.3.6.

(i) Whatever the buffer size is, you should help t c p by writing in chunks of at least that size, *e.g.* by using a BufferedOutputStream or a ByteBuffer of at least that size.

The maximum throughput of a single t c p connection is limited at any one time to $W/(RTT)$, where W is the current receive 'window', whose maximum possible size is the receive buffer size, and r t t is the round-trip time over the connection for a packet and its acknowledgement. As you can't reduce r t t (it does tend to be outside your control!), you have to increase the window size, and therefore the receive buffer size, to compensate.

The optimum size of a send buffer depends on two factors: the bandwidth or data rate of the connection, and the r t t or delay time—the time for a packet to make a round-trip between endpoints. The buffer needs to be large enough to hold all data which has not yet been acknowledged, *i.e.* all data currently in flight, in case any of it needs to be re-transmitted. Waiting for an acknowledgement implies a round-trip. The buffer therefore needs to be as large as the nominal 'capacity' of the intervening network, given by:

$$capacity \text{ (bits)} = bandwidth \text{ (bits/sec)} \times delay \text{ (sec)} \qquad (\text{EQ 3.1})$$

This quantity is referred to as the 'bandwidth-delay product'. The bandwidth used in this calculation is the effective bandwidth over the entire connection, not just the bandwidth via which either endpoint is connected to the Internet, which may be much higher.

The bandwidth-delay product can be understood by thinking of the network as a cylindrical pipe as shown in Figure 3.4. The bandwidth of the network corresponds to the cross-sectional area of the pipe, and the delay of the network corresponds to the length of the pipe. A network can have high delay if it extends across a slow gateway or router, or a large number of either: some physical-layer technologies such as xD S L have inherently long delay. The bandwidth-delay

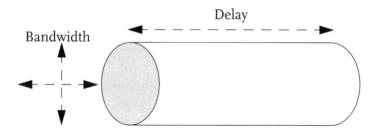

FIGURE 3.4. Bandwidth-delay product

product corresponds to the total volume of the pipe. As this volume consists of data which has been sent but not acknowledged, the sender needs to buffer it all locally so as to be able to re-send any or all of it if necessary. Using a buffer smaller than the bandwidth-delay product means not 'filling' the network, *i.e.* not using it to its maximum capacity. If you want maximum throughput, *e.g.* for a large file or a streaming video transfer, use a large enough buffer. If you don't want to be so selfish, use a smaller buffer. Controlling the size of the socket buffers in relation to the bandwidth-delay product provides a rough but effective means, indeed the only means, of 'choking' the output of a socket.

3.14 MULTI-HOMING

As we saw in section 2.2.5, a multi-homed host is a host which has more than one IP address. Multi-homing has non-trivial consequences for TCP servers, and trivial consequences for clients.

3.14.1 *Multi-homing—servers*

A TCP server normally listens at all local IP addresses, and such a server need not usually be concerned with the fact that it may be running in a multi-homed host. The following are situations in which a TCP server may need to be aware of multi-homing.

If the server is to service only one subnet, it should bind itself to the appropriate local IP address. This in turn may require use of the Server-Socket.setReuseAddress method discussed in section 3.3.5.

If the server supplies its own IP address to clients, it must return an IP address which the client can access. Typically the client doesn't have access to all the IP addresses of the server, but can only access it on one of them. If the client has already connected to the server, the simplest way to assure that a returned IP address is usable is to force it to the address the client used to connect, given by Socket.getLocalAddress for the accepted socket, as described in section 3.4.4.

In directory services when registering service descriptors, the server must advertise itself via an IP address which all clients can access. The best way to assure that advertised service addresses are most usable is to advertise the 'most public' IP address or hostname in each case.

3.14.2 *Multi-homing—clients*

A TCP client normally pays no attention to its local addresses, as we have seen in section 3.4.8. If for some reason it really cares about which network interface it uses to make connections, it should specify the local IP address when doing so, as discussed in section 3.4.4.

3.15 NAGLE'S ALGORITHM

Nagle's algorithm was a minor modification to TCP adopted in 1984 (RFC 896). It deters TCP from sending a sequence of small segments in circumstances when the data is being injected slowly by the application. By default, Nagle's algorithm is enabled, but it can be disabled by setting an option known as the 'no delay' option:

```
class Socket
{
  void      setTcpNoDelay(boolean noDelay)
                             throws SocketException;
  boolean  getTcpNoDelay() throws SocketException;
}
```

This can be confusing: remember that setTcpNoDelay(true) turns Nagle's algorithm *off*, and that its default state is *on*.

Nagle's algorithm operates simply by delaying the transmission of new TCP segments while any data remains unacknowledged, so that they can be coalesced into a smaller number of larger segments. It turns out that this has other benefits, such as preventing retransmissions to a dead host.

The original application of the algorithm was 'single-character messages originating at a keyboard', *e.g.* a Telnet session. Without Nagle's algorithm, this causes TCP to send each character in a separate segment, with one byte of data and 40 bytes of header, *i.e.* an overhead of 4000%. While this is unimportant on a lightly loaded LAN, it is a very inefficient use of a heavily loaded WAN or portion of the Internet; it can lead to premature saturation of the network; and it can be extremely expensive on a network which charges per IP packet.

There are very few situations in which you would want to turn this algorithm off. The X Window System is one such situation, because small mouse movements need to be transmitted more or less in 'real time' in order to keep the system responsive to the user (Stevens *TCP/IP* Vol. I §19.4). Java RMI disables

Nagle's algorithm, even though R M I buffers all data and flushes it promptly rather than writing little bits at a time to the network: presumably the intention is to ensure that the final segment of a call or reply is transmitted promptly, and that the small R M I 'ping' message is not delayed.

In almost all situations where you may think you want to disable the Nagle algorithm, the real answer is to use a BufferedOutputStream with a buffer size at least equal to the largest request or reply size: set the socket send and receive buffers to at least this size as discussed in section 3.13.2, and write the entire request or reply out in one operation with the BufferedOutputStream.flush method. The entire buffer will be transmitted in a single T C P segment, which is a much better use of the network than tranmitting the same data in many small segments.

According to R F C 1122, implementations 'should' support Nagle's algorithm, but 'must' support an application interface to turn it off for an individual connection; this is what the Socket.setTcpNoDelay method is for when noDelay is true. The R F C does *not* require an application interface to *re-enable* the algorithm, *i.e.* to set noDelay to false in the Java A P I. This means that the setTcpNoDelay method may do nothing if the noDelay argument is false.

> The Socket.setTcpNoDelay method is equivalent to setting the TCP_NODELAY option via the Berkeley Sockets *setsockopt()* A P I.

> In rare circumstances, mostly involving large M T U s, the combination of Nagle's algorithm and T C P's 'delayed A C K' algorithm can cause T C P to get *almost* 'stuck': specifically, to degrade to less than 1% of possible throughput. This can be avoided as long as the socket send buffer is *either* at least as large as the receive buffer at the other end *or* larger than three MSS segments, as discussed in section 3.13.2.

3.16 LINGER ON CLOSE

The Socket.setSoLinger method controls the behaviour of T C P when a socket is closed:

```
class Socket
{
  void setSoLinger(boolean linger, int timeout)
                     throws SocketException;
  int  getSoLinger() throws SocketException;
}
```

where timeout is specified in seconds.[24] A return value of -1 from the getSoLinger method indicates the default setting (linger = false).

T C P defines three different behaviours for 'linger on close', which are shown in Table 3.3.

TABLE 3.3 TCP 'linger' settings

linger	timeout	Description
false	ignored	Default. When the socket is closed,[a] the closing thread is not blocked but the socket is not destroyed immediately: it first enters a CLOSING state while any remaining data is transmitted and the FIN-ACK close protocol is exchanged with the other end; the socket then enters the TIME-WAIT state, which lasts for twice the maximum lifetime of a TCP segment, to ensure that further data transmissions to the socket are rejected with a TCP RST, the interval being chosen so that TCP can retransmit the final part of the close protocol if necessary, and so that the local and remote endpoint pair which define the connection are not reused during the TIME-WAIT period, so that any delayed data segments from the closed connection won't be delivered to the new connection. When TIME-WAIT expires the socket is destroyed.[b]
true	$\neq 0$	'Linger'. When the socket is closed,[a] the closing thread is blocked ('lingers') while any pending data is sent and the close protocol is exchanged, or the timeout expires, whichever occurs first; the thread then continues. If the timeout expires, either: *(i)* the connection is 'hard-closed' as described below,[c] or *(ii)* any remaining data remains queued for delivery, after which the connection is closed via FIN-ACK as described above.[d] These semantics are platform-dependent (Java cannot overcome them). In Java, *timeout* is an *int* specifying seconds, limiting it to $2^{31} - 1$ seconds; some platforms further limit it to $(2^{15} - 1)/100 = 32.767$ seconds, by using an internal 16-bit signed quantity representing hundredths of a second.[e]
true	0	'Hard close'. When the socket is closed,[a] any pending data is discarded and the close protocol exchange (FIN-ACK) does not occur: instead, an RST is issued, causing the other end to throw a SocketException 'connection reset by peer'.

a. *i.e.* via any of Socket.close, Socket.getXXXStream.close, or Socket.shutdownOutput.

b. Many implementations unnecessarily prevent reuse of the local port during the TIME-WAIT period as well, even when connecting to a different remote endpoint.

c. This behaviour is required by the WINSOCK 2 specification §3.4.

d. This behaviour was required by a Posix.1g draft (quoted in the comp.unix.bsd newsgroup by W. R. Stevens, 22 May 1996), but not by IEEE Std 1003.1-2001, which leaves it undefined.

24. Chan, Lee, & Kramer, *The Java Class Libraries*, 2nd Edition, Volume 1, incorrectly specifies milliseconds.

e. If the timeout expires, the Berkeley Sockets and W I N S O C K APIs both set E W O U L D B L O C K and return -1, although this is not specified in I E E E Std 1 0 0 3 . 1 - 2 0 0 1 . As at J D K 1.4.2, Java ignores all this anyway, so you can't tell in Java at the closing end whether the timeout expired or not. The author has requested an enhancement for Socket.close to throw an InterruptedIOException in this circumstance (Bug Parade id 4631988).

It is rarely if ever necessary to alter this option from its default setting, and normally you should not do so. Some T C P implementations don't support the various non-default linger options; some ignore the timeout; and the behaviour if the timeout expires is platform-dependent. You should avoid this feature for these reasons alone.

Circumstances *appear* to exist in which the default setting is unsuitable. Consider the case where data is written and the socket is then closed. Under the default setting, the application may resume from the Socket.close method before the data in transit has been transmitted, and the application has no way of telling whether it was ever read by the other end. In this case one solution would be to linger for a reasonable period of time while the close is in progress. If the transmission is so critical, it is more to the point to wait for an application-defined reply, rather than just sending it off into the ether.

If it is genuinely necessary to abort a connection rather than terminate it gracefully, the 'hard close' can be used.

Recommendations are occasionally seen to use this option to allow servers to re-use a listening port quickly after they exit, especially during development. The correct answer to this problem is the 'reuse address' option, which appears in Java as the ServerSocket.setReuseAddress methods described in section 3.3.5.

Recommendations are also seen to use this option to overcome the problem of lots of closed sockets in the TIME-WAIT state at clients. Again, a better answer is the Socket.setReuseAddress method described in section 3.4.9, although really you should leave the TIME-WAIT state well alone: it exists for the very good reason described in Table 3.3.

3.17 KEEP-ALIVE

T C P 'keep-alive' is a technique which probes an active T C P connection to ensure that the other end is still alive.

If the other end is alive, it will acknowledge the probe. If a keep-alive probe is not acknowledged after a small number of retries, the socket is put into a 'reset' state, which will cause a SocketException to be thrown on the next read, write, or close operation on the socket.

Keep-alive is a controversial option in T C P, for several reasons:

(a)   It is implemented via a protocol 'trick' rather than by a dedicated protocol element.[25]

(b) It is somewhat against the spirit of T C P, which was purposely designed to allow intermediate routers to fail (*i.e.* to allow optimum routes to change) during the lifetime of a connection *without causing the connection itself to fail*: keep-alive can therefore cause an otherwise live connection to fail.

(c) It consumes bandwidth, and indeed costs money on networks that charge by the packet.

(d) It doesn't keep anything alive, so it is misnamed: the name suggests that it keeps a connection alive, which is completely unnecessary in T C P; what it actually does is detect, unreliably, whether the other party is still alive.

(e) Because of the limitations imposed on its implementation, described below, its actual usefulness is rather limited.

R F C 1122 specifies a number of constraints on keep-alive implementations:[26]

(a) Keep-alive is an optional feature of T C P, not a mandatory one.

(b) If supported, it must be off by default.

(c) The interval between successful keep-alive probes must default to at least two hours: usually, this interval can only be changed globally, typically only by a super-user or administrator on platforms where they exist.

(d) It must be specifically enabled by any end-point which wants to *send* keep-alives, *i.e.* possibly by both ends of a connection; in other words, whether keep-alive is on or off is a property of each endpoint, not of the connection as a whole.

(e) It is primarily intended for use by servers, to avoid long-term loss of resources for clients which have terminated; however it can be used by clients.

In Java, T C P keep-alive is controlled with the Socket.setKeepAlive method:

```
class Socket
{
  void      setKeepAlive(boolean keepAlive)
                          throws SocketException:
  boolean   getKeepAlive()  throws SocketException;
}
```

---

25. For details see Stevens Vol. I §23.3. The 'trick' consists in sending a T C P segment with a byte-offset which has already been acknowledged, *i.e.* appearing to be a duplicate: this causes the other end to issue an A C K specifying the next byte-offset it is expecting.

26. Braden, *Requirements for Internet Hosts—Communication Layers*, I E T F R F C 1122, 1989.

where keepAlive is true if keep-alive is to be enabled, otherwise false. These methods both throw SocketException if keep-alive control is not supported by the current platform, or if some underlying TCP error occurs.

Telnet servers typically enable keep-alive where possible. Sun's implementation of RMI enables keep-alive at clients if supported by the underlying platform.

Keep-alive should be viewed as a kind of 'court of last resort' for finally terminating dead connections after two hours if it is available. It should not be relied on as a substitute for sensible use of timeouts. You should consider using application-level connection probes ('pings') where connections are expected to be of long duration.

3.18 URGENT DATA

JDK 1.4 introduced APIs for sending and receiving TCP 'urgent' or 'out-of-band' (OOB) data:

```
class Socket
{
  void      sendUrgentData(int data)  throws IOException;
  void      setOOBInline(boolean on)  throws IOException;
  boolean   getOOBInline()            throws IOException;
}
```

Urgent data is sent with the Socket.sendUrgentData method. This sends one byte of urgent data on the socket, from the low-order eight bits of data. Urgent data is sent after any data already written to the socket output stream, and before any data subsequently written to the socket output stream.

The operation is primarily intended to support *sending* urgent data to non-Java recipients, to comply with existing application protocols such as Telnet.

Java provides only limited support for *receiving* urgent data: you can only receive urgent data in Java in-line, which you must first enable with the Socket.setOOBInline method with on = true.

When this state is *enabled*, urgent data is received inline with normal data. No means is provided in JDK 1.4 of distinguishing urgent data from non-urgent data at the receiver.

> Doing so would require implementing a method for the SIOCATMARK operation of *ioctl*() or the corresponding Posix.1g *sockatmark*() API. Implementing out-of-line reception of urgent data would require implementing the MSG_OOB flag of *recv*() somehow.

When this state is *disabled* (the default), urgent data is received 'out-of-line' *and silently discarded* by Java.

Obviously receiving out-of-band data in-line is something of an absurdity.

3.19 TRAFFIC CLASS

IP supports an optional 'traffic class' socket attribute. This attribute is a hint to the network about the type of service required for packets originating from the socket.

The traffic-class for a socket can be managed with the methods:

```
class Socket
{
  int setTrafficClass(int tc) throws SocketException;
  int getTrafficClass()       throws SocketException;
}
```

The Socket.getTrafficClass method may return a different value from the one last set, because the underlying network implementation may have ignored it.

The traffic class attribute primarily affects the path chosen through the network. The underlying network implementation, including any intermediate router or host, may ignore the value specified. The value has no effect on the local TCP protocol stack, but it acts as a hint to the nearest router, instructing it about the type of dataflow required by this connection. The router may propagate the information to neighbouring routers, and may alter the setting as required to implement the requested class of service.

The meaning of the attribute varies between IPV4 and IPV6 as described in section 3.19.1 and section 3.19.2. This is one of the few places in the Java networking API where you need to be aware of differences between IPV4 and IPV6.

3.19.1 IPV4 type-of-service

In IPV4, the value supplied to and returned by these methods is the eight-bit TOS (type of service) field defined in RFC 791. The lowest-order bit, with value 0x01, is reserved and must be zero.The value is usually zero or one of the RFC 1349 TOS values shown in Table 3.4.

TABLE 3.4 IPV4 type-of-service values

Name	Value	Description
–	0	Normal service
IPTOS_LOWCOST	0x02	Minimise monetary cost
IPTOS_RELIABILITY	0x04	Maximise reliability
IPTOS_THROUGHPUT	0x08	Maximise throughput
IPTOS_LOWDELAY	0x10	Minimise delay

These are known as the 'D T R C' bits, an acronym from the initial letters of 'delay', 'throughput', 'reliability', and 'cost'. Java provides no symbolic constants for these values. Other values are possible: however, a value other than those above does not necessarily imply one or more of the above attributes, even though the corresponding bit(s) may be set in the value.

> The J D K 1.4.0 and 1.4.1 documentation incorrectly states: 'The T O S field is [a] bitset created by bitwise or-ing values'. This was the case as of R F C 791–5, which were rescinded in this respect by R F C 1349, the R F C referenced by the J D K documentation. This says 'because this specification redefines T O S values to be integers rather than sets of bits, computing the logical OR of two T O S values is no longer meaningful. For example, it would be a serious error for a router to choose a low delay path for a packet whose requested T O S was 1110 simply because the router noted that the former "delay bit" was set.' However, 'although the semantics of values other than the five listed above are not defined by this memo, they are perfectly legal T O S values.'

The three highest-order bits, *i.e.* those masked by oxco, are a 'precedence' or priority field representing 'an independent measure of the importance of the datagram or segment'.

These options affect routing paths as well as priority in the router. For example, a satellite link would be a good choice to maximize throughput, but a bad choice for minimizing latency. The options are often set asymmetrically: for example, an application sending bulk data might choose to maximize throughput; on the other hand the receiving application might choose to minimize latency on its sent packets so that acknowledgements are sent quickly.

3.19.2 I P V 6 *traffic class*

In I P V 6, the value supplied and returned by these methods is the eight-bit T C (traffic class) field defined in R F C 2460. At the time of writing, the usage and semantics of this field were still the subject of experiment and were not yet defined, although presumably the values defined in Table 3.4 will continue to be supported with the same meanings.

> According to BugID 4529569, the I P V 6 'flow label' field, another traffic-shaping parameter, is always set to zero. This BugID is a request for further socket APIs: to control the flow label; to return the flow label of an individual packet; and to set T O S / T C on a per-packet basis, presumably for U D P packets.

3.19.3 *Differentiated Services*

R F C 2474 obsoletes the previous RFCs mentioned above, and redefines the T O S and traffic-class fields as the Differentiated Services Codepoint (D S C P), or D S for short. This is a value field which maps inside the router to a 'per-hop behaviour' (P H B), a behaviour which can be composed of all sorts of router-dependent things including one or more or the attributes above, selection of actual queuing algorithms, and so forth, according to the router setup. The router may write this field based on a router-specific traffic classification scheme, and it may rewrite the field to something the next router understands.

3.19.4 *Conclusion*

If you don't have a router at all, *i.e.* you have a closed LAN, there is no point in setting this option at all, as only routers take any notice of it.

Applications such as FTP still use the RFC 1345 definitions. Basically, applications can use any value the nearest router understands, and if these happen to be the RFC 1349 TOS values, we are all in luck. The RFC 1349 values seem like a good start if one or more of the following are true:

(a)   You have a pre-RFC 2474 router.

(b)   You have an RFC 2474-compliant router which is programmed to understand the RFC 1349 values, or

(c)   You aren't sure.

The RFCs mentioned in this section are summarized in Table 3.5.

TABLE 3.5 TOS & traffic-class RFCs

RFC	Supercedes/updates	Comment
791		Defines TOS 'along the abstract parameters [of[precedence, delay, throughput, and reliability'.
795		Defines delay, throughput, and reliability as per Table 3.4; values to be OR-ed together bitwise.
1349	791–5	Adds 'cost', so all four 'DTRC' values are now defined; redefines TOS as integers rather than sets of bits, so removes ability to OR values together bitwise.
1455		Experimentally adds the TOS value oxfo for 'physical link security'.
2460		Defines the IPv6 'traffic class' field for IPv6.
2474	1349, 1455	Redefines TOS and traffic class as 'differentiated services' as described in section 3.19.3.

3.20 PERFORMANCE PREFERENCES

In JDK 1.5 the 'performance preferences' for a socket can be expressed via the method:

```
class Socket
{
  void setPerformancePreferences
    (int connectionTime, int latency, int bandwidth)
      throws SocketException;
}
class ServerSocket
{
  void setPerformancePreferences
    (int connectionTime, int latency, int bandwidth)
      throws SocketException;
}
```

where the three parameters indicate the relative importance of short connection time, low latency, and high bandwidth respectively.

This feature is intended for use with multi-protocol implementations of Java where TCP is not the only available protocol, and provides hints as to how to select among the available protocols. If this operation is performed on a Socket, it must be called before connecting the socket, and invoking it afterwards has no effect. No 'get' method is provided. If this operation is performed on a ServerSocket, it must be called before the ServerSocket is bound.

3.21 PUTTING IT ALL TOGETHER

A revised TCP server which implements the improvements suggested above is shown in Example 3.6.

```
class ConcurrentTCPServer implements Runnable
{
  public static final int  BUFFER_SIZE= 128*1024;// 128k
  public static final int  TIMEOUT    = 30*1000; // 30s
  ServerSocket    serverSocket;

  ConcurrentTCPServer(int port) throws IOException
  {
    // (Don't specify localAddress for ServerSocket)
    serverSocket = new ServerSocket(port);
    // Set receive buffer size for accepted sockets
    // before accepting any, i.e. before they are connected
    serverSocket.setReceiveBufferSize(BUFFER_SIZE);
    // Don't set server socket timeout
  }
```

```
public void run()
{
  for (;;)
  {
    try
    {
      Socket socket = serverSocket.accept();
      // set send buffer size
      socket.setSendBufferSize(BUFFER_SIZE);
      // Don't wait forever for client requests
      socket.setSoTimeout(TIMEOUT);
      // despatch connection handler on new thread
      new Thread(new ConnectionHandler(socket)).start();
    }
    catch (IOException e)
    {
      /*Exception handling, not shown … */
    }
  } // end for (;;)
} // end run()
} // end class
```

EXAMPLE 3.6 Improved TCP server

Further server architectures are discussed in Chapter 5 and Chapter 12.

A revised TCP client which implements the improvements suggested above is shown in Example 3.7.

```
public class TCPClient implements Runnable
{
  public static final int  BUFFER_SIZE= 128*1024;// 128k
  public static final int  TIMEOUT    = 30*1000; // 30s
  Socket socket;

  public TCPClient(String host, int port) throws IOException
  {
    this.socket = new Socket();
    // Set receive buffer size before connecting
    socket.setReceiveBufferSize(BUFFER_SIZE);
    // connect to target
    socket.connect(new InetSocketAddress(host, port));
    // Set send buffer size and read timeout
    socket.setSendBufferSize(BUFFER_SIZE);
    socket.setSoTimeout(TIMEOUT);
  }
```

```
public void run()
{
  try
  {
    // prepare to send request
    OutputStream out =
      new BufferedOutputStream(socket.getOutputStream(),
        BUFFER_SIZE);
    // send request data, not shown …
    // flush request
    out.flush();
    // prepare to read reply
    InputStream in =
      new BufferedInputStream(socket.getInputStream(),
        BUFFER_SIZE);
    // receive reply & process it, not shown …
  }
  catch (IOException e)
  {
    /*…*/
  }
  finally
  {
    try
    {
      if (socket != null)
        socket.close();
    }
    catch (IOException e)
    {
      // ignored
    }
  } // end finally
} // end run()
} // end class
```

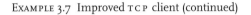

EXAMPLE 3.7 Improved T C P client (continued)

Scalable I/O

THIS CHAPTER DISCUSSES the new I/O features introduced in J D K 1.4. These new features are contained in the new java.nio package and its sub-packages, and in a small number of complementary revisions made to the java.io and java.net packages.

We will discuss these features along general lines, mainly insofar as they affect network I/O. Subsequent chapters delve into the detail, discussing scalable T C P and scalale U D P respectively.

4.1 INTRODUCTION

'New I/O' was introduced into J D K 1.4 to 'provide new features and improved performance in the areas of buffer management, scalable network and file I/O, character-set support, and regular-expression matching'.

The specification was developed in the Java Community Process as J S R 51. The major components of J S R 51 for advanced network programming are stated as:

(a) Scalable I/O, in the form of 'non-blocking mode' and 'multiplexing', and

(b) Fast buffered binary and character I/O.

Non-blocking mode and multiplexing make it possible to write 'production-quality web and application servers that scale well to thousands of open connections and can easily take advantage of multiple processors'.[1] This is mainly because in T C P and U D P servers using non-blocking I/O and multiplexing, a separate Java

---

1. All quotations in this section are from the J D K 1.4 documentation and the J S R-51 specification unless indicated otherwise.

thread is not required for every open connection, unlike the TCP servers we have seen in Chapter 3.

Fast buffered binary and character I/O make it possible to write 'high-performance, I/O-intensive programs that manipulate streams or files of binary data'.

4.1.1 *Comparison with stream I/O*

'Traditional' Java I/O—the java.io package—is provided as a hierarchy of 'stream' classes which share and extend a common API. A Java stream is an object derived from InputStream or OutputStream which represents an open connection, or data path, to an external data source or sink. Streams are unidirectional, *i.e.* can be used for either input or output but not both. Streams can be chained together so as to form I/O filter chains: for example, a DataInputStream is often chained to a BufferedInputStream, which in turn is often chained to an input stream obtained from a Socket or a FileInputStream:

```
Socket     socket = new Socket("localhost",7);
InputStream in    = socket.getInputStream();
// Add buffering to input
in = new BufferedInputStream(in);
// Add data-conversion functions to input
DataInputStreamdataIn = new DataInputStream(in);
```

As this example shows, various types of stream exist which together combine the functions of input-output, buffering, and data conversion.

Traditional streams provided buffering as an optional feature, rather than a built-in part of the I/O mechanism; this design made it possible to run multiple buffers, whether deliberately or inadvertently. The technique used for chaining streams together can imply a data copy operation at each stream junction, especially when doing data conversions. All these factors can lead to inefficient I/O in Java programs.

In Java 'new I/O', these three functions have been separated. Input-output is provided by a new abstraction called a 'channel'; buffering and data conversion is provided by a new abstraction called a 'buffer'. There is a hierarchy of channel classes and a separate hierarchy of buffer classes.

The rationale behind the new I/O is clear. Separating the I/O functions into channel operations and buffer operations allowed the Java designers to:

(a) Require that a channel must always be associated with a single buffer.

(b) Specify the ways that channels and buffers can be fitted together.

(c) Do so via the type system so you can't even compile an incorrect program.

(d) Provide reliable and portable semantics for asynchronous closing and interruption of I/O.

(e) Extend the channel and buffer classes in different directions without being 'imprisoned' by the Java type system.

(f) Extend the channel and buffer classes to provide higher-level functions, such as polling and non-blocking I/O in channels, direct buffers, and character-set conversion buffers.

4.1.2 Overview of New I/O

New I/O is performed via channels and buffers. A 'channel' is connected to an external data source and/or sink (*e.g.* a file or network socket), and has read and/or write operations. A 'buffer' holds data within the program, and provides 'get' and 'put' operations. Reading from a channel reads data from the source and puts it into the buffer; conversely, writing to a channel gets data from the buffer and writes it to the sink.

More powerful channel classes exist which support multiplexing as well as reading and writing. Different buffer classes exist for different primitive types.

4.2 CHANNELS

A Java channel represents an open data path, possibly bidirectional, to an external data source or sink such as a file or a socket.

By contrast with streams, channels can be bidirectional, *i.e.* can perform both input and output, if the external data object (the source or sink) permits. Channels cannot be chained together like I/O streams: instead, channels are confined to actual I/O operations. Buffering and data conversion features are provided in java.nio by *buffers*, discussed in section 4.3.

4.2.1 Channel hierarchy

The complete tree of channel interfaces and classes is shown in Table 4.1.

TABLE 4.1 Hierarchy of channels

Inheritance tree	Interfaces implemented
Channel	
∟ *InterruptibleChannel*	*Channel*
∟ *ReadableByteChannel*	*Channel*
∟ ∟ *ScatteringByteChannel*	*ReadableByteChannel*
∟ *WritableByteChannel*	*Channel*
∟ ∟ *GatheringByteChannel*	*WritableByteChannel*
∟ *ByteChannel*	*ReadableByteChannel, WritableByteChannel*

TABLE 4.1 Hierarchy of channels (continued)

Inheritance tree	Interfaces implemented
AbstractInterruptibleChannel[a]	*Channel, InterruptibleChannel*
└ FileChannel	*ByteChannel, ScatteringByteChannel, GatheringByteChannel*
└ SelectableChannel	*Channel*
└ AbstractSelectableChannel[a]	
└ DatagramSocketChannel	*ByteChannel, ScatteringByteChannel, GatheringByteChannel*
└ Pipe.SinkChannel	*WritableByteChannel, GatheringByteChannel*
└ Pipe.SourceChannel	*ReadableByteChannel, ScatteringByteChannel*
└ ServerSocketChannel	*Channel*
└ SocketChannel	*ByteChannel, ScatteringByteChannel, GatheringByteChannel*

a. in java.nio.channels.spi: an implementation detail.

Each concrete channel implementation is associated with exactly and only the I/O operations it is capable of. For example, ServerSocketChannel implements SelectableChannel, whose purpose we will encounter in section 4.5, but the only I/O operation it supports is closure. By contrast, SocketChannel implements ByteChannel: therefore, indirectly, it also implements ReadableByteChannel and WritableByteChannel, so it supports simple reads and writes; it also implements ScatteringByteChannel and GatheringWriteChannel, so it supports gathering reads and scattering writes (both to be described later).

4.2.2 *Channel interfaces and methods*

java.nio.Channel is the root of the hierarchy of channel interfaces. The Channel interface only exports a close operation and an isOpen query:

```
interface Channel
{
  boolean  isOpen();
  void     close() throws IOException;
}
```

The ReadableByteChannel interface exports a simple read operation:

```
interface ReadableByteChannel extends Channel
{
  // returns the number of bytes read
  int   read(ByteBuffer destination) throws IOException;
}
```

The WritableByteChannel interface exports a simple write operation:

```
interface WritableByteChannel extends Channel
{
  // returns the number of bytes written
  int   write(ByteBuffer source) throws IOException;
}
```

The ByteChannel interface unifies the readable and writable interfaces:

```
interface ByteChannel
  extends ReadableByteChannel, WritableByteChannel
{
}
```

The ScatteringByteChannel interface exports scatter-read methods, whereby data is read with one underlying operation and scattered into multiple buffers (targets):

```
interface ScatteringByteChannel extends ReadableByteChannel
{
  // Both methods return the number of bytes read
  long  read(ByteBuffer[] targets) throws IOException;
  long  read(ByteBuffer[] targets, int offset, int length)
                                  throws IOException;
}
```

The GatheringByteChannel interface exports gather-write methods, whereby the data to be written is gathered up from multiple buffers (sources) and written with one underlying operation:

```
interface GatheringByteChannel extends WritableByteChannel
{
  // Both methods return the number of bytes written
  long  write(ByteBuffer[] sources)  throws IOException;
  long  write(ByteBuffer[] sources, int offset, int length)
                                  throws IOException;
}
```

In both cases, offset and length refer to the ByteBuffer[] array itself, not to any individual ByteBuffer.

> The 'scatter-read' and 'gather-write' methods correspond to the Berkeley Sockets *readv()* and *writev()* APIs. Note that the methods of these interfaces return longs rather than ints. This was a late change in the java.nio specification: longs are required because there can be up to $2^{32} - 1$ elements in the ByteBuffer[] array, each of which can contain up to $2^{32} - 1$ bytes; the total size of the transfer can therefore be up to $2^{64} - 1$ bytes, which is too many to be represented in an int.

The InterruptibleChannel interface identifies channels which can be closed and interrupted asynchronously:

```
interface InterruptibleChannel extends Channel
{
  void close() throws IOException;
}
```

An interruptible channel may be closed asynchronously: *i.e.* a thread may invoke the InterruptibleChannel.close method while another thread is executing a blocking I/O operation on the channel. This causes the blocked thread to incur an AsynchronousCloseException.

An interruptible channel may be interrupted asynchronously: *i.e.* a thread may invoke Thread.interrupt on another thread which is executing a blocking I/O operation on the channel. This closes the channel, and causes the blocked thread to incur a ClosedByInterruptException.[2]

4.2.3 Obtaining a channel

A channel can be obtained from a FileInputStream, a FileOutputStream, or a RandomAccessFile:

```
FileChannel  FileInputStream.getChannel();
FileChannel  FileOutputStream.getChannel();
FileChannel  RandomAccessFile.getChannel();
```

A channel can also be obtained from a Socket, ServerSocket, or DatagramSocket, but only if the socket was created from a channel, so the operation is circular.

---

2. This may surprise. We might have expected the channel to remain open and the blocked thread to get an InterruptedIOException. The close semantics are dictated by the requirement to provide the same semantics across the various supported platforms, specifically, the strange behaviour of Linux when a thread blocked in a socket operation is interrupted asynchronously.

Instead of getting the channel from the socket, it is usually more to the point to get the socket from the channel:

```
SocketChannel          channel  = SocketChannel.open();
Socket                 socket   = channel.socket();

ServerSocketChannel    channel  =
  ServerSocketChannel.open();
ServerSocket           serverSocket   = channel.socket();

DatagramChannel        channel  = DatagramChannel.open();
DatagramSocket         datagramSocket= channel.socket();
```

A MulticastSocketChannel class was reportedly planned for J D K 1.5 but did not appear.

Finally, a channel can also be obtained from a java.nio.Pipe:

```
Pipe                   pipe             = Pipe.open();
Pipe.SinkChannel       sinkChannel      = pipe.sink();
Pipe.SourceChannel     sourceChannel    = pipe.source();
```

The channel associated with a file input or output stream, random access file, socket, or pipe is unique: repeated calls of getChannel, Pipe.sink, or Pipe.source always return the same object.

4.2.4 *Channel conversions—the Channels class*

The Channels class provides static methods to convert between streams and channels:

```
class Channels
{
  // convert streams to channels
  static ReadableByteChannel    newChannel(InputStream is);
  static WritableByteChannel    newChannel(OutputStream os);

  // convert channels to streams
  static InputStream
    newInputStream(ReadableByteChannel ch);
  static OutputStream
    newOutputStream(WritableByteChannel ch);
}
```

It also provides methods to convert channels into Readers and Writers which are not discussed further in this book. The streams, readers, and writers delivered by these methods have a number of special properties:

(a)   They are not buffered.

(b)   They do not support the mark/reset mechanism.

(c)   They are thread-safe.

(d)   They can only be used in blocking mode: if used in non-blocking node (to be discussed later), their read and write methods will all throw an IllegalBlockingModeException.

(e)   Closing them causes the underlying channel to be closed.

Property (d) is important. It means that you can only read and write Java datatypes via methods of DataInput and DataOutput, or serialize Java objects via methods of ObjectInput and ObjectOutput on a channel which is in blocking mode.

The following code fragments will throw an IllegalBlockingModeException at the places indicated:

```
SocketChannel    channel = SocketChannel.open();
channel.connect(new InetSocketAddress("localhost",7));
channel.configureBlocking(false);

InputStream      in = Channels.newInputStream(channel);
ObjectInputStream   objIn = new ObjectInputStream(in);

// The next line throws an IllegalBlockingModeException
Object object = objIn.readObject();

OutputStream     out = Channels.newOutputStream(channel);
ObjectOutputStream    objOut
  = new ObjectOutputStream(out);

// The next line throws an IllegalBlockingModeException
objOut.writeObject(object);
```

4.3 BUFFERS

A channel can only perform input-output in conjunction with a buffer.

A java.nio 'buffer' is a container for data of a single primitive type. A buffer class is provided for each of the primitive types byte, char, short, int, long, float, and double (but not for boolean). Buffers have finite capacities.

In addition to data, buffers also contain four interdependent state attributes: *capacity, limit, position,* and *mark*:

(a)   The *capacity* of a buffer is the number of elements it contains. What this represents in bytes depends on the size of the datatype supported by the buffer. The capacity is immutable: it is fixed when the buffer is created.

(b) The *limit* of a buffer is the index of the first element that should not be read or written. The limit is mutable.

(c) The *position* of a buffer is the index of the next element that should be read or written. The position is mutable.

(d) The *mark* of a buffer is the index to which its position will be restored if its reset method is invoked. The mark is mutable: it is not always defined but it can be defined and subsequently modified by program operations. It is undefined when a buffer is first created. The mark is discarded (*i.e.* becomes undefined) if the position or the limit is adjusted to be less than the current mark.

Capacity, limit, position, and *mark* always satisfy the invariant:

$$0 \leq mark \leq position \leq limit \leq capacity \qquad (\text{EQ 4.1})$$

which is preserved by all operations on the buffer.

The amount of remaining data or space in a buffer is given by:

$$limit - position \qquad (\text{EQ 4.2})$$

The position, limit, and capacity of a buffer are illustrated in Figure 4.1.

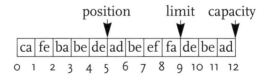

FIGURE 4.1. Buffer attributes

Operations are provided for allocation of new buffers (*allocate*) and creating buffers from existing buffers (*duplicate, slice, wrap*), as we will see in section 4.3.2.

Buffers provide type-specific *put* and *get* operations which add data to them and remove data from them respectively: these are the basic functions of a buffer. The *put* and *get* operations are invoked by the channel *read* and *write* operations respectively. It's important to understand this, and to get it the right way around. When writing data, a channel has to *get* it from a buffer; when reading data, a channel has to *put* it into a buffer.

Buffers also provide simple operations which directly modify their internal state (*mark, position, limit,* and *capacity*), as we will see in section 4.3.4, and compound operations (*clear, flip, rewind, compact*) which modify more than one of these items at a time, as we will see in section 4.3.5 &ff.

4.3.1 *Buffer hierarchy*

The complete tree of buffer classes is shown in the tree diagram of Table 4.2.

TABLE 4.2 Hierarchy of buffers

Buffer
∟ ByteBuffer
∣ ∟ MappedByteBuffer
∟ CharBuffer
∟ DoubleBuffer
∟ FloatBuffer
∟ IntBuffer
∟ LongBuffer
∟ ShortBuffer

To simplify the discussion, we introduce a meta-notation along the lines of the JDK 1.5 'Generics' language feature,[3] using *T* to indicate any primitive type for which a buffer implementation is provided, for example:

```
class Buffer<T> extends Buffer
{
  // this is a buffer for objects of primitive type T
}
```

4.3.2 *Obtaining a Buffer*

Buffers are not constructed but obtained.[4] Each concrete buffer implementation for a primitive type *T* exports methods for the creation of buffers:

```
class Buffer<T> extends Buffer
{
  static Buffer<T>   allocate(int capacity);

  Buffer<T>          asReadOnlyBuffer();
  boolean            isReadOnly();
```

---

3. To be clear, buffers are not actually defined in JDK 1.5 this way (because the types concerned are primitive types). I am just using this notation to avoid describing seven or eight structurally identical classes.

4. This is because they are specified as abstract classes and implemented via hidden classes returned by an object factory, to support the NIO SPI (service provider interface).

```
Buffer<T>        duplicate();
Buffer<T>        slice();
static Buffer<T>  wrap(T[] array);
static Buffer<T>  wrap(T[] array, int offset, int length);
}
```

The static allocate method is really a factory method which returns a new empty buffer of the specified *capacity* and associated type *T*. *Capacity* is specified as the desired number of items of type *T*, not as a number of bytes (if different).

The static wrap methods return a new buffer wrapped around an array of data.

The asReadOnlyBuffer, duplicate, and slice instance methods return buffers whose internal data mirrors that of the current buffer, but whose internal state settings differ in various ways.

The asReadOnlyBuffer method returns a read-only buffer which shares the current buffer's data, but not its *mark, position,* or *limit,* although these are initially identical. Changes to the current buffer's data are reflected in the read-only buffer (but not *vice versa:* a read-only buffer is immutable). The isReadOnly method returns the read-only status of a buffer.

The duplicate method returns a buffer which shares the current buffer's data, but not its *mark, position,* or *limit,* although these are initially identical. Changes to the current buffer's data are reflected in the new buffer and vice versa. The new buffer is read-only if and only if the current buffer is read-only; ditto 'direct'.

The slice method returns a buffer whose content is a shared sub-sequence—a 'slice'—of the source buffer's content, extending from the source buffer's *position* to its *limit.* Changes to the current buffer's data will be reflected in the new buffer and vice versa. The new buffer's *mark, position,* and *limit* are independent of those of the current buffer The new buffer is read-only if and only if the current buffer is read-only; ditto 'direct'.

The initial settings of the buffers returned by each of the above methods are summarized in Table 4.3.

TABLE 4.3 Initial N I O buffer settings

Method	capacity	position	limit	mark
allocate(capacity)	= capacity	zero	= capacity	undefined
wrap(array)	= array.length	zero	= capacity	undefined
wrap(array, offset, length)	= length	= offset	= offset + length	undefined
asReadOnlyBuffer	initially as source, not mirrored			
duplicate	initially as source, not mirrored			
slice	= source capacity	zero	= source limit − source position	initially as source

4.3.3 Buffer data operations: 'get' and 'put'

Each concrete buffer implementation for a primitive type T exports methods which get items of type T from the buffer; it also exports methods which put items of type T into the buffer:

```
class Buffer<T> extends Buffer
{
    T          get();                // Get one T, relative
    Buffer<T>  get(T[] buffer);      // Get bulk T, relative
    Buffer<T>  get(T[] buffer, int offset, int length);
    Buffer<T>  get(int index);       // Get one T, absolute

    Buffer<T>  put(T data);          // Put one T, relative
    Buffer<T>  put(T[] buffer);      // Put bulk T, relative
    Buffer<T>  put(T[] buffer, int offset, int length);
    Buffer<T>  put(int index, T data);    // Put one T, absolute
    // Put remaining T from source into 'this'
    Buffer<T>  put(Buffer<T> source);
}
```

The get and put methods which take array parameters provide bulk operations. The get and put methods which take index parameters provide 'absolute' operations which do not depend on or disturb the *position* of the buffer.

All the other methods are 'relative' operations which operate at *position* and then advance it by the number of items transferred (*not* the number of bytes transferred, if different).

The absolute *get* operation gets a single data item from the buffer at the specified *index*, without disturbing the buffer's *position*, after checking that the invariant:

$$0 \le index < position \qquad\qquad (\text{EQ } 4.3)$$

holds, throwing an IndexOutOfBoundsException if not.

The relative *get* operation first checks to see if the amount of remaining data given by Equation 4.2 is enough to satisfy the request, throwing a BufferUnderflowException if not. If the operation specifies a data array, offset, and length, it also checks that the following invariant holds:

$$0 \le length + offset \le data.length \qquad\qquad (\text{EQ } 4.4)$$

throwing the unchecked IndexOutOfBoundsException if not; otherwise it transfers the data starting at the current *position*, and finally advances *position* by the number of data items transferred.

The put methods are optional operations. A read-only buffer does not allow them: if they are invoked they throw a ReadOnlyBufferException. This is a Java RuntimeException, *i.e.* an unchecked exception.

A buffer is either read-only or read-write. Any buffer can be converted into a read-only buffer of the same type and mirroring the same data with the asReadOnly method described in section 4.3.2.

The absolute put operation puts a single data item into the buffer at the specified *index*, without disturbing the buffer's *position*, after checking that the invariant of Equation 4.3 holds, throwing an IndexOutOfBoundsException if not.

The relative *put* operation first checks to see if the amount of remaining space given by Equation 4.2 is sufficient to satisfy the request, throwing a BufferOverflowException if not. If the operation specifies a data array, offset, and length, it also checks that the invariant of Equation 4.4 holds , throwing the unchecked IndexOutOfBoundsException if not. Otherwise it transfers the data starting at the current *position*, and finally advances *position* by the number of data items transferred.

The effect on buffer attributes of a relative *get* or *put* of one item is shown in Figure 4.2.

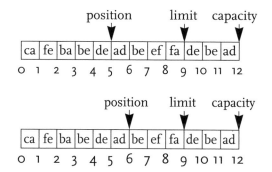

FIGURE 4.2. Buffer before and after one-item relative get or put

4.3.4 *Simple buffer state operations*

The abstract Buffer class exports methods which modify its state and which are inherited by the concrete type-specific buffer classes:

```
class Buffer
{
  int      position();           // get position
  int      limit();              // get limit
  int      capacity();           // get capacity

  Buffer   position(int position);  // set position
  Buffer   limit(int limit);        // set limit

  boolean  hasRemaining();
  int      remaining();

  Buffer   mark();
  Buffer   reset();
}
```

The hasRemaining method returns true if and only if the buffer has data elements between the current *position* and the current *limit*. The remaining method returns the number of such data elements (*not* the number of bytes, if different). The mark method sets the buffer's *mark* to the current *position*. The reset method resets *position* to the current *mark* if any, otherwise it throws an InvalidMarkException. This operation is used when re-reading or overwriting data.

4.3.5 *Compound buffer state operations*

The following methods operate on the *mark*, *position*, and *limit* at a higher level:

```
class Buffer
{
  Buffer   clear();
  Buffer   flip();
  Buffer   rewind();
}
```

These operations are discussed in detail in the following subsections.

4.3.6 *'Clear' operation*

The clear operation clears the buffer logically (*i.e.* without disturbing the data contents). This is usually done prior to a *put* operations:

```
buffer.clear();
buffer.put(…);
```

or a channel *read* operation, which is equivalent from the buffer's point of view:

```
buffer.clear();
channel.read(buffer);
```

The clear operation sets *position* to zero and *limit* to *capacity*, as shown in Figure 4.3.

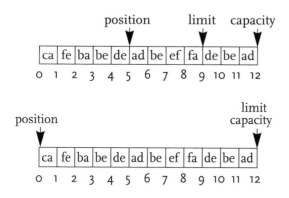

FIGURE 4.3. Buffer before and after clear

4.3.7 'Flip' operation

The curiously named flip operation makes data which has just been 'put' into the buffer available for 'getting'. It is used after putting data into the buffer and before getting it out again:

```
buffer.put(…);
buffer.flip();
buffer.get(…);
```

Because of the equivalence of *read* with *put*, and *write* with *get*, the flip operation is used in both directions of I/O. Consider a channel write operation:

```
buffer.put(array);
buffer.flip();
channel.write(buffer);
```

or a channel read operation:

```
channel.read(buffer);
buffer.flip();
buffer.get(array);
```

The flip operation can be thought of as flipping the buffer from *put/read* mode to *get/write* mode. The flip operation sets *limit* to *position* and *position* to zero, as shown in Figure 4.4.

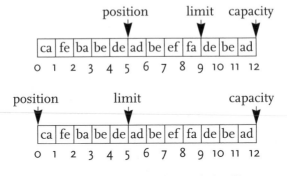

FIGURE 4.4. Buffer before and after flip

4.3.8 'Rewind' operation

The rewind operation rewinds the buffer, assuming that *limit* has been set appropriately. It should be performed when getting or writing the same data more than once:

```
channel.write(buffer);      // write data
buffer.rewind();
buffer.get(array);          // get what was written
```

or:

```
buffer.get(array);          // get what's to be written
buffer.rewind();
channel.write(buffer);      // write it
```

or:

```
channel1.write(buffer);     // write data to channel 1
buffer.rewind();
channel2.write(buffer);     // write same to channel 2
```

The rewind operation sets *position* to zero and does not alter *limit*, as shown in Figure 4.5.

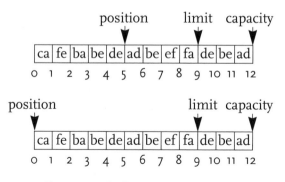

FIGURE 4.5. Buffer before and after *rewind*

4.3.9 'Compact' operation

Each concrete buffer implementation for a primitive type *T* exports a method for compacting buffers:

```
class Buffer<T> extends Buffer
{
  Buffer<T>        compact();
}
```

The compact operation compacts the buffer after a get operation (*e.g.* a channel write) so that any 'un-got' data is now at the beginning of the buffer, and that a subsequent put will place new data after this data, with maximum space being available for the put.

The compact operation is generally performed in conjunction with the flip operation when reading and writing, as shown in the following rather neat copy operation:

```
buffer.clear();
// Loop while there is input or pending output
while (in.read(buffer) >= 0 || buffer.position() > 0)
{
  buffer.flip();
  out.write(buffer);
  buffer.compact();
}
```

This example illustrates several key concepts:

(a) The read operation executes; if it returns a negative value, end-of-stream has been reached.

(b) At this point, *position* is the count of data items remaining to be written starting from position zero; if *position* is zero, nothing remains to be written.

(c) The flip operation readies the buffer for the write operation.

(d) The write operation writes as much as can be written.

(e) The compact operation readies the buffer for the next read operation. which will append new data to the end of the buffer.

(f) The loop iterates while new data is read (read() > 0) or there is still pending data to write (buffer.position() > 0).

Note that once end-of-stream has been reached, the iterations consist of write operations only; in other words, the sequence:

```
while (buffer.position() > 0)
{
  buffer.flip();
  out.write(buffer);
  buffer.compact();
}
```

is equivalent to the sequence

```
while (buffer.hasRemaining())
  out.write(buffer);
```

although the latter is more efficient, as it doesn't move the data around. If maximum efficiency is required, the copy example above can be rewritten thus:

```
buffer.clear();
// Loop while there is input
while (in.read(buffer) >= 0)
{
  buffer.flip();
  out.write(buffer);
  buffer.compact();
}
// final flush of pending output
while (buffer.hasRemaining())
  out.write(buffer);
```

These copying examples work equally well in blocking mode or non-blocking mode (discussed in section 4.4), although it is preferable to use a Selector to detect pending input and available output space as discussed in section 4.5.

Like the put operation, the compact operation is optional, and is not supported by read-only buffers: if invoked on a buffer which doesn't support it, a ReadOnlyBufferException is thrown. This is a Java RuntimeException, *i.e.* an unchecked exception.

The compact operation proceeds as follows:

(a) It discards any data which has already been 'got', *i.e.* any data before *position*.

(b) It moves any remaining data (between *position* and *limit*) to the beginning of the buffer.

(c) It sets *position* to *limit – position* (*i.e.* the index after the last data item moved),[5] and sets *limit* to *capacity*.

This is illustrated in Figure 4.6.

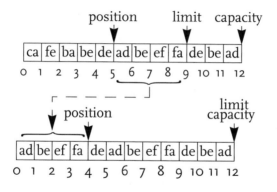

FIGURE 4.6. Buffer before and after *compact*

4.3.10 Byte buffers

Byte buffers exhibit all the behaviour describe above, but the ByteBuffer class is more powerful than the other type-specific classes in a number of ways.

You will have noticed that all the channel read and write methods operate on a ByteBuffer rather than a Buffer. This makes ByteBuffer the foundation of channel I/O.

---

5. The JDK 1.4.0 online documentation incorrectly had *position ← limit – 1 – position*; this was corrected in JDK 1.4.1.

This may surprise. Why not define read and write to take a Buffer parameter instead? The reason seems to be that I/O really does transfer physical bytes, rather than transferring some abstraction whose semantics could satisfactorily be expressed by the abstract Buffer class. Transforming the transferred bytes to and from other datatypes is a separate issue, and it is programmed separately and explicitly in Java new I/O.

The ByteBuffer class exports methods to get all the supported primitive datatypes, *i.e.* all the Java primitive types other than boolean. For example, for type float:

```
class ByteBuffer extends Buffer
{
    float        getFloat();
    float        getFloat(int index);

    ByteBuffer   putFloat(float data);
    ByteBuffer   putFloat(int index, float data);
}
```

In our meta-notation, the following methods are supported for each type *T*:

```
class ByteBuffer extends Buffer
{
    T            getT();
    T            getT(int index);

    ByteBuffer   putT(T data);
    ByteBuffer   putT(int index, T data);
}
```

In each case, as you would expect, the buffer *position* is advanced by the correct amount for the size of the datatype concerned,[6] although the index parameters are specified in terms of byte offsets, not offsets of items of type *T*.

Byte buffers can be allocated as 'direct' buffers:

```
class ByteBuffer extends Buffer
{
    static ByteBuffer   allocateDirect(int capacity);
}
```

A *direct* buffer is one upon which the JVM 'will make a best effort to perform native I/O operations directly', *i.e.* avoiding intermediate copy steps into and out

---

6. Datatype sizes are platform-independent: they are defined in *The Java Language Specification*, 3rd edition, section 4.2. Java programs have little need to be aware of the sizes of primitive types, as this design exemplifies.

of the JVM. Such buffers typically have much higher allocation and deallocation costs than normal (indirect) buffers, but perform much more quickly when in use. They are typically used for large, long-lived buffers. If a direct buffer is used, not a single bit of data enters the JVM.

4.3.11 View buffers

A byte buffer can also create one or more 'views' of itself. A *view* is a buffer of another datatype, whose content mirrors that of the data remaining in the source buffer. View buffers have the following advantages over the type-specific get/put methods described in section 4.3.10:

(a) They are indexed in terms of datatype entry offsets rather than byte offsets.

(b) They provide bulk operations into and out of arrays.

(c) View buffers can be 'direct' as just described: view buffers are the only way that direct buffers for types other than byte can be allocated.

View buffers are allocated by the methods:

```
class ByteBuffer extends Buffer
{
  CharBuffer      asCharBuffer();
  DoubleBuffer    asDoubleBuffer();
  FloatBuffer     asFloatBuffer();
  IntBuffer       asIntBuffer();
  LongBuffer      asLongBuffer();
  ShortBuffer     asShortBuffer();
}
```

When a view buffer is allocated, changes to the shared data in either buffer are mirrored in the other. The two buffers' *mark, position,* and *limit* are independent. The new *mark* is undefined; the new *position* is zero; and the new *limit* and *capacity* are initially equal to the amount of data remaining in the source buffer, adjusted for the new datatype length.

> This means dividing by two for char or short; dividing by four for int or float; dividing by eight for double or long.

A view buffer is direct if and only if it was allocated from a direct byte buffer, and read-only if and only if it was allocated from a read-only byte buffer.

The use of view buffers can be demonstrated by example. A FloatBuffer view of a ByteBuffer can be used to receive large arrays of floats from a channel:

```
ByteBuffer   byteBuffer = ByteBuffer.allocate(…);
channel.read(byteBuffer);
byteBuffer.flip();
FloatBuffer  floatBuffer = byteBuffer.asFloatBuffer();
float[]  floats = new float[FloatBuffer.remaining()];
floatBuffer.get(floats);
```

This is efficient, particularly if the byte buffer is a direct buffer: the array of floats is received and copied exactly once, in the last line of the example. We can't improve on this: the data has to get into the JVM some time, and doing it with a bulk channel operation is the most efficient way to do it.

The converse operation—writing float data—is more problematic. We need a ByteBuffer to perform channel I/O, and as we saw in section 4.3.10, ByteBuffer doesn't have bulk methods for non-byte data. We could use the one-at-a-time ByteBuffer.putFloat(float) method:

```
float[]      floats     = new float[] {…};
ByteBuffer   byteBuffer = ByteBuffer.allocate(…);
for (int i = 0; i < floats.length(); i++)
  byteBuffer.putFloat(floats[i]);
byteBuffer.flip();
channel.write(byteBuffer);
```

This solution is slow, which rather defeats the purpose of using new I/O at all. We can put the float data in bulk into a FloatBuffer easily enough:

```
float[]      floats     = new float[] {…};
FloatBuffer  floatBuffer = FloatBuffer.wrap(floats);
```

However we still need a ByteBuffer to perform channel I/O, and no methods are provided to convert a FloatBuffer into a ByteBuffer.[7] View buffers provide the solution: construct the FloatBuffer as a view of a ByteBuffer and put the data in bulk into the float buffer, whose data is mirrored in the underlying byte buffer:

```
float[]      floats     = new float[] {…};
ByteBuffer   byteBuffer = ByteBuffer.allocate(…);
FloatBuffer  floatBuffer = byteBuffer.asFloatBuffer();
floatBuffer.put(floats);
floatBuffer.flip();
```

This is still inadequate. As we saw in section 4.3.10, the *position* and *limit* of these buffers are independent, so although the data we put into the float buffer is mir-

---

7. as at JDK 1.5. The feature has been requested.

rored in the byte buffer, the *position* and *limit* are not: in fact, the byte buffer still appears to be empty. We need to adjust the *position* and *limit* of the byte buffer to agree with those of the float buffer, taking the different datatype lengths into account. We can avoid hardwiring the datatype lengths into this calculation by using the ratio of the respective capacities of the byte buffer and float buffer as the datatype-length 'factor', as shown below:

```java
// continuing on from previous block ...
int   factor =
   byteBuffer.capacity()/floatBuffer.capacity();
int   byteBufferLimit = floatBuffer.limit()*factor;
byteBuffer.limit(byteBufferLimit);
channel.write(byteBuffer);
```

because the ratio between the capacities is the inverse of the ratio between the datatype lengths. Clearly some sort of synchronize method seems to be required to restore the relationship between the *position* and *limit* of a view buffer and its underlying buffer.

A helper class with a generic Buffers.synchronize method is shown in Example 4.1.

```java
import java.nio.*;
public final class Buffers
{
  private Buffers() {} // non-constructable
  /**
   * Synchronize position and limit of <code>target</code>
   * with those of its view buffer <code>view</code>,
   * taking into account datatype item size differences.
   *
   * @param view source buffer, e.g. FloatBuffer
   * @param target the ByteBuffer underlying the view.
   */
  public static void   synchronize(final Buffer view,
                                   ByteBuffer target)
  {
    int factor = target.capacity()/view.capacity();
    target.limit(view.limit()*factor);
    target.position(view.position()*factor);
  }
}
```

EXAMPLE 4.1 Buffers.synchronize helper method

The completed bulk output example is shown in Example 4.2.

```
float[]        floats = new float[] {…};
ByteBuffer     byteBuffer = ByteBuffer.allocate(…);
FloatBuffer    floatBuffer = byteBuffer.asFloatBuffer();
floatBuffer.put(floats);
floatBuffer.flip();
Buffers.synchronize(floatBuffer, byteBuffer);
channel.write(byteBuffer);
```

EXAMPLE 4.2 Bulk output of float[] (improved)

4.3.12 Buffers and threads

Buffers are not safe for use by multiple threads unless appropriate synchronization is performed by the threads, *e.g.* by synchronizing on the buffer itself.

4.4 NON-BLOCKING I/O

The normal Java I/O mode is *blocking*: input-output blocks the calling thread from further execution until a non-empty data transfer has taken place. Satisfying the non-emptiness rule may involve waiting on an external data source or sink to produce or consume data respectively.

New I/O channels provide *non-blocking* input-output, which has no non-emptiness rule, and therefore never needs to wait on an external data source or sink.

4.4.1 Purpose

The fundamental purpose of non-blocking I/O is to avoid blocking the calling thread, so that it can do something else useful instead of just waiting for data to arrive or depart. This means that one endpoint (*e.g.* server or client thread) never blocks awaiting an action by the other endpoint (*e.g.* client or server thread). For example, it allows a network client to be written to a message-driven model rather than an R P C (remote procedure call) model.

Another advantage is that a single thread can handle multiple tasks (*e.g.* multiple non-blocking connections) rather than having to be dedicated to a single network connection: this in turn economizes on threads, and therefore memory; or, conversely, it allows a given number of threads to handle much more than that number of network connections.

4.4.2 Characteristics of blocking I/O

Channels are initially created in blocking mode, and streams—even those with channels—can only be operated in blocking mode.

A blocking *read* operation blocks until *at least some* data is available, although not necessarily all the data requested. It may transfer less than the data count requested, *i.e.* may return a lesser value. A read from a network stream or channel blocks while there is no data in the socket receive-buffer. As soon as *any* amount of data becomes available in the socket receive-buffer, it is transferred and execution is resumed. If no data is available, a blocking read may therefore have to wait for the other end to send something.

A blocking *write* operation blocks until *at least some* data can be transferred, although not necessarily all the data requested. A write operation on a channel may transfer less than the data count requested, *i.e.* may return a lesser value, although it always transfers something, *i.e.* never returns zero.[8] A write on a network channel blocks until *at least some* socket send-buffer space is available. As soon as space becomes available, that amount of data is transferred and execution is resumed. As send-buffer space depends on space in the receive buffer at the other end, a blocking write may therefore have to wait for the other end to create space in its receive buffer by reading some data out of it.

The blocking *connect* operation is described for TCP channels in section 5.2.1. The connect operation for UDP channels never blocks, as described in section 10.1.3.

A channel in blocking mode cannot be used with a Selector as described in section 4.5.[9]

4.4.3 Characteristics of non-blocking I/O

Non-blocking I/O can only be performed with JDK 1.4 channels.

A non-blocking *read* operation—unlike a blocking read—may return zero, indicating that no data was available. A non-blocking read on a network channel transfers only the data, if any, that was already in the socket receive-buffer at the time of the call. If this amount is zero, the read transfers no data and returns zero.

A non-blocking *write* operation—unlike a blocking write—may return zero, indicating that no space was available. A non-blocking write operation on a network channel transfers only as much data as could currently be appended to the socket send-buffer at the time of the call. If this amount is zero, the write transfers no data and returns zero.

The channel *connect* operation for non-blocking TCP channels is described in section 5.2.2, and for UDP channels, both blocking and non-blocking, in section 10.1.3. A channel in non-blocking mode can be used with a Selector as described in section 4.5.

---

8. However, write operations on *streams* block until the transfer is complete or an exception occurs. This is implemented via an internal loop, and is implied by the fact that the OutputStream.write methods all return void: an incomplete transfer cannot be notified to the calling application.

9. Otherwise an IllegalBlockingModeException is thrown. This may surprise Berkeley Sockets programmers, who can use *select()* on both blocking and non-blocking sockets.

4.4.4 *Methods*

Non-blocking I/O can be performed with any channel derived from SelectableChannel: these include DatagramChannel, Pipe.SinkChannel, Pipe.SourceChannel, ServerSocketChannel, and SocketChannel, as shown in Table 4.1. The blocking mode of such a channel is set and tested via the methods:

```
class SelectableChannel implements Channel
{
    // Test and set blocking mode
    boolean          isBlocking();
    SelectableChannel configureBlocking(boolean block)
                      throws IOException;
}
```

Non-blocking I/O is performed with the read and write methods defined in section 4.2.2. The only difference from blocking mode is that in non-blocking mode they return zero, indicating that no data was transferred, if the channel wasn't ready for the operation, *i.e.* if no incoming data has been buffered for a read operation, or no outgoing buffer space is available for a write operation.

> This is not the only reason these methods can return zero: they also do so if no actual transfer was requested, *e.g.* if there is no room in the buffer when reading, or nothing to write when writing, in both cases because *position = limit*. This can occur in blocking mode as well as non-blocking mode.

If a channel is in non-blocking mode and a stream I/O operation is attempted on it, an IllegalBlockingModeException is thrown, as shown in section 4.2.4.

4.5 MULTIPLEXING

Multiplexed I/O allows a thread to manage multiple I/O channels at the same time by means of event notifications: the thread registers the channels of interest with a 'selector' object and then calls a selector method which returns when one or more channels is is ready for an I/O operation, or after a specified timeout period.

Multiplexing is somewhat like being directly driven by hardware interrupts from the network controller.

The difference between managing a single channel in blocking mode and managing (multiplexing) multiple channels is illustrated in Figure 4.7.

For some reason which Sun have not made clear, multiplexing must be used in conjunction with non-blocking I/O.[10]

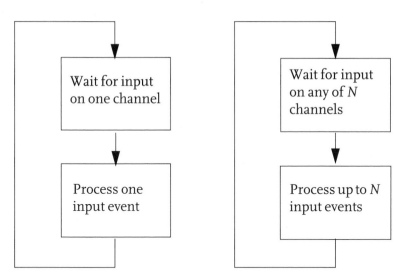

FIGURE 4.7. Blocking I/O *vs.* multiplexing

Multiplexing is familiar to Berkeley Sockets and W I N S O C K programmers as the *select*() API, and to Unix System V 'streams' programmers as the *poll*() API.

4.5.1 *Multiplexing and scalability*

Multiplexing provides the scalability in the Java new I/O subsystem. Instead of using blocking I/O, requiring one thread per channel, an application can use non-blocking I/O and multiplexing to manage multiple channels in a single thread. This approach scales much better when the number N of of simultaneously open channels is large, say in the hundreds or thousands, because it reduces the number of threads required from N to N/M where M is the number of channels managed by each thread. M can be adjusted within the application as required to suit its mix of resource constraints and its requirements for responsiveness.

---

10. Up to the latest J D K 1.5. This semantic restriction seems unnecessary. All Java platforms I am acquainted with support multiplexing in blocking mode via the Berkeley Sockets *select*() A P I. The W I N S O C K *WSAAsyncSelect()* and *WSAEventSelect()* APIs require non-blocking mode, and one of these seems to be used by the J D K 1.4 Win32 implementation, which if true would explain both the semantic restriction and BugId 4628289 on the Bug Parade. Fixing the bug would also appear to make it possible to remove the semantic constraint.

We will see server and client architectures for exploiting multiplexing in Chapter 12.

4.5.2 *Classes for multiplexing*

In Java, I/O multiplexing is done with the Selector class, the SelectionKey class, and channel classes derived from SelectableChannel.

As shown in Figure 4.1, and as we have just seen in section 4.4, classes derived from SelectableChannel include DatagramChannel, Pipe.SinkChannel, Pipe.SourceChannel, ServerSocketChannel, and SocketChannel.

4.5.3 *The Selector class*

The heart of I/O multiplexing is the Selector class, which exports methods for opening and closing a selector:

```
class Selector
{
  static Selector open()    throws IOException;
  boolean         isOpen();
  void            close()   throws IOException;
}
```

Once a selector is obtained, any selectable channel can be *registered* with it:

```
class SelectableChannel extends Channel
{
  boolean        isRegistered();
  SelectionKey   register
    (Selector selector, int  operations)
                throws ClosedChannelException;
  SelectionKey   register(Selector selector, int operations,
                      Object attachment)
                throws ClosedChannelException;
}
```

The operations parameter specifies the *interest set*: a bit-mask of the I/O operations of interest, whose values are defined in the SelectionKey class:

```
class SelectionKey
{
  static final int  OP_ACCEPT;
  static final int  OP_CONNECT;
```

```
static final int  OP_READ;
static final int  OP_WRITE;
}
```

For example, registering for OP_READ and OP_WRITE can be done thus:

```
Selector   sel = Selector.open();
channel.register
  (sel, SelectionKey.OP_READ|SelectionKey.OP_WRITE);
```

The valid values for the operations parameter can be obtained from the channel via the validOps method:

```
class SelectableChannel extends Channel
{
  int   validOps();
}
```

However you should *not* code as follows:

```
Selector   sel = Selector.open();
channel.register(sel, channel.validOps());
```

especially in a server. A server is not interested in OP_CONNECT and should not register for it. The validOps of a SocketChannel always include OP_CONNECT, even for a SocketChannel resulting from ServerSocketChannel.accept. Such a SocketChannel is already connected and OP_CONNECT will therefore always be ready. This will cause Selector.select to return immediately and probably hard-loop. Further, in either clients or servers, as discussed in in section 5.3, you should never register for OP_CONNECT and OP_WRITE at the same time, or for OP_ACCEPT and OP_READ at the same time.

Selectable I/O operations are discussed further in section 4.5.4. Selection keys are discussed in section 4.5.5. The optional attachment parameter is described in section 4.5.6.

A channel can be registered with an empty *interest set, i.e.* an operations parameter of zero. Such a channel is never selected. The interest set of a channel's registration key can be modified at any time by calling the SelectionKey.interestOps method. This affects the *next* selection operation discussed in the next subsection. On some platforms this method is synchronized against concurrent executions of Selector.select and friends, and it has been found best to call it only from the same thread that calls Selector.select.

4.5.4 *Selectable I/O operations*

Registering a channel means wanting to be notified when the channel becomes ready for one or more types of I/O operation. A channel is *ready* for an I/O operation if the operation *would not block* if performed in blocking mode, or, in non-blocking mode, if it *would not* return a zero, false, or null result.[11] It might return a result indicating success, or some failure condition such as end-of-stream; or it might throw an exception.

Obviously, 'would not block', 'would not return zero' etc. can only mean 'would not have blocked, returned zero, etc *if it had been executed at the time the select method returned*'. Computers cannot predict the future. If another thread operates on the socket immediately after the select call, the ready status resulting from the select may no longer be valid. Robust network programs must deal correctly with zero, false, or null results from I/O operations, even if the select method selected them as ready.

The selectable I/O operations and their meanings when ready are specified in Table 4.4.

TABLE 4.4 Selectable I/O operations

Name	Meaning when ready
OP_ACCEPT	ServerSocketChannel.accept would not return null.
OP_CONNECT	SocketChannel.finishConnect would not return false.
OP_READ	A read operation on the channel would not return zero.
OP_WRITE	A write operation on the channel would not return zero.

Further information about these operations is given for TCP in Table 5.1, and for UDP in Table 10.1.

4.5.5 *Selection keys*

The result returned by SelectableChannel.register is a SelectionKey, which is simply a representation of the registration. This design allows a channel to be registered with more than one selector: each registration produces a unique registration key, which can be used to cancel the registration without affecting other registrations of the same channel with other selectors.

The SelectionKey class exports the manifest constants shown in section 4.5.4, and exports the following methods:

---

11. Berkeley Sockets and WINSOCK programmers will recognize this as the EWOULDBLOCK and WSAEWOULDBLOCK conditions respectively.

```
class SelectionKey
{
    // return the channel whose registration produced this key
    SelectableChannel  channel();

    // return the selector which produced this key
    Selector           selector();

    // return the operations-of-interest set
    int                interestOps();

    // return the set of operations which are now ready
    int                readyOps();

    boolean            isAcceptable();    // OP_ACCEPT ready
    boolean            isConnectable();   // OP_CONNECT ready
    boolean            isReadable();      // OP_READ ready
    boolean            isWritable();      // OP_WRITE ready

    // Alter the operations-of-interest set
    SelectionKey       interestOps(int ops);

    // cancel the registration
    void               cancel();
    boolean            isValid();   // ⇒ not closed/cancelled

    // get/set the attachment
    Object             attachment();
    Object             attach(Object object);
}
```

4.5.6 Selection key attachments

A selection key 'attachment' essentially provides an application-defined context object for the key and channel. It is an arbitrary object which remains associated with the selection key which results from the registration, and which can be set, unset, and retrieved subsequently:

```
class SelectionKey
{
    Object attachment();                // get the attachment
    Object attachment(Object object);   // set the attachment
}
```

The attachment setter method attaches an object to the key in the same way as the third parameter to SelectableChannel.register described above. An object can be detached by attaching either another object or null. The method returns the previous attachment if any, otherwise null.

4.5.7 *The select operation*

The primary multiplexing operation is the select method of the Selector class, which comes in three forms:

```
class Selector
{
  int   select()                 throws IOException;
  int   select(long timeout)     throws IOException;
  int   selectNow()              throws IOException;
}
```

These methods select channels which are ready for at least one of the I/O operations in their interest set (defined in section 4.5.3). For example, a channel registered with an interest set of {OP_READ} is selected when a read operation would not return zero; a channel registered with an interest set of {OP_WRITE} is ready when a write operation would not return zero; a channel registered with an interest set of {OP_READ, OP_WRITE} is ready when *either* a read method or a write method would not return zero.

The selectNow method does not block. The select method with no arguments blocks until at least one channel is selected or the selector is woken up asynchronously with the Selector.wakeup method. The select(long timeout) method blocks until at least one channel is selected, the selector is woken up asynchronously with the Selector.wakeup method, or the timeout period expires, where timeout is either a positive number of milliseconds or zero, indicating an infinite wait as in select with no arguments.

The select operation adds the keys of channels which have become ready to the *selected-key set*, and returns the number of channels which have become ready, *i.e.* the number of keys selected: this may be zero.

The set of registered keys and the current set of selected keys are returned by the methods:

```
class Selector
{
  Set   keys();              // currently registered keys
  Set   selectedKeys();      // currently selected keys
}
```

The selected channels are obtained via the selected-keys set, and can be processed individually as shown in the following example:

```
Selector    selector = Selector.open();
channel.register(selector, channel.validOps());
int         selectedCount = selector.select();
Iterator    it = selector.selectedKeys().iterator();
```

```
while (it.hasNext())
{
  SelectionKey          key = (SelectionKey)it.next();
  it.remove();
  SelectableChannel     selCh = key.channel();
  if (key.isAcceptable())
    handleAcceptable(key);    // not shown …
  if (key.isConnectable())
    handleConnectable(key);   // not shown …
  if (key.isReadable())
    handleReadable(key);      // not shown …
  if (key.isWritable())
    handleWritable(key);      // not shown …
}
```

Note that the application must remove each SelectionKey from the selected-key set, otherwise it will show up again next time after Selector.select or Selector.selectNow returns, because the selector never clears the selected-keys set. As long as this practice is followed, the size of the selected-key set is the same as the value returned by the select operation:

$$\text{selector.select(...)} == \text{selector.selectedKeys().size()} \qquad (\text{EQ } 4.5)$$

$$\text{selector.selectNow()} == \text{selector.selectedKeys().size()} \qquad (\text{EQ } 4.6)$$

Leaving a key in the selected-key set would only make sense if the key wasn't processed on this iteration, *i.e.* the associated I/O operation was skipped for some reason; this might occur if one iteration was devoted solely to I/O and a separate iteration with a different priority was devoted to accepting connections. However, in such a case it would make more sense to use multiple selectors.

The selected-key set is *partially* immutable. Although keys can be removed from the selected-key set as shown, keys cannot be explicitly added to it. Only Selector.select and Selector.selectNow may add keys to the selected-key set. If the application attempts to do so, an UnsupportedOperationException is thrown.

4.5.8 *Selection and timeouts*

If the select operation returns a result of zero, one or more of the following have occurred:

(a) The timeout specified has expired.

(b) The selector was woken up asynchronously (see section 4.6.4).

(c) A registered key was cancelled asynchronously (see section 4.6.5).

When the selection result is zero, the set of selected keys is empty, so the following invariant holds:

```
selector.selectedKeys().size() == 0;
```

and nothing of interest has occurred to any of the registered channels. *If and only if* we can assume no asynchronous operations, the channels have all timed out. In this case, the set of timed-out channels is the entire set of registered channels, which is available via the set of registered keys returned by the keys method, and can be processed for timeout individually as shown below.

```
int   selectedCount = selector.select(TIMEOUT);
if (selectedCount > 0)    // process ready channels
{
  Iterator   readyKeys =
    selector.selectedKeys().iterator();
  while (readyKeys.hasNext())
  {
    SelectionKey        readyKey =
      (SelectionKey)it.next():
    it.remove();
    SelectableChannel   readyChannel = readyKey.channel();
    // 'readyChannel' is ready …
  }
}
else // timeout
// Precondition: no asynchronous operations
{
  // process idle channels
  Iterator   it = selector.keys().iterator();
  while (it.hasNext())
  {
    SelectionKey        key = (SelectionKey)it.next();
    SelectableChannel   idleChannel = key.channel();
    // 'idleChannel' has timed out - process it …
  }
}
```

This technique is simple but flawed. First, the precondition may not hold: the assumption of no asynchronous operations may be invalid. Second, the selection operation may not return zero frequently enough for timely processing of idle channels. If even one channel become ready in each timeout period, the timeout block is *never* executed, and any timeouts on the remaining channels are never processed.

We need a technique which works for any return value of Selector.select, and which allows for asynchronous wakeups. In general, we cannot assume that the selection operation has blocked for the entire timeout period. We must keep track of elapsed time explicitly:

```
long timeout    = 180*1000L;
long startTime  = System.currentTimeMillis();
int  selectCount= selector.select(timeout);
long endTime    = System.currentTimeMillis();
```

As Selector.select may not have returned zero, we cannot assume as we did before that all registered channels were idle. The idle channels are obtained from the set-algebraic difference of the set of registered keys and the set of selected keys, as follows:

```
// copy registered keys
Set idleKeys = new HashSet(selector.keys());
// subtract ready keys
idleKeys.removeAll(selector.selectedKeys());
// now iterate over idle keys,
// calling SelectionKey.channel() on each …
```

Obviously we had to copy the registered-key set to form the set of idle keys, rather than modifying the set directly. In fact the registered-key set returned by Selector.keys is immutable: the only way to remove a key from the set is to cancel its registration with SelectionKey.cancel.

Note also that the registered-key set is not thread-safe, and therefore neither is the clone; neither is the selected-key set; neither is a HashSet. We can make a thread-safe set from any set if necessary:

```
idleKeys = Collections.synchronizedSet(idleKeys);
```

If we are just using timeouts to detect channels which have gone idle for any reason, without being interested in strict enforcement of timeout periods, *i.e.* if we don't mind idle channels being unprocessed for longer periods than the timeout, we could use an increased timeout value and an 'idle-threshold' equal to the original timeout:

```
long threshold  = 60*1000L;
long timeout    = threshold*3;
```

and process channels which have remained idle for the threshold period:

```
long elapsedTime = endTime - startTime;
if (elapsedTime > threshold)
{
  // ...
}
```

The complete selection process with this method of timeout processing looks something like this:

```
static final long   THRESHOLD = 60*1000L;// 60 seconds
static final long   TIMEOUT = THRESHOLD*3;
Selector selector = Selector.open();
// ...
long startTime  = System.currentTimeMillis();
int  readyCount = selector.select(TIMEOUT);
long endTime    = System.currentTimeMillis();
long elapsed    = endTime - startTime;
// process ready channels
Iterator readyKeys = selector.selectedKeys().iterator();
while (readyKeys.hasNext())
{
  SelectionKeyreadyKey = (SelectionKey)it.next():
  it.remove();
  SelectableChannelreadyCh = readyKey.channel();
  // 'readyCh' is ready.
  // ...
}
if (elapsed >= THRESHOLD)
{
  // Process idle channels
  Set        idleKeys = (Set)selector.keys().clone();
  idleKeys.removeAll(selectedKeys);
  Iterator   it = idleKeys.iterator();
  while (it.hasNext())
  {
    SelectableChannel   idleCh =
      (SelectableChannel)it.next();
    // 'idleCh' has been idle for >= THRESHOLD ms ...
  }
}
```

The threshold technique is still not really good enough. The select operation may still return too frequently for the threshold ever to to be triggered. We can tune the timeout/threshold ratio to reduce this problem, but we cannot eliminate it. If we must process idle channels with 100% reliability, or enforce timeouts strictly, we need a solution along these lines:

(a) Each registered channel is associated with an idle-time, initially zero.

(b) After each selection operation, clear the idle-time of all *ready* channels, and scan all *non-ready* channels adding the elapsed time calculated above to their idle-time: a channel has timed out if its idle-time equals or exceeds the time-out value.

The elaboration of this scheme is left as an exercise for the reader.

4.6 CONCURRENT CHANNEL OPERATIONS

The design of 'new I/O' allows for multiple threads to operate on channels simultaneously. A channel may be read by multiple threads simultaneously; may be written by multiple threads simultaneously; and may be simultaneously read to and written from. A selector may be operated on by multiple threads simultaneously. I/O operations on certain channels can be interrupted. Selection operations can be interrupted or woken up.

4.6.1 Concurrent reading and writing

Multiple threads can read from and write to the same channel.

If a concurrent read operation is in progress on a channel, a new read operation on the channel blocks until the first operation is complete. Similarly, if a concurrent write operation is in progress on a channel, a new write operation on the channel blocks until the first operation is complete. In both cases, this occurs *regardless* of the blocking mode of the channel, because the block is enforced by Java object synchronization rather than by the underlying I/O system.

A channel may or may not support concurrent reading and writing: if it does, a read operation and a write operation may or may not proceed concurrently (without blocking), depending on the type of the channel.[12]

However, as we saw in section 4.3.12, buffers are not thread-safe. Concurrent I/O operations on a channel can only use the same buffer if appropriate synchronization is performed, *e.g.* by synchronizing on the buffer itself.

---

12. Socket channels support concurrent reading and writing without blocking; file channels support it with blocking which is partially platform-dependent.

4.6.2 Interrupts

As described in section 4.2.2, a thread which is blocked in a read or write operation on a channel which implements the InterruptibleChannel interface may be interrupted by calling the Thread.interrupt method.

A thread which is blocked in a select operation on a Selector may be interrupted by calling the Thread.interrupt method.

The semantics of interrupts for InterruptibleChannels and Selectors are different: see Table 4.5.

4.6.3 Asynchronous closure

An interruptible channel can be closed asynchronously. Any thread blocked in a read or write operation on the closed channel is thrown an AsynchronousCloseException. If any selection operation including the closed channel is in progress, see section 4.6.5.

Similarly, if a selector is closed asynchronously, any thread blocked in a select operation on a Selector behaves as though woken up as described in section 4.6.4, with the exception that the closure can be detected by a false result from Selector.isOpen.

The semantics of asynchronous closure for InterruptibleChannels and Selectors are different: see Table 4.5.

4.6.4 Wakeup

A selection operation can be 'woken up' asynchronously by the Selector.wakeup method. If any threads are concurrently blocked in the selection operation on that selector, the thread which *first* blocked returns immediately. Otherwise, wakeup causes the *next* selection operation to return immediately, regardless of timeout value, including Selector.selectNow (which does not block).

The effect of wakeup is cleared by any selection operation including Selector.selectNow. To express this in Java, the following returns immediately:

```
selector.wakeup();
selector.select(timeout);// no block here
```

but the following blocks:

```
selector.wakeup();
selector.selectNow();
selector.select(timeout);// blocks here
```

(assuming no concurrent operations on the selector). In either case, the return value of the selection operation and the selected-key set of the selector reflect the status of the operation at the time it returned: in particular, the return value may be zero or non-zero and the selected-key set may be correspondingly empty or non-empty. If the return value is non-zero, there is *no way* for the woken-up thread to detect that wakeup was called; if the return value is zero, the woken-up thread can detect the wakeup by comparing the elapsed time to the specified timeout value, as described in section 4.5.8: if *elapsed < timeout*,[13] the selector has been woken up.

Invoking the wakeup method more than once between selection operations has the same effect as invoking it once, *i.e.* it sets a boolean status: this status is cleared by any selection operation.

For the remaining semantics of the *wakeup* operation, see Table 4.5.

TABLE 4.5 Semantics of asynchronous operations

Blocking operation	Asynchronous operation	Semantics
read or write on an InterruptibleChannel	Thread.interrupt	The channel is closed. Channel.isOpen == false. The blocked thread is thrown a ClosedByInterruptException.[a] Thread.isInterrupted == true.
	close on an InterruptibleChannel	The channel is closed. Channel.isOpen == false. The blocked thread is thrown an AsynchronousCloseException. Thread.isInterrupted == false.
Selector.select[b]	Thread.interrupt	Selector.wakeup is called. The selector is not closed. Selector.isOpen == true. The blocked thread returns immediately. Thread.isInterrupted == true.
	Selector.close	Selector.wakeup is called. The selector is closed. Selector.isOpen == false. The blocked thread returns immediately. Thread.isInterrupted == false.

13. That is, if *elapsed* is *significantly* less than *timeout*, allowing for granularity in the timers, scheduling delays, *etc.* For the same reasons, if no channels become ready and no asynchronous selector operations occur, the elapsed time will normally be *at least* the specified timeout value, depending on the characteristics of the underlying platform.

TABLE 4.5 Semantics of asynchronous operations (continued)

Blocking operation	Asynchronous operation	Semantics
	Selector.wakeup	The selector is not closed. Selector.isOpen == true. The first of any blocked threads returns immediately with Thread.isInterrupted == false. If there are no blocked threads, the *next* select operation returns immediately.

a. N.B. not an InterruptedIOException or an InterruptedException, which may surprise.

b. Although Selector supports interrupt and asynchronous-close semantics, it does *not* implement InterruptibleChannel. Firstly, it isn't a Channel. Second, its semantics for these operations are different, as shown in the table.

4.6.5 Concurrency and selectors

While a select operation is in progress, all sort of actions relevant to it can be performed concurrently: channels can be registered or closed, or their registrations with the selector can be modified or cancelled. This is described at length in the J D K online documentation in terms of mechanism: the following describes the semantics.

A new channel may be *registered* with a Selector while a select operation is in progress. Similarly, the registration can be *modified*, *i.e.* the interest-operation set of a selection key can be changed, while a select operation is in progress. In both cases, the change is not taken into account in the current select operation, but becomes effective in the *next* select operation.

A registration, *i.e.* a selection key, may be *cancelled*, or its channel closed, while a select operation is in progress. Such a key will not be included in the selected-set or counted in the return value of the select operation. The select operation may return a zero value: as we saw in section 4.5.8, this cannot safely be taken to imply that the timeout period has expired.

However, regardless of these semantics of the selection operation itself, a selection key may be cancelled or its channel closed at any time, so the presence of any key in any of a selector's key sets cannot be taken to imply that the key is valid or that its channel open. Applications which perform asynchronous processing must be careful to synchronize their operations on key sets, and to check the SelectionKey.isValid condition (which implies the Channel.isOpen condition) when processing selection keys. For example:

```
int        selectedCount = selector.select();
Set        selectedKeys = selector.selectedKeys();
// Synchronize on the set of selected keys.
```

```
// Any asynchronous operations on the selector or set
// must also synchronize on the set …
synchronized (selectedKeys)
{
  Iterator   it = selectedKeys.iterator();
  while (it.hasNext())
  {
    SelectionKeykey = (SelectionKey)it.next();
    it.remove();
    // Check for asynchronous close or cancel
    if (!key.isValid())
      continue;
    // …
  }
}
```

As remarked in section 4.5.4, if parallel operations on a channel are in progress, it cannot be assumed that a channel is ready even though a selector has selected it: the ready state may already have been dealt with by another thread between the return from Selector.select and the processing of the channel. Processing of ready channels must be robust—must cope with the possibility of a channel read or write returning zero (*i.e.* doing nothing), or an accept or connect operation returning null.

4.6.6 WIN 32 and JDK 1.4.0

Multiplexing in J D K 1.4.0 for W I N 3 2 platforms is broken:

(a) Selector.select doesn't wake up every time a channel becomes ready, only the first time.

(b) Sometimes a selection key is reported as being updated when it is really just a key already in the selected set that is still ready.

(c) There is a limit of 63 registered channels per Selector.

See the Java Developer Connection Bug Parade, bug IDs 4469394, 4530007, and 4503092. Some of these problems are corrected in J D K 1.4.1, and the feature appears to work as advertised in 1.4.2 and subsequent versions of the J D K.

4.7 EXCEPTIONS IN NEW I/O

The exceptions that can arise during operations on channels and buffers, and their meanings, are listed in Table 4.6.

TABLE 4.6 Exceptions in new I/O

Name	Meaning	
AlreadyConnectedException	Thrown by SocketChannel.connect if the channel is already connected.	U
AsynchronousCloseException	Thrown by any blocking operation on a channel when it is closed by another thread.	C
BufferOverflowException	Thrown by any relative Buffer.put operation if the buffer's limit is reached.	U
BufferUnderflowException	Thrown by any relative Buffer.get operation if the buffer's limit is reached.	U
CancelledKeyException	Thrown by any attempt to use a cancelled SelectionKey.	U
CharacterCodingException	Thrown when a character encoding or decoding error occurs.	C
ClosedByInterruptException	Thrown by a blocking operation on a channel if the invoking thread is interrupted by another thread with Thread.interrupt. The channel is now closed, and Thread.isInterrupted is true of the thread which receives the exception. Not thrown by FileChannel.lock: see FileLockInterruptionException.	C
ClosedChannelException	Thrown by any channel operation if the channel is already closed, or by SocketChannel.write if the socket has been shutdown for output, or SocketChannel.read if the socket has been shutdown for input.[a]	C
ClosedSelectorException	Thrown by any method of Selector if the selector has been closed.	U
ConnectionPendingException	Thrown by SocketChannel.connect if the channel already has a pending connecting.	U
FileLockInterruptionException	Thrown by FileChannel.lock if the invoking thread is interrupted by another thread (with Thread.interrupt); Thread.isInterrupted is true of the thread which receives the exception.	C

TABLE 4.6 Exceptions in new I/O (continued)

Name	Meaning	
IllegalBlockingModeException	Thrown by any blocking-mode-specific operation on a channel if the channel is not in the correct mode, *e.g.* read and write on a stream obtained from the channel if the channel is in non-blocking mode.	U
IllegalCharsetNameException	Thrown when using a charset name of illegal format, as defined in the J D K documentation.	U
IllegalSelectorException	Thrown by SelectableChannel.register if the channel and selector weren't created by the same SelectorProvider.[b]	U
InvalidMarkException	Thrown by any reset operation on a Buffer if the mark is undefined.	U
MalformedInputException	Thrown when an input byte sequence is not legal for a given charset, or an input character sequence is not a legal 16-bit Unicode sequence.	C
NoConnectionPendingException	Thrown by SocketChannel.finishConnect if no connection is pending, *i.e.* if SocketChannel.connect has not been called successfully.	U
NonReadableChannelException	Thrown by any read method on a channel not opened for reading.	U
NonWritableChannelException	Thrown by any write method on a channel not opened for writing.	U
NotYetBoundException	Thrown by any I/O operation on a ServerSocketChannel which has not been bound to a local port.	U
NotYetConnectedException	Thrown by any I/O operation on a SocketChannel which has not been connected.	U
OverlappingFileLockException	Thrown by FileChannel.lock or FileChannel.tryLock if the specified region overlaps a region which is either already locked by the same J V M or which another thread in the same J V M is already waiting to lock.	C

Table 4.6 Exceptions in new I/O (continued)

Name	Meaning	
ReadOnlyBufferException	Thrown by any read, put or compact operation, *i.e.* any operation which mutates the content as opposed to just the *mark, position,* or *limit,* on a Buffer which is read-only.	U
UnmappableCharacterException	Thrown when an input character (or byte) sequence is valid but cannot be mapped to an output byte (or character) sequence.	C
UnresolvedAddressException	Thrown by any attempt to use an unresolved socket address for a network operation (*e.g.* bind or connect, as opposed to a local operation).	U
UnsupportedAddressTypeException	Thrown by any attempt to bind or connect to a socket address of an unsupported type.	U
UnsupportedCharsetException	Thrown when no support is available for a requested charset.	U

a. This may surprise Berkeley Sockets and WINSOCK programmers, who are used to read operations returning an EOF condition if the socket has been shutdown for input.

b. This provider class is found in the package java.nio.channels.spi. This exception can only happen if you are using a non-default NIO provider. Providers and Service Provider Interfaces of all kinds are for service implementors and are beyond the scope of this book.

In this table, the right-hand column has 'C' for checked exceptions and 'U' for unchecked exceptions (*i.e.* exceptions derived directly or indirectly from java.lang.RuntimeException, which are not checked by the Java compiler as being caught or thrown by methods in which they can occur).

CHAPTER 5

Scalable *T C P*

IN THIS CHAPTER we discuss Java NIO —scalable I/O—as applied to TCP.

5.1 CHANNELS FOR TCP

Scalable I/O over TCP is performed with the ServerSocketChannel and SocketChannel classes we encountered in passing in section 4.2.1.

Like all channels, these channels are intially created in blocking mode.

5.1.1 *Import statements*

The following Java import statements are assumed in the examples throughout this chapter.

```
import java.io.*;
import java.net.*;
import java.nio.*;
import java.nio.channels.*;
import java.nio.channels.spi.*;
import java.util.*;
```

5.1.2 *ServerSocketChannel*

The ServerSocketChannel class provides channel I/O for server sockets:

```
class ServerSocketChannel
{
  static ServerSocketChannel open()    throws IOException;
```

```
  ServerSocket              socket() throws IOException;
  SocketChannel             accept() throws IOException;
}
```

ServerSocketChannels are created, and the associated ServerSocket can be obtained, as follows:

```
ServerSocketChannel channel  = ServerSocketChannel.open();
ServerSocket        serverSocket = channel.socket();
```

The associated server socket is created unbound, and must be bound with the ServerSocket.bind method described in section 3.3.7 before being used for any network operation.

The accept method corresponds to the method ServerSocket.accept, with two differences:

(a)   It returns a SocketChannel rather than a Socket.

(b)   It can be executed in non-blocking mode, in which case it can return null if no incoming connection is available.

We *must* use ServerSocketChannel.accept rather than ServerSocket.accept under the following circumstances:

(a)   If we are performing the accept operation in non-blocking mode, or

(b)   if we intend to perform non-blocking channel operations on the accepted socket.

5.1.3 SocketChannel

Similarly, the SocketChannel class provides channel I/O for sockets:

```
class SocketChannel
{
  static SocketChannel  open()
    throws IOException;
  static SocketChannel  open(SocketAddress address)
    throws IOException;
  Socket                socket()
    throws IOException;
}
```

SocketChannels are created, and the associated Socket obtained, as follows:

```
SocketChannel  channel= SocketChannel.open(...)
Socket          socket = channel.socket();
```

If the no-argument form of the open method is used, the associated socket is created unconnected, otherwise the socket is created and connected to the remote SocketAddress specified. For example:

```
String host = "localhost";
int    port = 7; // echo port
SocketAddress address =
  new InetSocketAddress(host, port);
SocketChannelchannel = SocketChannel.open(address);
```

5.2 TCP CHANNEL OPERATIONS

As we saw in section 5.1, a SocketChannel is created in blocking mode. It can be put into non-blocking mode using:

```
class SocketChannel
{
  SelectableChannel configureBlocking(boolean block)
    throws IOException;
  boolean            isBlocking();
}
```

where blocking is true for blocking mode and false for non-blocking mode.

An unconnected TCP channel can be connected to a target with the SocketChannel.connect method:

```
class SocketChannel
{
  boolean  connect(SocketAddress address)
    throws IOException;
  boolean  isConnected();
  boolean  isConnectionPending();
  boolean  finishConnect()
    throws IOException;
}
```

The isConnected method tells whether the *local* socket has been connected to the target yet: it doesn't tell anything about the other end of the connection, as discussed in section 3.4.10.

The isConnectionPending and finishConnect methods are mainly used in non-blocking mode as described in section 5.2.2.

5.2.1 *Blocking* TCP *connection*

If the channel being connected is in *blocking* mode:

(a) The connect method blocks until the connection is complete or has been refused, i.e. is equivalent to calling Socket.connect with an unspecified or infinite timeout.

(b) The finishConnect method need not be called: it returns true immediately if the channel is connected, or throws a NoConnectionPending if the channel is not connected.

(c) The isConnectionPending method never returns true.

5.2.2 *Non-blocking* TCP *connection*

If the channel being connected is in *non-blocking* mode:

(a) The connect method immediately returns true if the connection can be made immediately, as sometimes happens with a local connection; otherwise, it returns false and the connection must be completed later with the finishConnect method, while the connection protocol continues asynchronously.

(b) The finishConnect method returns true if the connection has been completed successfully; returns false if it is still pending; or throws an IOException if the connection could not be made for any reason: most commonly, the connection was refused by the remote target because nothing was listening at the specified port, which is manifested as a ConnectException.

(c) The isConnectionPending method returns true if connect has been called but finishConnect has not yet been called, otherwise false.[1]

Relating this to the TCP connection protocol, finishConnect returns false and isConnectionPending returns true until the SYN/ACK segment has been received from the server, as shown in the sequence diagram of Figure 5.1.

A simple non-blocking TCP client connect operation is illustrated in Example 5.1.

```
SocketAddress address =
  new InetSocketAddress("localhost",7);
SocketChannel channel = SocketChannel.open();
channel.configureBlocking(false);
if (!channel.connect(address))
```

---

1. That is, it does *not* try to predict the result of finishConnect.

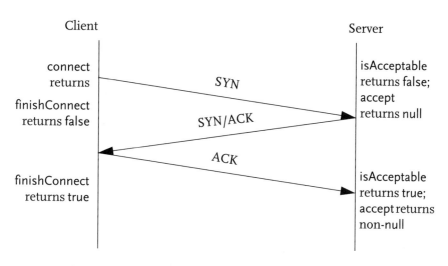

FIGURE 5.1. TCP segment exchanges for non-blocking connect

```
{
    // connection was not instantaneous, still pending
    while (!channel.finishConnect())
    {
        // connection still incomplete: do something useful ...
    }
}
```

EXAMPLE 5.1 Simple non-blocking TCP client connection

5.2.3 Read operation

In blocking mode, a TCP channel read blocks until *at least some* data is available, although not necessarily the amount of data requested.

In non-blocking mode, a TCP channel read never blocks. If the connection has been closed by either end, or shutdown for reading at this end, an exception is thrown. If data is present in the socket receive-buffer, that data is returned, up to the amount requested or the data's own size, whichever is smaller. If no data is present, the operation does nothing and returns zero.

If no exception is thrown, the return value indicates how much data was read, possibly zero.

5.2.4 *Write operation*

In blocking mode, a TCP channel write blocks until *at least some* space is available in the socket send-buffer, although not necessarily the amount of space required by the data written.

> How much space? Most TCP implementations support a 'low-water mark' which by default is 2KB: a write only transfers data if at least this much space is available in the send buffer. The low-water mark, even if supported by the TCP implementation, cannot be controlled from Java as at JDK 1.5.

In non-blocking mode, a TCP channel write never blocks. If the connection has been closed by either end, or shutdown for writing at this end, an exception is thrown. If space is available in the socket send-buffer, data is transferred up to the amount specified or space available, whichever is less. If space is unavailable the operation does nothing and returns zero.

If no exception is thrown, the return value indicates how much data was written, possibly zero.

A simple non-blocking TCP I/O sequence is illustrated in Example 5.2.

```
ByteBuffer      buffer = ByteBuffer.allocate(8192);
SocketChannel  channel;// initialization as in Example 5.1
channel.configureBlocking(false);
buffer.put(...);
buffer.flip();
while (channel.write(buffer) == 0)
  ; // do something useful ...
buffer.clear();
while (channel.read(buffer) == 0)
  ; // do something useful ...
```

EXAMPLE 5.2 Simple non-blocking TCP client I/O

As the comments say, the programs should be doing useful work, or at least sleeping, instead of spinning mindlessly while the connection is incomplete in Example 5.1 or the I/O transfers return zero in Example 5.2.

5.2.5 *Close operation*

A SocketChannel is closed via the close method:

```
class SocketChannel
{
  void    close() throws IOException;
}
```

However, the documentation of SelectableChannel, the base class of SocketChannel and ServerSocketChannel (and DatagramChannel), rather obscurely states:

> 'Once registered with a selector, a channel remains registered until it is deregistered. This involves deallocating whatever resources were allocated to the channel by the selector.

> A channel cannot be deregistered directly; instead, the key representing its registration must be cancelled. Cancelling a key requests that the channel be deregistered during the selector's next selection operation.'

This means that closing a SelectableChannel which is currently registered is internally implemented in two phases:

1. An operation to prevents further operations on the channel, executed in the SelectableChannel.close method, which also cancels any keys associated with the channel, and

2. a deferred operation which really closes the socket: this takes place in the next execution of a Selector.selectXXX method on the appropriate Selector.

This is 'as intended',[2] but it can cause problems in TCP clients using non-blocking channel I/O. Generally, a client will exit its select loop after closing a channel, so phase 2 never occurs. The symptom of this behaviour is that the local socket stays in the CLOSE-WAIT state.[3] The simplest solution is to call Selector.selectNow immediately after closing the channel:

```
Selector      sel;
SocketChannel sch;
// ...
sch.close();
sel.selectNow();
```

Generally, there isn't a great deal of point in using non-blocking I/O in clients: it saves threads, but clients rarely deal with enough different servers (or connections) for it to be worth the trouble.

---

2. See Bug Parade id 5073504.

3. CLOSE-WAIT means that TCP is waiting for the local end to close the socket after a remote close has been received. See Appendix A: TCP port states.

5.3 Multiplexing in tcp

In addition to the OP_READ and OP_WRITE operations, multiplexing in tcp deals with 'readiness' of the OP_ACCEPT and OP_CONNECT operations. The selectable I/O operations supported by tcp are shown in Table 5.1.

Table 5.1 Selectable I/O operations in tcp

Operation	Meaning
OP_ACCEPT (ServerSocketChannel)	ServerSocketChannel.accept would not return null: either an incoming connection exists or an exception is pending.
OP_CONNECT (SocketChannel with connection pending)	SocketChannel.finishConnect would not return false: either the connection is complete apart from the finishConnect step or an exception is pending, typically a ConnectException.
OP_READ (connected SocketChannel)	read would not return zero: either data is present in the socket receive-buffer, end-of-stream has been reached, or an exception is pending. End-of-stream occurs if the remote end has closed the connection or shut it down for output, or if the local end has shut it down for input.[a]
OP_WRITE (connected SocketChannel)	write would not return zero: either space exists in the socket send-buffer, the connection has been closed or shutdown for input at the remote end,[b] or an exception is pending.

a. In addition to end-of-stream, the *javadoc* for java.nio.channels.SelectionKey.OP_READ up to jdk 1.4.2 redundantly specifies 'has been remotely shut down for further reading': this refers to a remote execution of Socket.shutdownOutput, which is already covered by the end-of-stream condition, as are the omitted cases of remote closure and local shutdown for input. See section 3.7.1 and section 3.7.2.

b. The *javadoc* for java.nio.channels.SelectionKey.OP_WRITE up to jdk 1.4.2 also specifies 'has been remotely shut down for further writing': this refers to a remote execution of Socket.shutdownInput, but be warned that the propagation of this effect is platform-dependent: see section 3.7.2.

In reality—in the underlying native *select()* api—there are not these four but only *two* events:

(a) A 'readable' event, which signals both the existence of data in the receive-buffer *and* the availability of an incoming connection to the accept method. In other words, under the covers, OP_ACCEPT and OP_READ are the same thing.

(b) A 'writable' event, which signals both the existence of space in the send-buffer *and* completion of a client Socket connection. In other words, under the covers OP_CONNECT and OP_WRITE are also the same thing, even more so than above, as both simply mean that space is available in the send-buffer—a condition which of course first occurs when the connection is complete.

The identity of OP_ACCEPT and OP_READ in Java presents no problem, as OP_ACCEPT is only valid on ServerSockets, for which OP_READ is invalid.

However, the identity of OP_CONNECT and OP_WRITE does cause problems. OP_CONNECT and OP_WRITE are both valid on client Sockets, so an ambiguity exists between these 'events': indeed some of the JDK 1.4 implementations mis-behave if you try to use both of OP_CONNECT and OP_WRITE at the same time. See for example Bug Parade bugs 4850373, 4960791, 4919127c. You must there-fore proceed as follows:

(a) Only use OP_CONNECT on unconnected sockets: OP_CONNECT must be removed from the interestOps as soon as it becomes ready for a channel.

(b) Only use OP_WRITE on connected sockets.

This confusion could have been avoided if Sun hadn't tried to distinguish events that are not distinct in their NIO specification.

Further, you should only use OP_WRITE when you have something to write *and* you've already failed to write it completely (by getting a short or zero-length result from a write method). Once the connection is complete, OP_WRITE is al-most always ready, except for the moments during which space is unavailable in the socket send-buffer. (This moment may be protracted if the remote end is slower at reading data than the local end is at writing it.)

It is only *useful* to select for OP_WRITE if you have data ready to be sent, and it is only *recommended* if you have also just encountered a short write on the chan-nel (*i.e.* the previous write operation didn't write the full amount requested).

In other words, you should assume that a connected channel is ready for writ-ing until you actually find that it isn't. Whenever you have nothing to write, or whenever a write operation succeeds completely, you should immediately stop selecting for OP_WRITE.

5.3.1 *Example*

A simple multiplexing TCP echo server is shown in the following example. This server never blocks in I/O, only in Selector.select. The server makes use of a key attachment to maintain a separate ByteBuffer per accepted connection. This is a simple example of a more general attachment technique for connection contexts which we will explore more fully in Chapter 12.

```
public class NIOEchoServer implements Runnable
{
  public static final int TIMEOUT= 5*1000;// 5s
  public static final int BUFFERSIZE= 8192;
```

```java
private ServerSocketChannel  serverChannel;

// Constructor
public NIOEchoServer(int port) throws IOException
{
  this.serverChannel = ServerSocketChannel.open();
  serverChannel.configureBlocking(false);
  serverChannel.socket().bind
    (new InetSocketAddress(port));
}

// Runnable.run method
public void run()
{
  try
  {
    Selector selector = Selector.open();
    serverChannel.register(selector,
      serverChannel.validOps());

    // loop while there are any registered channels
    while (selector.keys().size() > 0)
    {
      int keyCount = selector.select(TIMEOUT);
      Iterator selectedKeysIterator =
        selector.selectedKeys().iterator();
      // loop over selected keys
      while (selectedKeysIterator.hasNext())
      {
        SelectionKey key =
          (SelectionKey)selectedKeysIterator.next();
        // Remove from selected set and test validity
        it.remove();
        if (!key.isValid())
          continue;
        // dispatch:
        if (key.isAcceptable())
          handleAcceptable(key);
        if (key.isReadable())
          handleReadable(key);
        if (key.isWritable())
          handleWritable(key);
      } // end iteration
    } // end while selector.keys().size() > 0
```

```
    }
    catch (IOException e) { /*...*/ }
} // end run()

// handle acceptable key
void handleAcceptable(SelectionKey key)
{
  try
  {
    ServerSocketChannel srvCh =
      (ServerSocketChannel)key.channel();
    SocketChannel        channel = srvCh.accept();
    channel.configureBlocking(false);
    // allocate a buffer to the conversation
    ByteBuffer buffer =
      ByteBuffer.allocateDirect(BUFFERSIZE);
    // register the accepted channel for read,
    // with the buffer as the attachment
    channel.register
      (key.selector(), SelectionKey.OP_READ,buffer);
  }
  catch (IOException e)
  {
    /*...*/
  }
} // end handleAcceptable()

// handle readable key
void handleReadable(SelectionKey key)
{
  try
  {
    SocketChannel channel = (SocketChannel)key.channel();
    ByteBuffer      buffer = (ByteBuffer)key.attachment();
    int count = channel.read(buffer);
    // Echo input to output, assuming writability
    // (see Table 5.1)
    handleWritable();
    if (count < 0)
    {
      // EOF - flush remaining output and close.
      while (buffer.position() > 0)
      {
        buffer.flip();
        channel.write(buffer);
```

```
            buffer.compact();
          }
          key.cancel();
          channel.close();
        }
      }
      catch (IOException e)
      {
        /*...*/
      }
    } // end handleReadable()
    // handle writable key
    void handleWritable(SelectionKey key)
    {
      try
      {
        SocketChannel channel = (SocketChannel)key.channel();
        ByteBuffer      buffer = (ByteBuffer)key.attachment();
        buffer.flip();
        int count = channel.write(buffer);
        buffer.compact();
        // Register or deregister for OP_WRITE depending on
        // success of write operation (see Table 5.1).
        int ops = key.interestOps();
        if (buffer.hasRemaining())
          ops |= SelectionKey.OP_WRITE;
        else
          ops &= ~SelectionKey.OP_WRITE;
        key.interestOps(ops);
      }
      catch (IOException e)
      {
        /*...*/
      }
    } // end handleWritable()
} // end of NIOEchoServer
```

EXAMPLE 5.3 Simple multiplexing TCP echo server

CHAPTER 6   *Firewalls*

IN OUR DISCUSSIONS OF NETWORKS so far, we have omitted the topic of firewalls.[1] We have implicitly assumed only the existence of a TCP/IP local area network (LAN). This chapter describes the implications of deploying TCP and UDP servers over the Internet, or over large intranets containing firewalls. If you intend to develop applications which are to be deployed across such networks, you must read this chapter.[2]

From one point of view, the Internet is nothing but an extremely large TCP/IP wide area network (WAN). However, making the jump from a LAN to the Internet is not a trivial exercise. There are significant complications.

In order to prevent office-wide LANs becoming part of the global Internet, a 'firewall' is normally placed at the gateway between the LAN and the Internet proper. Like a physical firewall, an Internet firewall's purpose is to provide a high level of security to those on the protected side by preventing dangerous elements from entering, *i.e.* to block all except authorized communications between the Internet and the inner LAN.

Figure 6.1 shows a simple view of a firewall.

6.1 Types of firewall

Firewalls are of two types, usually paired together:

---

1. Parts of this chapter first appeared in Pitt & McNiff, *java.rmi: The Guide to Remote Method Invocation*, Addison Wesley 2001, and are used by permission.

2. The discussion is by no means intended to provide complete coverage of firewalls or network perimeter security techniques in general. This is a large topic. For further information, see Cheswick and Bellovin, Firewalls and Internet Security.

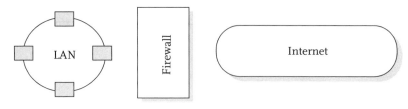

FIGURE 6.1. Simple view of firewall

(a)   Transport firewalls

(b)   Application firewalls.

6.1.1 *Transport firewalls*

Transport firewalls are generally hardware boxes. They only understand a general transport protocol, typically I P (including T C P and User Datagram Protocol (U D P)), and operate simply by allowing or disallowing connection requests based on the source and target I P address and port number.

Transport firewalls generally block all T C P and U D P ports except certain 'well-known' ones, such as S M T P (25), H T T P (80), P O P 3 (110), N N T P (119), S N M P (120), and I M A P (143). The ports for F T P (20–21) are sometimes blocked, sometimes not. Other well-known ports such as Telnet (23) are usually blocked.[3] 'Anonymous' application-defined ports (1024 and up) are generally blocked, including the ports for *rmid* (1098) and the R M I registry (1099), and all ports allocated by the R M I system for remote objects.

> F T P is the Internet File Transfer Protocol. S M T P is the Simple Mail Transfer Protocol used between e-mail servers. Telnet is a protocol and application suite which provides remote terminal access. P O P stands for the Post Office Protocol used by e-mail clients. N N T P is the Network News Transfer Protocol. I M A P is the Internet Message Access Protocol, an e-mail retrieval protocol used by e-mail clients. H T T P is the HyperText Transfer Protocol, the transport protocol associated with H T M L. It is the communications protocol observed between Web browsers and Web servers. It is not to be confused with H T M L itself, which is the page markup language of the World Wide Web, and which is transported via H T T P.

---

3. The 'well-known' ports for T C P are defined in R F C 1700, as amended.

6.1.2 *Application firewalls*

Application firewalls are also known as *proxies*. An application firewall understands a particular application protocol, such as FTP and HTTP, and interposes itself in the conversation between a client behind the transport firewall and a server outside it. To the client, it appears to be the server; to the real server, it appears to be the client. The application firewall ensures that what is going over the connection really is a conversation in the application protocol concerned, and it is controlled by an application-specific configuration which permits or denies access to the outside based on application-specific considerations.

Figure 6.2 illustrates the relationship between transport firewalls and application firewalls.

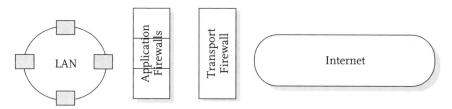

FIGURE 6.2. Application and transport firewalls

Transport firewalls generally restrict outgoing connections to those originated by an application firewall. An installation's total effective firewall consists of the transport firewall and all application firewalls.

6.1.3 HTTP *proxies*

The best-known type of application firewall is the HTTP proxy.

Applications such as Web browsers can be configured to send HTTP requests via an HTTP proxy server. The functions of the HTTP proxy server are *(i)* to ensure that the data is indeed HTTP requests and responses, *(ii)* to control which target sites and ports are allowed, and *(iii)* to forward the request to the target port. By this means, 'harmless' applications such as Web browsers can be configured to penetrate the firewall—as long as what is going through it really is HTTP.

The restriction to HTTP works because the HTTP proxy server really is a Web server, and only understands the HTTP protocol.

> HTTP proxies usually also provide a cache service for Web pages: this service is outside the scope of this discussion.

For the purpose of this discussion, HTTP proxy services either:

(a) allow HTTP to be sent to any port on the target host, or

(b)   allow H T T P to be sent only to the well-known H T T P port 80 on the target
      host.

Java clients can be configured to send H T T P requests via an H T T P proxy server,
by setting the system properties http.proxyHost and http.proxyPort. These properties control the operation in Java of java.net.URL and java.net.URLConnection objects having "http" as the protocol; they also control the operation of R M I clients,
as we shall see.

6.1.4 Firewall configuration and control

Firewall configurations are under the control of network administrators. In theory, network administrators can be persuaded to 'open' certain ports in order to
support specific application protocols such as C O R B A I I O P or Java R M I. In
practice, they are generally rather hard to convince about this: firewall policy crit-
ically affects corporate security.

6.2 S O C K S

S O C K S is the title of another 'peephole' through the firewall. Logically speaking,
a S O C K S server is a general-purpose application proxy, often called a 'S O C K S
proxy'. It provides a means of encapsulating an authenticated conversation between a known client inside the firewall and a S O C K S server at the firewall. It
permits the client to connect to a service outside the firewall on an arbitrary port,
while allowing the network administrator to control which clients may access
this service, and without exposing arbitrary client-side ports through the firewall.[4]

> The conversation between the client and the S O C K S server is authenticated. However,
> don't assume that this secures the conversation in any way. The conversation between
> the S O C K S server and the other end is not authenticated, and that is the part that takes
> place over the Internet.

Java clients which use java.net.Socket to connect to servers will automatically
conduct a S O C K S-based conversation if the system property socksProxyHost is set,
This means that Java clients can use S O C K S to get through their own firewalls
and communicate with servers in the public internet.

---

4. S O C K S v5 is specified in R F C 1928.

6.2.1 *Limitations of* SOCKS

SOCKS is an excellent solution for the client side. SOCKS can also be used within limits on the server side or for client-side callbacks, although server-side SOCKS is not supported in Java prior to JDK 1.4.0.

6.3 HTTP TUNNELLING

Most high-level protocols which attempt to solve the firewall issue use the 'HTTP tunnelling' technique, in which the communications are packaged inside HTTP requests and responses, and sent via the well-known HTTP port 80, which is normally left open in firewalls.

This is rather like enclosing a sealed addressed envelope inside another sealed addressed envelope, with the understanding that the inner envelope is to be posted to the inner addressee when received by the outer addressee (the recipient of the outer envelope). Consider the example of an over-supervised girl (Alice) trying to write to her boyfriend (Bob) when her outgoing mail is scrutinized by her parents. Alice seals a letter to her boyfriend inside a letter to an approved girlfriend (Tracey). The letter to Tracey gets through the parental "firewall", and Tracey posts the inner envelope to Bob on receipt.

HTTP tunnelling only works through firewalls with HTTP proxies.

6.3.1 *Limitations of* HTTP *tunnelling*

HTTP tunnelling is a client-side solution only:

(a) It cannot address the problem of a server behind its own firewall.

(b) It cannot handle client-side callbacks: servers outside a firewall cannot execute callbacks to clients located behind a firewall via SOCKS.

(c) It cannot address the problem of a server behind a firewall.

(d) An HTTP server must be present at the server end, and an HTTP proxy server is required at the client-side firewall.

6.4 JAVA SOLUTIONS

The solutions available via Java code are as follows:

(a) Set http.proxyHost and http.proxyPort to get HTTP tunnelling in RMI or HttpURLConnection.

(b) Set socksProxyHost and socksProxyPort to use a SOCKS proxy for a Socket.

(c) Use the J D K 1.5 java.net.Proxy class when constructing a Socket. This over-rides either of the above, and can provide either a direct connection, an H T T P tunnel, or a connection mediated by s o c k s. This technique makes for simpler programming when the actual firewall technique required is not known in advance.

6.5 NETWORK ADDRESS TRANSLATION

Network Address Translation, usually referred to as N A T, is a function present in many firewalls and routers, often in conjunction with D H C P (Dynamic Host Configuration Protocol). N A T is a technique for sharing a single I P address among multiple internal hosts. The N A T device presents a single I P address to the world outside it, and provides multiple I P addresses to the subnet it controls. N A T performs all the necessary address translation on I P, T C P, and U D P head-ers to allow hosts inside its subnet to communicate with hosts outside it. The outside hosts think they are communicating with the public ip address of the N A T device.

N A T works well, and pretty transparently, for T C P clients and U D P senders, as long as they don't attempt to provide their own I P addresses to hosts inside data payloads, as N A T doesn't attempt to rewrite payloads, not knowing anything about application protocols. Application protocols which do provide ip address information in payloads are therefore problematic within N A T-controlled sub-nets. Java R M I is one such example.

N A T can get in the way of T C P servers and U D P receivers operating within its subnet, as by default it won't have T C P listeners or U D P receivers operating at the ports involved. N A T devices can usually provide the required port-forwarding to make this work, but special configuration is required, and this is generally static: this means that use of dynamically-allocated port numbers for T C P listen-ers or U D P receivers is problematic within N A T-controlled subnets.

CHAPTER 7

Secure Sockets

THIS CHAPTER DISCUSSES secure sockets, which provide privacy and integrity for network communications.

Secure sockets appear in Java in the javax.net and javax.net.ssl packages, which were formerly known as the Java Secure Sockets Extension (JSSE).

We will examine the origins and current specifications of secure sockets; we will discuss the level of security they provide; and we will discuss their implementation and use in Java.

7.1 A BRIEF INTRODUCTION TO SECURITY

In brief, the security of a network communication depends on four things:

(a) Authenticating the identity of each party to the conversation.

(b) Authorizing that identity to participate in the conversation.

(c) Ensuring the privacy of the conversation.

(d) Ensuring the integrity of each delivered message.

Authentication of the identity of an endpoint to the satisfaction of the other endpoint must ultimately be proven by an exchange of information previously known to both ends, or acquired from a trusted third party, typically X.509 certificate chains.

Authorization requires the application to decide whether the authenticated identity is the one it wants to talk to in this conversation. I emphasise again that authorization is inevitably a decision that can only be taken by the application: I have never seen a way in which authorization can be satisfactorily delegated to an API or framework.

Privacy assures that the data cannot be read in transit by eavesdroppers, *i.e.* protects the conversation from passive attacks. It is accomplished via encryption and decryption, again using a key known only to the parties to the conversation.

Integrity assures that the message is delivered intact and has not been injected or tampered with in transit, *i.e.* protects the conversation from active attacks. It is usually achieved by sending and checking a *message digest*, a cryptographically secure annotation, delivered with the message, formed by a computation over the original message contents. The computation is repeated on receipt, to check that the received and computed digests are equal. The digest itself is cryptologically secure, because it is computed with a key known only to the parties to the conversation.

Note the order in which I have placed these factors. Security is too often thought of only as cryptography, but it's really not much use having a beautifully encrypted and decrypted conversation unless you're sure you know who you're talking to, and unless you can detect interpolations, forgeries, and replays.

Typically the keys used for signing message digests and encrypting messages are short-lived keys agreed specifically for that conversation, to guard against key leakage and replay attacks: these are known as 'session keys'.

Encryption techniques are of two kinds: *symmetric* and *asymmetric*. In symmetric encryption, the same key is used to both encrypt and decrypt the message. In asymmetric encryption, a *key pair* is used, of which one is publicly known, and one is private to the receiving entity: the public key is used to encrypt the message, but only the private key will decrypt it; conversely, when computing message digests, the digest is formed with the private key and checked with the public key, which assures that only the holder of the private key could have computed the digest.

Encryption keys are chosen so that guessing them, or trying to crack the message by brute-force enumeration of possible keys, is computationally infeasible, *i.e.* would take longer than the lifetime of interest of the message or key. The degree of privacy is related directly to the length of the key: this is why there are 40-bit keys, 56-bit keys, and so on up to (presently) 1024-bit keys. The longer the key, the stronger the encryption.[1]

7.2 INTRODUCTION TO SSL

Secure Sockets Layer (SSL) is the name of a family of protocols layered over TCP and the Sockets API which provides authentication, integrity, and privacy services.

---

1. An account of encryption and key-distribution techniques intelligible to the layman is given in Singh, *The Code Book*, chapter 6. A complete professional guide and reference to modern cryptography is given in Schneier, *Applied Crytogrgraphy*, 2000.

RFC 2246 defines an Internet standard called the Transport Security Protocol (TLS).[2] As this was developed from earlier specifications by Netscape of a protocol called Secure Sockets Layer or SSL,[3] the entire topic is often generically referred to as 'secure sockets' or SSL.

The TLS protocol and its SSL predecessors share a primary goal: 'to provide privacy and data integrity between two communicating applications'. The protocol 'allows client/server applications to communicate in a way that is designed to prevent eavesdropping, tampering, or message forgery'. The TLS and SSL protocols are widely implemented, *e.g.* by popular Web browsers and servers, and by the javax.net.ssl package. All implementations of of TLS and SSL complying with the specifications can interoperate with other complying implementations of the same protocol. The TLS 1.0, SSL 3.0, and SSL 2.0 protocols do not interoperate, but the setup phases of TLS and SSL 3.0 allow for clients and servers to negotiate the actual protocol to be used, so that for example an endpoint can announce its readiness to communicate via either TLS or SSLv3.[4]

Although there are differences in detail between TLS and SSL, the protocols all consist of a 'record protocol', a 'handshake protocol', and an optional 'session resumption' feature. These are described briefly below. For further details see RFC 2246 or the SSL documents.

7.2.1 *Record protocol*

The lowest level is provided by the Record Protocol. This provides cryptographic connection security which is *private* and *reliable*.

Privacy is provided by data encryption via one of a number of symmetric cryptographic techniques such as RSA, DES, RC4, *etc.* Encryption keys are generated uniquely for each connection, based on a secret negotiated by another protocol (such as the Handshake Protocol). The Record Protocol can also be used without encryption.

Reliability is provided via a message integrity check using a keyed Message Authentication Code (MAC). Various secure hash functions (*e.g.* SHA, MD5, etc.) can be used for MAC computations.

The Record Protocol is used for encapsulation of higher level protocols, including *(i)* the Handshake Protocol described below and *(ii)* whatever application protocol is being transported.

The operating environment of the record protocol consists of a compression algorithm, an encryption algorithm, and a MAC algorithm.

---

2. Dierks & Allen, RFC 2246: *The TLS Protocol Version 1.0*, January 1999.

3. Hickman & Kipp, *The SSL Protocol*, Netscape Communications Corp., Feb 9, 1995; Frier, Karlton, & Kocher, *The SSL 3.0 Protocol*, Netscape Communications Corp., Nov 18, 1996. See also Schneier & Wagner, *Analysis of the SSL 3.0 Protocol*.

4. This is described in Appendix E of RFC 2246.

7.2.2 Handshake protocol

The Handshake Protocol allows the server and client to authenticate each other and to negotiate an encryption algorithm and secret cryptographic keys before the application protocol transmits or receives its first byte of data. The Handshake Protocol is itself secure, having the properties of authentication, privacy, and integrity:

(a) The peer's identity can be authenticated using asymmetric (public key) cryptography (e.g. RSA, DSS, etc.). This authentication can be made optional, but it is generally required for at least one of the peers. See also the security analysis in section 7.2.6 below.

(b) The negotiation of a shared secret is private: the negotiated secret is unavailable to eavesdroppers (passive attackers); and, provided at least one endpoint of the connection is authenticated, the secret cannot be obtained even by an attacker who can place himself in the middle of the connection (an active attacker).

(c) The negotiation messages have integrity: no attacker can modify the negotiation communications without being detected by the parties to the communication.

The handshake protocol results in a *session*, which establishes security parameters for use by the Record Layer when protecting application data. The handshake protocol can be initiated at any time.

SSL uses asymmetric encryption to establish identity and trust, and then establishes a symmetric 'session key' via an RSA or Diffie-Helman key exchange: the parties to the conversation exchange a series of numbers leading to a number known to both ends but which is neither observable nor computable by an eavesdropper. This number, or session key, is then used for symmetric encryption of the conversation.

7.2.3 Sessions

An SSL *session* is a collection of security parameters agreed between two peers—two parties to a conversation—as a result of a handshake. It includes the peer identities (if established), the encryption and compression methods to be used between the peers, and the private and public keys and master secrets used by these methods.

An SSL session can outlive the connection which produced it, and can be 're-sumed' by a subsequent or simultaneous connection between the same two peers. This 'session resumption' feature of SSL allows the security parameters associated with a single secure session to be used for multiple conversations (TCP connections) 'sequentially or concurrently', *i.e.* for connections formed one after the other or at the same time. This technique saves on network transmission times for the T C P connection handshake: most of the handshake protocol is avoided when resuming an existing session; only the part which changes the current cipher keys is executed, saving a significant amount of computation and network transmission.

7.2.4 Session keys

The term 'session key' is generally used in cryptography to refer to a temporary key used to exchange between two endpoints. Using this term in s s l would be confusing, as it would suggest incorrectly that session keys are part of the session and are shared by all connections using that session. In fact, a unique key is used for each direction of each distinct s s l connection—i.e. a unique key for each distinct SSLSocket in the distributed system. These two keys are therefore better termed the 'cipher keys' for the connection. In this chapter we will use the term 'cipher keys' to denote the encryption keys used on a connection.

As we will see, the cipher keys for the connection can be changed as often as desired by either end.

7.2.5 Cipher suites

T L S and s s l support a variety of key exchange, bulk encryption, and message authentication techniques. These are grouped into 'cipher suites'. Each cipher suite specifies an algorithm for each of key exchange, bulk encryption (including secret key length), and message authentication. Cipher suites are identified by names of the general form:

TLS_KEYEXCHANGE_WITH_CIPHER_HASH

or

SSL_KEYEXCHANGE_WITH_CIPHER_HASH

where T L S or s s l specifices the protocol, *keyexchange* specifies the key-exchange algorithm, *cipher* specifies the encryption algorithm, and *hash* specifies the message authentication algorithm.

The set of techniques is open-ended, as is the set of cipher suites. T L S and s s l clients and servers negotiate a common cipher suite for the connection being created. The most secure of the combinations available to both client and server is chosen. If no common cipher suite can be found, no session is established.

7.2.6 Security analysis

T L S and s s l 3.0 provide security against passive attacks (eavesdropping) and replay attacks. To be secure against active attacks (man-in-the-middle), they *must*

have strong server authentication. The following security analysis is quoted from
RFC 2246.

Warning: completely anonymous [non-authenticated] connections only provide pro-
tection against passive eavesdropping. Unless an independent tamper-proof channel
is used to verify that the finished messages were not replaced by an attacker, server
authentication is required in environments where active man-in-the-middle attacks
are a concern.

For TLS to be able to provide a secure connection, both the client and server systems,
keys, and applications must be secure. In addition, the implementation must be free
of security errors.

The system is only as strong as the weakest key exchange and authentication algo-
rithm supported, and only trustworthy cryptographic functions should be used. Short
public keys, 40-bit bulk encryption keys, and anonymous servers should be used with
great caution. Implementations and users must be careful when deciding which cer-
tificates and certificate authorities are acceptable; a dishonest certificate authority
can do tremendous damage.

Similar wording appears in the SSL 3.0 document. Complete security analyses
appear in Appendix F of RFC 2246 (TLS) and appendix F of the SSL 3.0 specification. SSL 2.0 is obsolete, and is being 'phased out with all due haste'. It is vulner-
able to a number of active attacks, some of which are described in the SSL 3.0
specification. SSL and the security environment it needs to be embedded in are
discussed in Schneier, *Secrets and Lies*, 2000. See also §§4.2 and following in the
frequently-asked questions list (FAQ) of the SSL Talk List, available online at
http://www.faqs.org/faqs/computer-security/ssl-talk-faq/.

7.2.7 Non-repudiation

A 'non-repudiable' message is one which the sender cannot deny sending, having a similar legal status to a paper document signed by the author. In computer
cryptology, this is accomplished by a *digital signature,* a secure computation performed with the sender's private key which accompanies the message and which
can be verified later with his public key (compare with encryption, which is performed with the public key and reversed with the private key).

When receiving messages from an authenticated peer, SSL and TLS perform
all the necessary steps to establish non-repudation of messages *except* the last:
they don't preserve any evidence which can be introduced into a court of law.
They don't preserve the original message, the decryption, the signature, or the
peer's certificate. For this reason, SSL and TLS by themselves are not inherently
non-repudiable protocols.

7.3 SECURE SOCKETS IN JAVA

Implementations of s s l for Java have been available for some years from third-party vendors. In 1999 Sun introduced the Java Secure Sockets Extension (j s s e), which supports t l s 1.0, s s l 3.0, w t l s, and related protocols. This became a standard part of Java from j d k 1.4.

j s s e consists of the packages javax.net and javax.net.ssl. It is designed to support a variety of security protocols including but not limited to t l s and s s l 3.0. Like many other parts of Java, these packages define an a p i for use by programmers and a Service Provider Interface or s p i for use by implementors: Sun provide a 'reference' implementation. This means that the implementations available from other vendors can be operated via the standard a p i as long as the vendor provides a suitable implementation of the s p i. Sun's implementation offers useable performance and facilities, but the specialist vendors may add value by offering extra features and superior performance.

Sun's Java implementation complies with the relevant standards, as should those by third-party vendors, so they should interoperate with each other and with compliant non-Java implementations.

7.3.1 Import statements

Throughout the rest of this chapter the following Java import statements are assumed:[5]

```
import java.io.*;
import java.net.*;
import java.security.*;
import java.security.cert.*;
import javax.net.*;
import javax.net.ssl.*;
```

7.3.2 Installation

One of the peculiarities of j s s e is that it doesn't run 'out of the box'. j s s e is quite tricky to install and configure correctly. You must perform some manual steps:

(a) If you use server or client authentication—server authentication is required in all the protocols enabled by default—you *must* install a 'keystore' and tell your application's j v m about it, as explained in section 7.3.3.

(b) You may need to install a 'truststore' as explained in section 7.3.3.

---

5. This chapter describes s s l and t l s as from j d k 1.4 onwards, not the earlier separate j s s e.

Follow the instructions provided with the J D K or your third-party implementation carefully. Some symptoms of an incorrect installation, generally encountered when trying to create a secure socket or server socket, are shown in Table 7.1.[6]

TABLE 7.1 J S S E installation problems

Symptom	Causes
The first secure socket takes a long time to create	This is normal. It can be masked as described in section 7.12.
SocketException: no s s l Server Sockets, or s s l implementation not available	*(i)* The security.policy file does not include the J S S E provider. *(ii)* The truststore or keystore password is incorrect. *(iii)* The truststore or keystore is in an unknown format or is corrupt.
SSLException: No available certificate corresponds to the s s l cipher suites which are enabled	*(i)* No keystore was defined for a server or client which needed to authenticate itself. Server authentication is enabled by default. See section 7.3.3. *(ii)* No certificate in the keystore matches any enabled cipher suite. For example, if only RSA cipher suites are enabled, an RSA keyEntry must be available in the keystore.

7.3.3 *Keystores and truststores*

The J S S E 'keystore' is a standard Java keystore created with the *keystore* tool, from which servers or clients obtain private-key certificates when authenticating themselves to peers. The simplest way to tell your application about the J S S E keystore is to set appropriate values for the system properties javax.net.ssl.keyStore and javax.net.ssl.keyStorePassword; other techniques are described in section 7.12.

If you are creating SSLServerSockets and you don't enable non-authenticating cipher suites, you *must* define a keystore: there is no default.

The J S S E 'truststore' is also a Java keystore, but it is used by peers which receive authentication certificates, to establish whether they can be trusted. Java is shipped with a truststore in the file named cacerts in the directory ${JAVA_HOME}/lib/security. J S S E automatically looks for this truststore and also for one named jssecacerts in the same directory. To use a different truststore, you can set the system property javax.net.ssl.trustStore appropriately. (The order of this processing is as follows: if javax.net.ssl.trustStore is set it is used, otherwise if jssecacerts exists it is used, otherwise cacerts.)

---

6. See also section 7.15 and Table 7.5. For this reason methods introduced in J D K 1.4 are not so marked as they are in the rest of this book.

The javax.net.ssl.trustStorePassword property specifies the truststore password, but normally this does not need to be set. The reason for this is described in section 7.12, along with other ways of establishing the keystore and truststore.

7.4 SOCKET FACTORY METHODS

The socket factory framework used by J S S E is defined by the javax.net factory classes:

```
class SocketFactory
{
    static SocketFactory getDefault();
    Socket createSocket()
      throws IOException;
    Socket createSocket(String host, int port)
      throws IOException, UnknownHostException;
    Socket createSocket(String host, int port,
                    InetAddress localAddress, int localPort)
      throws IOException, UnknownHostException;
    Socket createSocket(InetAddress host, int port)
      throws IOException;
    Socket createSocket(InetAddress host, int port,
                    InetAddress localAddress,
                    int localPort)
      throws IOException, UnknownHostException;
}
class ServerSocketFactory
{
    static ServerSocketFactory getDefault();
    ServerSocket createServerSocket()
      throws IOException;
    ServerSocket createServerSocket(int port)
      throws IOException;
    ServerSocket createServerSocket(int port, int backlog)
      throws IOException;
    ServerSocket createServerSocket(int port, int backlog,
                            InetAddress localAddress)
      throws IOException;
}
```

The static getDefault methods of these factory classes return factory instances which create standard Java Sockets and ServerSockets. The various socket-creation methods should look familiar, as they correspond precisely to the con-

structors for ServerSockets and Sockets which we have already encountered in
section 3.3.1 and section 3.4.1 respectively, and need no further explanation here.

With these factories, you can code an entire application using standard
sockets:

```
class Client
{
  SocketFactory  factory = SocketFactory.getDefault();
  Socket         socket;

  Client(String host, int port) throws IOException
  {
    this.socket = factory.createSocket(host, port);
  }
  // ...
}

class Server
{
  ServerSocketFactory factory =
    ServerSocketFactory.getDefault();
  ServerSocket           serverSocket;

  Server(int port) throws IOException
  {
    this.serverSocket = factory.createServerSocket(port);
  }
  // ...
}
```

and so on as we have seen many times before.

The javax.net.ssl factory classes extend the socket factory classes above. The
static getDefault methods of these factory classes return factory instances which
create secure sockets and server sockets:

```
class SSLSocketFactory extends javax.net.SocketFactory
{
  static SocketFactory getDefault();
}

class SSLServerSocketFactory
  extends javax.net.ServerSocketFactory
{
  static ServerSocketFactory getDefault();
}
```

To agree with the javax.net socket factory interfaces, the return types of these methods are declared as javax.net.SocketFactory and javax.net.ServerSocketFactory respectively, although what they actually return are objects of the derived classes javax.net.ssl.SSLSocketFactory and javax.net.ssl.SSLServerSocketFactory respectively. This is unimportant if you only want to call methods already defined above; but if you want to call s s l-specific methods on the socket factories, you must typecast the return values to SSLSocketFactory and SSLServerSocketFactory respectively.

Once you have instances of these factories, you can create secure sockets with their factory methods: these are identical to those exported by SocketFactory and ServerSocketFactory, *i.e.* correspond to constructors for Socket and ServerSocket.

By using the socket-factory technique, we can switch back and forth between standard sockets and secure sockets as often as we like, *e.g.* for development or debugging purposes—as long as we are sure to switch *both* ends: standard sockets do not interoperate with secure sockets (of course!—otherwise the secure sockets would not be secure).

At this point, provided you have installed j s s e correctly, we have enough information to convert the application classes above to s s l:

```
class Client
{
    // This is the only change for a client.
    SocketFactory factory = SSLSocketFactory.getDefault();
    Socket socket;

    Client(String host, int port) throws IOException
    {
        this.socket = factory.createSocket(host, port);
    }
    // ...
}

class Server
{
    // This is the only change required for a server.
    ServerSocketFactoryfactory =
        SSLServerSocketFactory.getDefault();
    ServerSocketserverSocket;

    static // initializer
    {
        System.setProperty("javax.net.ssl.keyStore", ...);
        System.setProperty("javax.net.ssl.keyStorePassword", ...);
    }
```

```
Server(int port) throws IOException
{
  this.serverSocket = factory.createServerSocket(port);
}
// ...
}
```

and so on (fill in the ellipses ... appropriately yourself). Note that the initialization of the factory variable is different in each case, plus the setting of the keystore properties for the server.

7.4.1 Connection layering

The SSLSocketFactory class exports the following connection-layering method in addition to those specified by javax.net.SocketFactory:

```
class SSLSocketFactory extends javax.net.SocketFactory
{
  Socket createSocket(Socket socket, String host,
                      int port, boolean autoClose)
    throws IOException;
}
```

This method is specific to SSLSocketFactory. It is used when the underlying Socket already exists and it is desired to transform it into a secure socket.

The autoClose parameter of this method controls whether closing the secure socket returned by the method also closes the underlying Socket supplied to the method. You could set this to false if you want to (dangerously) interleave secure communications over the SSLSocket with insecure (but faster) communications directly over the Socket, or if you want to (again dangerously) terminate the secure part of the conversation and continue it insecurely.

> In theory this method could also be used to wrap an SSLSocket inside another SSLSocket, thus obtaining multiple levels of encryption. I don't recommend it: the performance would be atrocious!

7.5 SECURE SOCKET OPERATIONS

As we already know what to do with a Socket and a ServerSocket, that's it! Stream input and output with J S S E sockets is exactly the same as the socket stream I/O techniques we have already encountered in section 3.6. (Channel I/O with J S S E sockets is discussed in section 7.9.) The only substantive differences you will notice are:

(a) The creation of the first SSLSocket or SSLServerSocket takes an appreciable amount of time, due to seeding of a secure random number generator.

(b) Using a BufferedOutputStream coupled to the socket's output stream is *essential*, otherwise the overhead of the record protocol is immense.[7]

(c) Sending urgent data, and getting or setting the OOBInline state are not supported (an unchecked UnsupportedOperationException is thrown).

(d) SSLSocket.getInputStream().available() always returns zero.

(e) For security reasons (to prevent truncation attacks), there is a close_notify message at the level of the record protocol, which must be responded to immediately with an outgoing close_notify (in other words, both sides of the connection must be closed at the same time); for this reason, the shutdownInput and shutdownOutput methods are not supported (an unchecked UnsupportedOperationException is thrown).

The factory methods above actually create objects of type SSLSocket and SSLServerSocket: these extend java.net.Socket and java.net.ServerSocket respectively, and therefore export the same methods. They also export additional methods to control many aspects of j s s e's behaviour.

Well, that's *almost* it. The rest of this chapter describes j s s e-specific programming techniques, including the handshake, the resulting session, client and server authentication, controlling the cipher suite and the protocol used (TLS, SSLv3, SSLv2Hello), the 'session context', session sharing, connection layering, the intersection of s s l and channel I/O, the intersection of s s l and r m i, session management, exceptions in s s l, s s l system properties, and a sample s s l client and server.

7.5.1 *The handshake*

As we saw in section 7.2.2, the s s l handshake negotiates security parameters with the peer. The handshake is initiated automatically when the first input or output operation is performed on the socket: it is deferred until then to give applications an opportunity to configure cipher suites, server/client mode, authentication requirements, and so on as described in the following sections. The handshake can be initiated manually with the method:

---

7. For example, writing 16 bytes one at a time (e.g. via DataOutputStream.writeBytes) results in 416 bytes of output; writing them at once (*e.g.* via DataOutputStream.writeBytes coupled to an intermedate BufferedOutputStream followed by a flush) results in 41 bytes of output.

```
class SSLSocket
{
    void startHandshake()  throws IOException;
}
```

Regardless of whether the handshake is initiated manually or automatically, there are several possibilities:

(a) No handshake has ever been performed between the peers. In this case the startHandshake method is synchronous, and returns when the initial hand-shake is complete or throws an IOException. This handshake establishes the session with its cipher suite and peer identities, as well as the cipher keys.

(b) A handshake has been performed between the same peers; neither the cli-ent or the server has invalidated the session that resulted; and session re-sumption is supported by the JSSE implementation. In this case, the startHandshake method is asynchronous and returns immediately. If data has already been sent on the connection, it continues to flow during the handshake. This handshake only establishes new cipher keys for the con-nection.

(c) The session has been invalidated and another valid session is available for resumption. If data has already been sent on the connection, it continues to flow during the handshake. This handshake only resumes an existing ses-sion with new cipher keys for the connection. In this case the startHandshake method is asynchronous and returns immediately. This case is not significanty different from case (b).

(d) The session has been invalidated, no other valid sessions are available (or session resumption is not supported), and session creation has *not* been dis-abled. In this case the handshake establishes a new session as in case (a); the handshake is asynchronous as in case (b).

(e) The session has been invalidated, no other valid sessions are available (or session resumption is not supported), and session creation has been disa-bled. In this case the handshake attempts to establish a new session as in case (a); the handshake is asynchronous as in case (b); the attempt will fail and the next read or write will throw an SSLException.

Regardless of whether the handshake is synchronous or asynchronous, the com-pletion of the handshake can be monitored immediately by using a handshake listener as discussed below.

If handshaking fails for any reason, the socket is automatically closed and can-not be used any further.

There is no need to start the initial handshake explicitly, as the first I/O on the connection will initiate the handshake and throw an IOException if it fails. How-ever, it can be useful to perform the initial handshake explicitly so that any exceptions arising out of it can be caught in one place rather than percolating all through the I/O code for the socket.

It is *very* useful for security purposes to perform *additional* handshakes, for example to establish new cipher keys after a certain period of time; to tune the cipher suites and authentication modes if those initially negotiated are unsatisfactory or need upgrading because the conversation is getting progressively more secret; or to establish a new session, *i.e.* to completely re-authenticate the peer and re-establish the cipher suites. If s s l connections are to be long-lived, it is standard security practice to change the encryption keys pretty frequently, and to expire sessions somewhat less frequently. r f c 2246 suggests an upper limit of 24 hours on session lifetimes.

It is clear from r f c 2246 §7.4 that either the client or the server may initiate a re-handshake. However some protocols may not support multiple handshakes on an existing socket, in which case an IOException may be thrown.

The completion of the handshake can be monitored by implementing and registering a HandshakeCompletionListener:

```
class SSLSocket
{
    // arguments may not be null …
    void addHandshakeCompletedListener
       (HandshakeCompletedListener listener);
    void removeHandshakeCompletedListener
       (HandshakeCompletedListener listener);
}
```

where the listener supplied implements the interface:

```
interface HandshakeCompletedListener extends EventListener
{
    void handshakeCompleted(HandshakeCompletedEvent event);
}
```

When a handshake completes successfully, a HandshakeCompletedEvent object is passed to the listener's handshakeCompleted method. This object provides access to the session parameters which have just been negotiated by the handshake: the cipher suite, the local certificates if any passed to the peer, the certificates if any passed by the peer, the SSLSession, and the SSLSocket on which handshaking has just completed. HandshakeCompletedEvent exports the following methods:

```
class HandshakeCompletedEvent extends EventObject
{
    String          getCipherSuite();
    Certificate[]   getLocalCertificates();
```

```
// @deprecated: use getPeerCertificates
X509Certificate[]
                getPeerCertificateChain()
                throws SSLPeerUnverifiedException;
Certificate[]  getPeerCertificates()
                throws SSLPeerUnverifiedException;
Principal      getPeerPrincipal()
                throws SSLPeerUnverifiedException;
SSLSession     getSession();
SSLSocket      getSocket();
}
```

Most of these methods are just shorthands for the corresponding methods of SSLSession, which are discussed in section 7.6. The inherited getSource method returns the same value as getSocket, but as an Object, not as an SSLSocket.

Good security practice *demands* that the identity of the peer be verified when the handshake completes: this is the application-defined authorization step referred to above.

```
X509Certificate cert = (X509Certificate)event
  .getPeerCertificates()[0];
X500Principal issuerDN = cert.getIssuerX500Principal();
// check issuerDN.getName() against that expected …
X500Principal subjectDN = cert.getSubjectX500Principal();
// check subjectDN.getName() against that expected …
```

ssl is responsible for checking the peer certificates for expiry, revocation, and trust: this establishes whether the certificate is a valid certificate leading to a trusted source of certificates, but it doesn't establish whether it represents the required identity. Only the application, or indeed the operator, knows that! As I observed above, it's not much use conducting an encrypted and authenticated conversation unless you know who you're talking to, and unless that is the person you want to utter these secrets to.

However, a HandshakeCompletionListener object's handshakeCompleted callback can't throw any checked exception, and throwing an unchecked exception is pointless (handshake listeners being despatched in a separate thread in Sun's implementation). If you dislike the peer's identity (or you don't like the negotiated cipher suite, or have some other problem with the handshake), all you can sensibly do inside the callback is either:

(a) close the socket, and perhaps notify the rest of your application somehow, or, less drastically

(b) disable session creation (see section 7.5.6); invalidate the session (see section 7.6.2), and request a new handshake: while keeping the socket open, this will cause it to become completely unusable, as any subsequent I/O operation will cause an SSLException or IOException.

For this reason it may be better to check the peer's identity (or the cipher suite or any other aspect of the handshake) from *outside* the handshakeCompleted callback, by getting and interrogating the SSLSession as discussed in section 7.6.

If you do like the peer's identity inside the handshake completion callback but don't like the negotiated cipher suite, you can change the enabled cipher suites on the socket, invalidate the session, and start a new handshake.

7.5.2 Client mode

By default, a client application creates sockets in 'client' mode and a server socket creates sockets in 'server' mode. This refers to the handshake protocol's concept of server and client when authenticating. Normally, servers are required to authenticate themselves; clients are not. In cases such as 'callbacks' where the client is also a server, this may need to be reversed, so that all authentication is provided by the same end of the connection: a client with a callback would use an SSLServerSocket in 'client' mode to accept the callback, while the server would use an SSLSocket with 'client' mode disabled (*i.e.* in 'server' mode) to initiate the connection to the callback. The FTP protocol is an example of this situation, which can also arise in applications built on Java RMI.

The 'client' mode of a socket is controlled by the methods:

```
class SSLSocket/class SSLServerSocket
{
    boolean   getUseClientMode();
    void      setUseClientMode(boolean useClientMode);
}
```

where the default value for a socket created by SSLSocketFactory.createSocket is true, and the default value for a socket created by SSLServerSocket.accept is inherited from the setting for the server socket, which in turn is false by default.

7.5.3 Client authentication

Unless you have enabled a non-authenticating cipher suite,[8] the server will authenticate itself to the client during the handshake. In addition to this, you can also request or require the client to authenticate itself to the server, by using these methods:

---

8. *i.e.* one of the suites containing the string '_anon_', which are disabled by default.

```
class SSLSocket/class SSLServerSocket
{
    boolean  getWantClientAuth();
    boolean  getNeedClientAuth();
    void     setWantClientAuth(boolean wantClientAuth);
    void     setNeedClientAuth(boolean needClientAuth);
}
```

These methods are only useful for sockets in the 'server' mode discussed in section 7.5.2: *i.e.* by default, sockets resulting from SSLServerSocket.accept. (From the point of view of authentication, it is only in server mode that the client is at the other end: if the socket is in client mode, the *server* is at the other end.)

If wantClientAuth is set, the client is requested to authenticate itself, but the handshake succeeds whether or not the client does so. In this case, client authentication is only requested if appropriate to the cipher suite which has been negotiated.

If needClientAuth is set, the client is *required* to authenticate itself: the handshake only succeeds if the client does so, otherwise negotiation ceases and the connection is dropped. Calling setWantClientAuth overrides any previous setting of setNeedClientAuth, and *vice versa*.

7.5.4 Cipher suite methods

The cipher suites supported by Java vary depending on your geographic location, because of u s a government restrictions on the export of cryptographic software. There are two sets of cipher suites: the *supported* cipher suites, *i.e.* the complete set available to the installation, and the *enabled* cipher suites, *i.e.* those enabled by default. Initially, Java only enables those cipher suites which provide confidentiality and which require server authentication; these constitute the minimum suggested configuration. The set of supported and enabled cipher suites can be obtained from static socket factory methods, or from a socket or server socket instance, and can be modified for a given socket or server socket instance, as shown in Table 7.2.

TABLE 7.2 Cipher suite methods

Classes	Method	Description
SSLSocketFactory, SSLServerSocketFactory, SSLServerSocket, SSLSocket	getSupportedCipherSuites	Return all cipher suites supported by the installation.
SSLSocketFactory, SSLServerSocketFactory	getDefaultCipherSuites	Return the cipher suites which are enabled by default.

TABLE 7.2 Cipher suite methods (continued)

Classes	Method	Description
SSLServerSocket, SSLSocket	getEnabledCipherSuites	Return all cipher suites enabled on this socket.
SSLServerSocket, SSLSocket	setEnabledCipherSuites	Change the set of cipher suites enabled on this socket.

All the enquiry methods return an array of String representing cipher suite names as described in section 7.2.5.

The enabled cipher suites for a socket or server socket can be altered via the setEnabledCipherSuites methods of SSLSocket and SSLServerSocket. These methods both take as argument an array of String representing the cipher suite names to be enabled, each of which must have been listed as being supported by the getSupportedCipherSuites method. These methods completely replace the previous enabled set. They only affect the ssl handshake operation, which occurs as described in section 7.5.1. The set of enabled cipher suites for a server socket is inherited by sockets resulting from ServerSocket.accept.

As we saw in section 7.2.5, the strongest common cipher suite is used for a secure connection. There are several reasons why an enabled cipher suite might not be used:

(a) It may not be enabled at the remote peer.

(b) Private keys or certificates of the format required by the cipher suite may not be available at both peers.

(c) The cipher suite may be anonymous but the remote peer requires authentication.

One way of *temporarily* getting round an incorrect installation is to enable all cipher suites on both client and server sides:

```
socket.setEnabledCipherSuites
   (socket.getSupportedCipherSuites());
```

This allows Java to use any supported cipher suite, including those which don't require server authentication: these are generally disabled because they are by definition insecure, for the reasons discussed in section 7.2.6. It can be useful for development purposes to use a less secure cipher suite, *e.g.* for temporary performance reasons at development time, or for testing prior to the acquisition of certificates. *However,* the problem solved by this technique is generally a missing, mis-installed, or expired server certificate, which should be corrected instead.

7.5.5 Protocol methods

The J S S E protocols supported by Java vary depending on the installation and vendor. There are two sets of protocols: the *supported* protocols, *i.e.* the complete set available to the installation, and the *enabled* protocols, *i.e.* those enabled by default. A protocol is identified by a string: in J D K 1.5, these are in order of decreasing strength, 'TLSv1' and 'SSLv3', as well as the pseudo-protocol 'SSLV2Hello'.[9] In each case, the protocol represents the *minimum* protocol level which can be negotiated. The set of supported and enabled protocols can be queried and modified for a socket instance by the following methods:

```
class SSLSocket/class SSLServerSocket
{
    // return all protocols supported by the installation
    String[] getSupportedProtocols();
    // return all protocols currently enabled on this socket
    String[] getEnablededProtocols();
    // set protocols enabled on this socket
    void    setEnabledProtocols(String[] protocols);
}
```

All the enquiry methods return an array of String representing protocol names. The enabled cipher suites for a socket or server socket can be altered via the setEnabledProtocols methods, which take an array of String representing the protocol names to be enabled, each of which must have been listed as being supported by the getSupportedProtocols method. These methods completely replace the previous enabled set. They only affect the s s l handshake, which occurs as described in section 7.5.1.

The enabled protocols for a server socket are inherited by sockets resulting from ServerSocket.accept.

The strongest common protocol is always negotiated for a secure conection. An enabled protocol can only be used if it is also enabled at the remote peer. As an example, the following code snippet ensures that the SSLv3 protocol is not used:

```
SSLSocket socket; // initialization not shown ...
String[] protocols = socket.getSupportedProtocols();
Arrays.sort(protocols);
int n = Arrays.binarySearch(protocols, "SSLv3");
if (n >= 0) // found
{
    List list = new ArrayList(Arrays.asList(protocols));
    list.remove(n);
```

---

9. 'SSLv2Hello' is a pseudo-protocol which allows Java to initiate the handshake with an SSLv2 'hello message'. This does *not* cause use of the SSLv2 protocol, which is not supported by Java at all. The necessity for this procedure is discussed in R F C 2246.

```
        socket.setEnabledProtocols
          ((String[])list.toArray(new String[0]));
    }
```

A similar technique can be used to disable the SSLv2Hello pseudo-protocol described above, which is not recognized by some SSL implementations.

7.5.6 Disabling session creation

Normally an SSLSocket can create a new session by invalidating its current session and starting a new handshake. This can be controlled with the methods:

```
class SSLSocket/class SSLServerSocket
{
    boolean  getEnableSessionCreation();// default = true
    void     setEnableSessionCreation(boolean enable);
}
```

where the setting for a server socket is inherited by sockets resulting from ServerSocket.accept. If session creation has been disabled, only existing non-invalidated sessions may be resumed: if no such sessions exist, no new handshakes can successfully occur. This facility has several uses:

(a) For an SSLSocket, you might disable this option before the first handshake if valid sessions with the same peer are known to exist.

(b) During a handshake listener callback, if you don't like the peer identity or the negotiated cipher suite, you can render the SSLSocket useless by disabling session creation, invalidating the session, and requesting a new handshake.

(c) A framework might want to prevent the application performing additional handshakes completely, by performing a manual handshake on each new SSLSocket and then disabling session creation.

(d) For an SSLServerSocket, disabling this option has the effect of disabling all accepted sockets except those accepted from peers who have already established sessions: this might be useful in certain closed environments.

7.6 Sessions

'In SSL, *sessions* are used to describe an ongoing relationship between two entities.'[10] An SSL session can outlive the connection which created it, and can be used simultaneously or sequentially by multiple connections between the same

---

10. *javadoc* for javax.net.ssl.SSLSession.

two entities. The session used on a connection may be replaced by a different session. Sessions are created or resumed as part of the s s L handshaking protocol.

An s s L session consists of a cipher suite and the identities of the client and server, if known. It is represented by the SSLSession interface:

```
interface SSLSession
{
  String            getCipherSuite();
  long              getCreationTime();
  byte[]            getID();
  long              getLastAccessedTime();
  Certificate[]     getLocalCertificates();
  // @deprecated: use getPeerCertificates
  X509Certificate[] getPeerCertificateChain()
    throws SSLPeerUnverifiedException;
  Principal         getPeerPrincipal()
    throws SSLPeerUnverifiedException;
  Certificate[]     getPeerCertificates()
    throws SSLPeerUnverifiedException;
  String            getPeerHost();
  String            getPeerPort();
  String            getProtocol();
  SSLContext        getSessionContext();
  Object            getValue(String name);
  String[]          getValueNames();
  void              invalidate();
  void              putValue(String name, Object value);
  void              removeValue
                      (String name, Object value);
}
```

The session currently associated with an s s L socket is obtained by the SSLSocket.getSession method. This method establishes the session if necessary by initiating the handshake and blocking till it completes. If an error occurred during the handshake, getSession returns an invalid SSLSession object whose cipher suite is 'SSL_NULL_WITH_NULL_NULL', an invalid value.[11]

The cipher suite negotiated for a session has already been described. The identifier associated with the session is created by the handshake protocol as defined by R F C 2246. The creation time and last-accessed time are automatically maintained by Java, and are held as milliseconds since midnight, January 1, 1970

---

11. This is a very strange piece of design. Throwing an SSLException would have been more conventional and certainly more convenient for the application programmer.

UTC. In this context, 'access' only means establishing a new connection via this session, and specifically excludes calling any of the SSLSession methods listed above. The last-access time is intended to be used in session management, *e.g.* invalidating sessions which have been unused for some period of time, or sorting sessions by age to optimize some task.

The *protocol* of a session is the standard protocol name negotiated by the handshake, e.g. 'TLSv1', 'SSLv3', as described in section 7.5.5.

For the server, the *peer host* is the client's host; and for the client, it is the server's host. The peer host may not be a fully qualified host name or even a host name at all, as it may represent a string encoding of the peer's network address. If a host name is desired, it might be resolved through a name service based on the value returned by this method. This value is not authenticated and should not be relied on for security purposes. It is mainly useful for non-legalistic logging and tracing.

Sessions support {*name, value*} pairs via the getValue, getValueNames, putValue, and removeValue methods. This facility is provided for application purposes like session management, and is not used internally: see also section 7.7.

The *session context* of an SSL session is described in section 7.8.

7.6.1 *Local and peer certificates*

The local certificate array returned by the getLocalCertificates method is the certificate chain which was actually sent to the peer during handshaking: the chain is selected from all available chains by the implementation's idea of the 'best' chain available, *e.g.* to comply with a format dictated by the cipher suite. The getLocalCertificates method returns null if no certificates were passed to the peer.

Similarly, the peer certificate array returned by the getPeerCertificates method is the certificate chain received from the peer during handshaking, selected by the peer in a similar way. The certificate arrays returned by these methods start with the local or peer entity's own certificate, followed by any certificate-authority certificates in order from leaf to root.

7.6.2 *Invalidating sessions*

A session can be *invalidated*. This prevents further connections being formed on this session, i.e. prevents resumption of this session by any new connection created between the same two peers. However, invalidating a session has no effect on existing connections in the session: specifically, it does *not* force a new handshake to occur on an existing connection; nor does it prevent that connection being used in future. A new handshake can be initiated as described in section 7.5.1. An SSL connection can be completely disabled by:

(a) Disabling creation of new sessions as discussed in section 7.5.6, and

(b) invalidating its session, and

(c)   requesting a new handshake.

An SSLSocket in this state cannot perform any I/O (except closure) without throwing an SSLException or IOException. (Alternatively, you *could* just close the socket ...)

7.6.3 *Session sharing*

If we create two or more SSLSockets connected to the same target, two distinct SSLSockets are returned by the SSLSocketFactory.createSocket method. However, s s l is able to use a single s s l session among all these SSLSockets. In other words, a single javax.net.ssl.SSLSession may be shared by multiple javax.net.ssl.SSLSockets connected to the same target: an s s l socket can share a previously established session with the same peer without having to do a complete handshake.

This can be rather confusing. The relationship between SSLSockets, SSLSessions, and SSLSessionContexts is depicted in the object graph shown in Figure 7.1 (this particular view results from a special case, as we will see later).

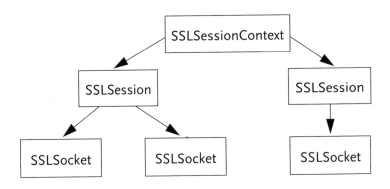

FIGURE 7.1. s s l object graph

Multiple SSLSockets can share the same SSLSession, and in fact this is the default behaviour:[12] if you create multiple SSLSockets connected to the same target, a single handshake is done, resulting in a single shared SSLSession. If you subsequently invalidate the session and start another handshake on any of the SSLSockets, the handshake will cause the SSLSocket to leave that session and either:

---

12. if session resumption is supported, as it usually is, except on some small mobile devices.

(a) resume an existing session, if another session between the same two peers exists which has not been invalidated, or

(b) create a new SSLSession via a complete renegotiation of cipher suites, authentication, and secret key, if new session creation hasn't been disabled for the socket as described in section 7.6, or

(c) fail.

This in turn means that a single SSLSocket may have multiple SSLSessions over its lifetime.

In other words, the object graph of Figure 7.1 must have resulted from the creation of three SSLSockets and the execution of a session invalidation and a new handshake on the third socket.

7.6.4 Session management

As a general principle, *clients* should use session sharing as much as possible up to the 24-hour limit mentioned earlier; *servers* need to balance the benefits of session-sharing against the cost of the memory concerned, probably by enforcing both a maximum session lifetime (measured in minutes rather than hours), and a lowish maximum size for the session-cache. See also section 7.13.

7.7 BINDING & BINDING LISTENERS

Objects can be *bound* to or *unbound* from an SSLSession, and obtained from it, via the methods:

```
interface SSLSession
{
    Object    getValue(String name);
    String[]  getValueNames();
    void      putValue(String name, Object value);
    void      removeValue(String name, Object value);
}
```

Session binding is provided for use by applications, *e.g.* to associate an application context with a remote user. Implementors of session managers may find some use for this feature.

Objects which want to know when they are being bound to or unbound from an SSLSession can implement the SSLSessionBindingListener interface:

```
interface SSLSessionBindingListener extends EventListener
{
  void valueBound(SSLSessionBindEvent event);
  void valueUnbound(SSLSessionBindEvent event);
}
```

The valueBound method of an object which implements SessionBindingListener is called whenever it is bound to a session via the SSLSession.putValue method. Similarly, the valueUnbound method of an object which implements SessionBindingListener is called whenever it is unbound from a session via the SSLSession.removeValue method.

Note that a SessionBindingListener is not explicitly registered or deregistered in any way: it is merely the *fact* that a bound or unbound object extends SSLSessionBindingListener which causes it to be notified.

7.8 SESSION CONTEXT

Each s s l session is bound to a *session context,* representing a set of s s l sessions associated with a single entity (a client or server) which participates in multiple concurrent sessions. Session contexts are not supported in all environments.

The session context of a session can be obtained via the method:

```
interface SSLSession
{
  SSLSessionContext getSessionContext();
}
```

In certain environments the session context may not be available, in which case the method returns null.[13] If a security manager is installed, the permission:

>   javax.net.ssl.SSLPermission("getSSLSessionContext")

is required, otherwise a SecurityException is thrown. A session context is really a kind of session manager with two policies:

(a)   It can enforce a uniform session timeout on all sessions in the context.

(b)   It can enforce a maximum number of sessions in the session cache (*i.e.* available for resumption).

---

13. For example, in devices with extreme memory limitations such that session resumption isn't desirable at all, or a j s s e implementation layered on another underlying s s l implementation which does not itself expose the ability to enumerate and manage the session cache.

Session contexts can also be queried to list all available session IDs, or to retrieve a specific session based on its ID. All these actions are controlled via the methods:

```
interface SSLSessionContext
{
    // Enumerate session IDs: returns Enumeration of byte[]
    Enumeration  getIds();

    // Get SSLSession by ID
    SSLSession   getSession(byte[] sessionId);

    // Get/set session cache size: zero means 'no limit'.
    int          getSessionCacheSize();
    void         setSessionCacheSize(int size);

    // Get/set session timeout in seconds:
    // zero means 'no limit'
    int          getSessionTimeout();
    void         setSessionTimeout(int seconds);
}
```

Session timeouts are expressed in seconds, where zero means no limit, which is also the default. If a finite timeout has been set, a session times out the indicated number of seconds after its creation time, after which it is invalidated as described in section 7.6. If the timeout is changed, all sessions are immediately checked for possible timeout. Note that this form of session timeout concerns only its total lifetime since creation: it has nothing to do with its usage or last-access time as returned by SSLSession.getLastAccessedTime.

The size of the cache used for storing sessions in a session context can be controlled by the setSessionCacheSize method. The default value of this parameter is zero, meaning no limit. The behaviour is unspecified when the limit has been reached, or reduced when full: in Sun's implementation, sessions are ejected from the cache according to a least-recently-used policy.[14] Ejected sessions are not invalidated, but they will not be re-used by new connections.

The sessions bound to a session context can be enumerated as follows:

```
SSLSessionContext ctx;   // initialization not shown ...
Enumeration       enum = ctx.getIds();
while (enum.hasMoreElements())
{
  byte[]     sessionId = (byte[])enum.nextElement();
```

---

14. See *java-security* mailing list, 13–16 April, 2002.

```
    SSLSession session = ctx.getSession(sessionId);
    // ...
}
```

7.9 JSSE AND CHANNEL I/O

You can do *blocking* channel I/O with secure sockets, using the stream-to-channel mapping facilities of the Channels class described in section 4.2.4:

```
SSLSocket socket; // initialization not shown
ReadableByteChannel rbc =
    Channels.newChannel(socket.getInputStream());
WritableByteChannel wbc =
    Channels.newChannel(socket.getOutputStream());
```

Neither of these channels is a SocketChannel, and so neither of them can perform the operations associated with a real SocketChannel, such as scatter-read, gather-write, non-blocking I/O, registration with Selectors, non-blocking connect, or asynchronous closure. Nor can the ReadableByteChannel perform writes, or the WritableByteChannel perform reads, again unlike a real SocketChannel.

However, these channels certainly are fully-fledged fair-dinkum ReadableByteChannels and WritableByteChannels respectively, and therefore support the corresponding operations: reading into a ByteBuffer, writing from a ByteBuffer, and synchronous closure.

Non-blocking JSSE I/O is discussed in Chapter 8.

7.10 SSL AND RMI

Neither the standard javax.net socket factory classes SocketFactory and ServerSocketFactory nor the SSL socket factory classes SSLSocketFactory and SSLServerSocketFactory described in section 7.4 implements the socket-factory interfaces defined in the java.rmi.server package (RMIClientSocketFactory and RMIServerSocketFactory), even though they export the required methods.[15]

In JDK 1.5, Sun finally provided built-in SslRMIClientSocketFactory and SslRMIServerSocketFactory classes in the javax.rmi.ssl package.

Prior to JDK 1.5, adapters must be written to use SSL socket factories with RMI. This is a fairly trivial exercise in the Adapter pattern, as long as we remember two important aspects of RMI socket factories:

---

15. This may possibly be to allow JSSE to fit into those Java Micro Edition profiles which do not contain RMI.

(a) R M I client socket factories must be serializable.

(b) R M I socket factories must provide a plausible implementation of the Object.equals method, *i.e.* an over-ride which takes R M I's serialization behaviour into account. Specifically, after beiung unmarshalled and deserialized by R M I, a single client socket factory instance at the server end becomes an instance per stub at the client end, and similarly the remote stub itself becomes multiple instances if returned by multiple remote calls.

This indicates that socket factory equality cannot be based on object identity (the default implemented by Object.equals) and instead should be at least based on equality of object *content*, or on class equality.[16]

The general technique for client socket factories is shown in Example 7.1.

```
public class SSLtoRMISocketFactoryAdapter
  implements RMIClientSocketFactory, Serializable
{
  public Socket createSocket(String host, int port)
    throws IOException
  {
    SocketFactory factory = SSLSocketFactory.getDefault();
    SSLSocket socket =
      (SSLSocket)factory.createSocket(host, port);
    // adjust cipher suites &c …
    return socket;
  }

  public boolean equals(Object that)
  {
    return that != null
    && that.getClass() == this.getClass();
  }
} // end class
```

EXAMPLE 7.1 R M I / S S L client socket factory

An RMI SSL server socket factory must also tell J S S E about the keystore via one of the techniques discussed in section 7.3.3 or section 7.12, unless another part of the application does so.

The general technique for server socket factories is shown in Example 7.2.

---

16. See Pitt & McNiff, *java.rmi: The Remote Method Invocation Guide*, §§11.4–11.5. This point was entirely overlooked by the R M I examples supplied by Sun with J S S E prior to J D K 1.5.

```
public class SSLtoRMIServerSocketFactoryAdapter
  implements RMIServerSocketFactory
{

  static // initializer
  {
    System.setProperty("javax.net.ssl.keyStore", …);
    System.setProperty("javax.net.ssl.keyStorePassword", …);
  }

  public Socket createServerSocket(int port)
    throws IOException
  {
    ServerSocketFactory factory =
      SSLServerSocketFactory.getDefault();
    SSLServerSocket serverSocket =
      (SSLServerSocket)factory.createServerSocket(port);
    // adjust cipher suites &c …
    return serverSocket;
  }

  public boolean equals(Object that)
  {
    return that != null
    && that.getClass() == this.getClass();
  }
} // end class
```

EXAMPLE 7.2 RMI/SSL server socket factory

7.11 DEBUGGING

JSSE includes a facility to trace its actions to System.out. This can be useful in debugging problems such as handshake failures or unexpectedly poor performance. The trace facility is 'not an officially supported feature of JSSE', but it is present in all Sun versions to date.

Using this facility, you can have JSSE trace its actions down to an excruciating level of detail.The choice of actions traced is controlled via keyword values set in the system property javax.net.debug. See the JDK documentation for current details.[17]

---

17. Guide to Features: Security: JSSE Reference Guide.

7.11.1 *Examples*

To debug 'MyApp' with some value of J S S E debugging:

```
java -Djavax.net.debug=XXX MyApp
```

where XXX is as follows:

(a)   To view all debugging messages:

```
-Djavax.net.debug=all
```

(b)   To view the hexadecimal dumps of each handshake message:

```
-Djavax.net.debug=ssl:handshake:data
```

(c)   To view the hexadecimal dumps of each handshake message, and to print trust manager tracing (the commas are optional):

```
-Djavax.net.debug=SSL:handshake:data:trustmanager
```

7.12 THE SSLContext

The true heart of the J S S E specification is the SSLContext class. This class establishes the factory classes which control the operation of J S S E :

(a)   the SSLSocketFactory and SSLServerSocketFactory, already encountered

(b)   the KeyManagerFactory, which supplies instances of the KeyManager interface which are called to provide authentication certificates and private keys to peers when they authenticate themselves to the remote peer

(c)   the TrustManagerFactory, which supplies instances of the TrustManager interface which are called to establishing trustworthiness of certificates received by peers when checking authentications received from the remote peer.

The SSLContext manages the SSLSessions associated with each instance of SSLSocketFactory or SSLServerSocketFactory, as well as the SecureRandom object used when generating session keys for these sessions.

Most of what the SSLContext class and its friends do is beyond the scope of this book, being for implementors of J S S E itself, or those doing fairly extraordinary security manoeuvres. The SSLContext A P I discussed here is shown below.

```
class SSLContext
{
    SSLSessionContext getClientSessionContext();
    SSLSessionContext getServerSessionContext();
    static SSLContext getInstance(String protocol)
      throws NoSuchAlgorithmException;
    String            getProtocol();
    SSLServerSocketFactory
                      getServerSocketFactory();
    SSLSocketFactory  getSocketFactory();
    void              init(KeyManager[] km,
                           TrustManager[] tm,
                           SecureRandom secure)
      throws KeyManagementException;
}
```

Note that the SSLContext maintains separate SSLSessionContexts for servers and clients.

7.12.1 *Using the SSLContext*

The SSLContext class and its friends can be used to control the authentication keystore and truststore other than via system properties, or to provide an existing SecureRandom object. If you are creating an SSLEngine as discussed in Chapter 8, you *must* create and initialize an explicit SSLContext.

An SSLContext is obtained via the static SSLContext.getInstance method shown above, where protocol is usually 'TLS' or 'SSL': for the complete list of supported protocols see Appendix A, 'Standard Names', in the J S S E Reference Guide provided with your J D K or your J S S E implementation.[18]

When an SSLContext is explicitly created, it must be initialized by the SSLContext.init method shown above. If the peer must authenticate itself (*i.e.* if it is a server, or a client of a server where needClientAuth has been set), the context *must* be initialized with a *non-null* KeyManager[] array.[19] The technique is shown in Example 7.3. The other parameters can be defaulted to null.

---

18. Two other getInstance methods not described here are used when a specific SSL implementation provider is required.

19. The J D K 1.5 *javadoc* documentation disagrees with its own J S S E Reference Guide on this point. The former states 'Either of the first two parameters may be null in which case the installed security providers will be searched for the highest priority implementation of the appropriate factory.' The latter states 'If the KeyManager[] parameter is null, then an empty KeyManager will be defined for this context. If the TrustManager[] parameter is null, the installed security providers will be searched for the highest-priority implementation of the TrustManagerFactory, from which an appropriate TrustManager will be obtained.' The latter is correct, and an SSLContext initialized with an empty KeyManager cannot authenticate itself.

```
KeyManagerFactory kmf =
  KeyManagerFactory.getInstance("SunX509");
KeyStore ks = KeyStore.getInstance("JKS");
File      keysFile = new File(…);
String    passphrase = …;
ks.load(new FileInputStream(keysFile),
  passphrase.toCharArray());
kmf.init(ks, passphrase.toCharArray());
SSLContext sslContext = SSLContext.getInstance("TLS");
sslContext.init(kmf.getKeyManagers(),
    /*TrustManager[]*/null,
    /*SecureRandom*/null);
SSLServerSocketFactory ssf =
  sslContext.getServerSocketFactory();
```

EXAMPLE 7.3 Hard-coded keystore setup

This technique might be preferred if, for example, you don't want to expose the keystore password globally as a system property. Note that the passphrase parameter of Keystore.load only causes the keystore to be checked for integrity on opening; the passphrase is really only required by the KeyManagerFactory.init method, to give it access to private key entries (i.e. to allow it to call the KeyStore.getKey method). This technique is entirely equivalent to the technique we encountered earlier using system properties, shown again for easy comparison in Example 7.4.

```
System.setProperty("javax.net.ssl.keyStore",
  keysFile.toString());
System.setProperty("javax.net.ssl.keyStorePassword",
  passphrase);
SSLServerSocketFactoryssf =
  (SSLServerSocketFactory)
    SSLServerSocketFactory.getDefault();
// at this point you might like to clear keyStorePassword
```

EXAMPLE 7.4 Keystore setup via system properties

You can use a similar technique to control the trust-store. The trust-store is supplied as the second parameter to the SSLContext.init method. The trust-store doesn't contain private key entries, so you don't need to supply its passphrase at all, for the reason discussed in the previous paragraph; therefore, the TrustManagerFactory.init method doesn't have a passphrase parameter. This technique is shown in Example 7.5.

The *third* parameter to the SSLContext.init method is a SecureRandom object. If you initialize one of these in parallel with your main initialization and then sup-

```
TrustManagerFactory tmf =
  TrustManagerFactory.getInstance("SunX509");
KeyStore ks = KeyStore.getInstance("JKS");
File trustFile = new File(…);
ks.load(new FileInputStream(trustFile), null);
tmf.init(ks);
SSLContext sslContext = SSLContext.getInstance("TLS");
sslContext.init(/*KeyManager[]*/null,
  tmf.getTrustManagers(),
  /*SecureRandom*/null);
SSLServerSocketFactory ssf =
  sslContext.getServerSocketFactory();
```

EXAMPLE 7.5 Trust-store setup via hard-coding

ply it to the SSLContext.init method, you can eliminate or at least reduce the annoying pause when creating the first SSLSocket or SSLServerSocket referred to in section 7.3.2. SSLContext initialization using all three parameters is demonstrated in Example 7.6.

7.13 RECOMMENDATIONS

Although the Java implementations of s s l work reasonably well by default once installed correctly, there are still better and worse ways to use s s l.

Unless you are writing a server which must support clients from anywhere (*e.g.* the entire Internet), you should limit the cipher suites you are prepared to use via the techniques discussed in section 7.5.4. The cipher suites you use should be commensurate with the value of your data.[20]

7.13.1 *General recommendations*

(a) Send data in the largest chunks possible: use buffered input and output streams over the streams obtained from the socket, with the largest possible buffer size, and flush the output as infrequently as possible, (ideally, only before reading. The buffer for the BufferedOutputStream should be at least 16384 bytes.

(b) *Clients* should use long session expiry times and a large or uncontrolled session cache size, as clients generally only deal with a few servers simultaneously.

---

20. For recommendations on s s l security and performance in greater detail in Rescorla, s s l *and* t l s, §§5.7, 6.8, & 6.18.

```
// Initialize key manager factory.
KeyManagerFactory kmf =
  KeyManagerFactory.getInstance("SunX509");
KeyStore ks = KeyStore.getInstance("JKS");
File     keysFile = new File(…);
String   passphrase = …;   // supply your own value
ks.load(new FileInputStream(keysFile),
  passphrase.toCharArray());
kmf.init(ks, passphrase.toCharArray());

// Initialize trust manager factory.
TrustManagerFactory tmf =
  TrustManagerFactory.getInstance("SunX509");
File trustFile = new File(…);// supply your own value
ks.load(new FileInputStream(trustFile), null);
tmf.init(ks);

// Initialize the source of secure random numbers.
// (You can do this asynchronously during startup to
// eliminate the delay creating the first
// SSLSocket/SSLServerSocket.)
SecureRandom   secureRandom = new SecureRandom();
secureRandom.nextInt();

// Get the SSL context instance.
SSLContext sslContext = SSLContext.getInstance("TLS");
// Initialize it
sslContext.init(kmf.getKeyManagers(),
  tmf.getTrustManagers(),
  secureRandom);

// Get the server socket factory.
SSLServerSocketFactory serverSocketFactory =
  sslContext.getServerSocketFactory();

// Get the client socket factory.
SSLSocketFactory  clientSocketFactory =
  sslContext.getSocketFactory();
```

EXAMPLE 7.6 SSLContext.init—all parameters

(c)   *Servers* should use a short session expiry time or a small session cache size, as they deal with a large number of clients simultaneously, and the time and space costs multiply rapidly.

(d)   If clients won't actually reconnect within the session expiry interval, *all* session management at the server is a waste of resources, so set the server's session cache size to one (zero means no limit).

(e) Use the shortest private keys compatible with your security requirements: 768 bits is strong enough for most commercial transactions, although 1536 bits is almost certainly too short for highly valuable data.

7.13.2 *For maximum performance*

(a) Use R S A for asymmetric algorithms.

(b) Use R C 4-128 for symmetric encryption.

(c) Use S H A-1 for message authentication.[21]

(d) Maximise connection pooling at the client.

(e) Maximise session resumption, and expire sessions at the maximum reasonable interval within the R F C recommendation of 24 hours.

(f) Change cipher suites at long intervals, say hours.

7.13.3 *For maximum security*

(a) Use R S A for asymmetric algorithms.[22]

(b) Use D E S 3 for symmetric encryption: this is more secure than R C-4, but about ten times as slow.

(c) Use S H A-1 for message authentication.

(d) Minimise connection pooling at the client.

(e) Minimize session resumption, or expire sessions frequently, say once or twice an hour.

(f) Change cipher keys at short intervals, say minutes.

7.14 HTTPS

As well as supporting secure T C P via a socket-level A P I, J S S E also supports the H T T P S protocol via the standard Java U R L A P I. This allows Java applications to be clients of, and to communicate securely with, T L S- or S S L-enabled web servers by using the 'https' U R L protocol and the java.net.URL class. Most of the common Web serverssupport 'https' U R L schemes, for example:

---

21. M D 5 is faster, but only by about 40%, and it is being phased out.

22. D S A is 2–10 times as slow as R S A, without being appreciably more secure, although this choice may actually be determined more by cost, compatibility requirements, intellectual property issues, or U S export restrictions.

```
https://www.verisign.com
```

J S S E provides an implementation for the 'https' U R L scheme. If you are using J D K 1.3 and J S S E, rather than J D K 1.4 or later where these are unified, you must enable this implementation by setting the system property java.protocol.handler.pkgs to com.sun.net.ssl.internal.www.protocol, either on the command line or programmatically. (This enables the relevant URLStreamHandler for the protocol scheme.) You can then use 'https' URLs in Java as shown in Example 7.7.

```
URL           url = new URL("https://www.verisign.com");
URLConnectionconn = url.openConnection();
InputStream in = conn.getInputStream();
// or, combining the two previous lines
InputStream in = url.openStream();
// etc as usual
```

EXAMPLE 7.7 HTTPS U R L usage

The URLConnection which was obtained in Example 7.7 is an object of type com.sun.net.ssl.HttpsURLConnection or javax.net.ssl.HttpsURLConnection, depending in a complex way on the J D K version and the value of the system property java.protocol.handler.pkgs as shown in Table 7.3.

TABLE 7.3 HttpsURLConnection type

J D K	java.protocol.handlers.pkgs value	HttpsURLConnection class
< 1.4 + J S S E	com.sun.net.ssl.internal.www.protocol	com.sun.net.ssl.HttpsURLConnection
≥ 1.4	com.sun.net.ssl.internal.www.protocol	com.sun.net.ssl.HttpsURLConnection
≥ 1.4	Not set	javax.net.ssl.HttpsURLConnection

The HttpsURLConnection class extends java.net.HttpURLConnection in both the packages com.sun.net.ssl and javax.net.ssl.

A different 'https' protocol implementation can be used by setting the system property java.protocol.handler.pkgs to the name of the supporting package name, as described in the *javadoc* for the java.net.URL class. Many common Web browsers support 'https' schemes.

The trust and key management for the 'https' U R L implementation is environment-specific, *i.e.* varies with the implementation.

7.15 EXCEPTIONS IN JSSE

The exceptions defined by JSSE form part of the inheritance tree shown in Figure 7.4.

TABLE 7.4 Hierarchy of JSSE exceptions

Exception

⎣ RuntimeException

⎣ IOException

⎣ ⎣ SSLException

⎣ ⎣ ⎣ SSLHandshakeException

⎣ ⎣ ⎣ SSLKeyException

⎣ ⎣ ⎣ SSLPeerUnverifiedException

⎣ ⎣ ⎣ SSLProtocolException

Exceptions thrown by JSSE are described in Table 7.5.

TABLE 7.5 Exceptions in SSL

Exception	Description
RuntimeException: no cipher suites in common	The intersection of the client's ciphersuite set with the server's ciphersuite set is empty. For example, Netscape Navigator and Internet Explorer only enable RSA-based cipher suites. If the server only enables DSA-based cipher suites, this condition will occur.
SocketException	'No SSL Server Sockets' or 'SSL implementation not available' both indicate incorrect installation: see section 7.3.2.
SSLException	'No available certificate corresponding to the SSL cipher suites which are enabled': the enabled cipher suites and available keystores do not match. An enabled cipher suite can only be used if the keystore contains a corresponding key entry: for example, if an RSA cipher suite is enabled, an RSA key entry must be available in the keystore, otherwise the RSA cipher suite cannot be used. If there are no available key entries for all of the cipher suites enabled, this exception is thrown.
SSLHandshakeException	The server and client could not negotiate the required level of security. The connection is now unusable.

TABLE 7.5 Exceptions in SSL (continued)

Exception	Description
SSLKeyException	A bad SSL key was encountered, usually indicating misconfiguration of the server or client certificate and private key.
SSLPeerUnverifiedException	The peer was not verified: thrown if the application attempts to retrieve peer certificates for a peer which did not authenticate itself, *e.g.* because the negotiated cipher suite did not support it, peer authentication (*e.g.* client authentication) was not established during the handshake, or no certificate existed at the peer.
SSLProtocolException	Indicate an error in the protocol operation. Normally this indicates an error in the local or peer implementation, but it can also occur if you deliberately violate the protocol, *e.g.* by connecting an ordinary Socket to an SSLSocket; wrapping a Socket in an SSLSocket as described in section 7.6.4 and then performing I/O with the Socket rather than the SSLSocket; or bypassing the record layer as discussed in section 7.9.

7.16 SSL SYSTEM PROPERTIES

The major system properties affecting the operation of SSL in Java are shown in Table 7.6.

TABLE 7.6 System properties in JSSE

Name	Values	Description
https.cipherSuites	no default	Comma-separated list of cipher suite names specifying which cipher suites to enable for use on objects of type HttpsURLConnection
https.protocols	no default	Comma-separated list of protocol suite names specifying which protocol suites to enable on objects of type HttpsURLConnection

TABLE 7.6 System properties in J S S E (continued)

Name	Values	Description
https.proxyHost	no default	Same as http.proxyHost but for 'https'
https.proxyPort	no default	Same as http.proxyPort but for 'https'
java.net.protocol.handler.pkgs	no default	See text in this section
javax.net.debug	See section 7.11	Controls debug tracing
javax.net.ssl.keyStore	filename, no default	Location of key store used by peers which authenticate themselves: by default this includes all J S S E servers
javax.net.ssl.keyStorePassword	no default	Key store password
javax.net.ssl.keyStoreType	default is given by KeyStore.getDefaultType	Key store implementation type, *e.g.* 'JKS'
javax.net.ssl.trustStore	filename: default is jssecacerts if it exists, otherwise cacerts	Location of trust store used by peers which request authentication: by default this includes all J S S E clients
javax.net.ssl.trustStorePassword	no default	Trust store password. Normally not needed: see section 7.12
javax.net.ssl.trustStoreType	default is given by KeyStore.getDefaultType	Trust store implementation type, *e.g.* 'JKS'

These properties are currently used by Sun's J S S E implementation: they are not guaranteed to be examined and used by other implementations, but if they are, they should behave in the same way as the J S S E implementation does. The table is accurate for J S S E 1.0.3 and J D K 1.5, but there is no guarantee that the properties will continue to exist or be of the same type (system or security) in future releases.

Other properties exist for customizing various security factories and algorithms: consult the J D K or J S S E documentation for these.

7.17 SAMPLE S S L CLIENT AND SERVER

The sample s s l client and server shown in this section exhibit good practice as described in section 7.13, *i.e.* practical session management and efficient use of buffering. The server can be further improved using the ideas of Chapter 12.

7.17.1 *Session-managing SSL Server*

```java
// SessionManagedSSLServer.java
public class SessionManagedSSLServer
  implements HandshakeCompletedListener, Runnable
{
  // Session management parameters.
  // In a practical implementation these would be defined
  // externally, e.g. in a properties file.
  // Cache up to four sessions

  static final int   SESSION_CACHE_SIZE = 4;
  // Time sessions out after 15 minutes.
  static final int   SESSION_TIMEOUT    = 15*60; // 15m

  private SSLContext             sslContext;
  private SSLServerSocketFactory serverSocketFactory;
  private SSLServerSocket        serverSocket;

  // Replace with your own local values ...
  static final File keysFile = new File("...","testkeys");
  static final String passPhrase = "passphrase";

  static // initialization
  {
// Alter as required
//  System.setProperty("javax.net.debug","ssl");
  }
  /**
    * Create new SessionManagedSSLServer
    * @param port Port to listen at
    * @exception IOException creating socket
    * @exception GeneralSecurityException initializing SSL
    */
  public SessionManagedSSLServer(int port)
    throws IOException, GeneralSecurityException
  {
    if (sslContext == null)
    {
      KeyManagerFactory kmf =
```

```
        KeyManagerFactory.getInstance("SunX509");
      KeyStore ks = KeyStore.getInstance("JKS");
      File    keysFile = new File(…);
      String  passphrase = …;
      ks.load(new FileInputStream(keysFile),
        passphrase.toCharArray());
      kmf.init(ks, passphrase.toCharArray());

      this.sslContext = SSLContext.getInstance("TLS");
      sslContext.init(kmf.getKeyManagers(),null,null);
      // Configure the server session context (1.4-specific)
      SSLSessionContext serverSessionContext =
        sslContext.getServerSessionContext();
      serverSessionContext
        .setSessionCacheSize(SESSION_CACHE_SIZE);
      serverSessionContext
        .setSessionTimeout(SESSION_TIMEOUT);
      this.serverSocketFactory =
        sslContext.getServerSocketFactory();
    }
    this.serverSocket =
      (SSLServerSocket)
        serverSocketFactory.createServerSocket(port);
  }

  /** handshakeCompleted callback.
   * Called whenever a handshake completes successfully.
   * Handshaking is usually asynchronous, but no I/O is done
   * on the socket until a handshake completes successfully,
   * so there is no need to synchronize anything with the
   * completion of this method.
   */

  public void handshakeCompleted
    (HandshakeCompletedEvent event)
  {
    String  cipherSuite = event.getCipherSuite();
    // Ensure cipher suite is strong enough, not shown …

    try
    {
      // (JDK 1.4)
      java.security.cert.Certificate[] peerCerts =
        event.getPeerCertificates();
      X509Certificate peerCert =
        (X509Certificate)peerCerts[0];
```

```
      // Verify distinguished name of zeroth certificate.
      Principal  principal = peerCert.getSubjectDN()
      // check principal.getName() &c against expectations,
      // not shown …
    }
    catch (SSLPeerUnverifiedException exc)
    {
      // do whatever is required, e.g. close the socket
    }
  } // handshakeCompleted()
  /** @see      java.lang.Thread#run() */
  public void run()
  {
    for (;;)
    {
      try
      {
        SSLSocket  socket =
          (SSLSocket)serverSocket.accept();
        socket.addHandshakeCompletedListener(this);
        new ConnectionThread(socket).start();
      }
      catch (IOException exc)
      {
        // …
      }
    } // for (;;)
  } // run()
  class ConnectionThread extends Thread
  {
    SSLSocket  socket;
    ConnectionThread(SSLSocket socket)
    {
      this.socket = socket;
    }
    public void run()
    {
      try
      {
//      Choose whichever of these suits your situation ...
//      socket.setWantClientAuth(true);
//      socket.setNeedClientAuth(true);
        InputStream  in =
          new BufferedInputStream
```

```java
        (socket.getInputStream(),8192);
      OutputStream    out =
        new BufferedOutputStream
          (socket.getOutputStream(),8192);
      // Handle the conversation ...
    }
    catch (SSLException exc)
    {
      // Treat this as a possible security attack ...
    }
    catch (IOException exc)
    {
      // Treat this as a network failure ...
    }
    finally
    {
      try
      {
        socket.close();
      }
      catch (SSLException exc)
      {
        // Handle possible truncation attack, not shown ...
      }
      catch (IOException exc)
      {
      }
    } // finally
  } // run()
} // class ConnectionThread
} // class SessionManagedSSLServer
```

EXAMPLE 7.8 Sample s s l server

7.17.2 *Session-managing SSL client*

```java
// SessionManagedSSLClient.java
public class SessionManagedSSLClient
  implements HandshakeCompletedListener
{
```

```
// Session management parameters.
// In a practical implementation these would be defined
// externally, e.g. in a properties file.
// Cache up to ten sessions

static final int  SESSION_CACHE_SIZE = 10;
// Time sessions out after 1 hour.
static final int  SESSION_TIMEOUT   = 60*60; // 1h

private SSLContext       sslContext;
private SSLSocketFactory socketFactory;
private SSLSocket        socket;

static // initializer
{
  // as required
  // System.setProperty("javax.net.debug","ssl");
}

/**
  * Create new SessionManagedSSLClient
  * @param host target host
  * @param port target port
  * @exception IOException creating socket
  * @exception GeneralSecurityException initializing SSL
  */
public SessionManagedSSLClient(String host, int port)
  throws IOException, GeneralSecurityException
{
  if (sslContext == null)
  {
    this.sslContext = SSLContext.getInstance("TLS");
    sslContext.init(null,null,null);
    // Configure client session context: JDK 1.4-specific
    SSLSessionContext clientSessionContext =
      sslContext.getClientSessionContext();
    clientSessionContext
      .setSessionCacheSize(SESSION_CACHE_SIZE);
    clientSessionContext
      .setSessionTimeout(SESSION_TIMEOUT);
    this.socketFactory = sslContext.getSocketFactory();
  }
  this.socket =
    (SSLSocket)socketFactory.createSocket(host,port);
  socket.addHandshakeCompletedListener(this);
}
```

```java
/** Handle conversation */
public void handleConversation()
{
  try
  {
    InputStream    in =
      new BufferedInputStream
        (socket.getInputStream());
    OutputStream   out =
      new BufferedOutputStream
        (socket.getOutputStream(),8192);
    // ...
  }
  catch (SSLException exc)
  {
    // Treat this as a possible security attack ...
  }
  catch (IOException exc)
  {
    // Treat this as a network failure ...
  }
  finally
  {
    try
    {
      socket.close();
    }
    catch (SSLException exc)
    {
      // Handle possible truncation attack, not shown ...
    }
    catch (IOException exc)
    {
      // ...
    }
    socket = null;
  } // finally
} // handleConversation()

/** handshakeCompleted callback.
 * Called whenever a handshake completes successfully.
 * Handshaking is usually asynchronous, but no I/O is done
 * on the socket until a handshake completes successfully,
```

```
* so there is no need to synchronize anything with
* the completion of this method.
*/
public void handshakeCompleted
   (HandshakeCompletedEvent event)
{
   String cipherSuite = event.getCipherSuite();
   // Ensure cipher suite is strong enough, not shown …

   try
   {
      // (JDK 1.4)
      java.security.cert.Certificate[] peerCerts =
         event.getPeerCertificates();
      X509Certificate peerCert =
         (X509Certificate)peerCerts[0];

      // Verify the distinguished name (DN)
      // of the zeroth certificate.
      Principal principal = peerCert.getSubjectDN()
      // check principal.getName() &c against expectation,
      // not shown …
   }
   catch (SSLPeerUnverifiedException exc)
   {
      // Handle this as required …
   }
} // handshakeCompleted()
} // class SessionManagedSSLClient
```

EXAMPLE 7.9 Sample SSL client

7.18 THE JAVA GSS-API

The JGSS-API or Java Genetic Security Services Application Programming Interface was introduced in JDK 1.4 as a standard part of the J2SE platform. JGSS is an implementation of RFC 2743, which defines the Generic Security Service Application Program Interface (GSS-API) as a language-independent specification, and RFC 2853 which defines a Java-specific language binding for it.[23]

The following is quoted from the abstract of RFC 2853:

---

23. Linn, J., RFC 2743, *Generic Security Service Application Program Interface Version 2, Update 1*, January 2000; Kabat *et al.*, RFC 2853, *Generic Security Service API Version 2: Java Bindings*, June 2000.

'*The Generic Security Services Application Program Interface (*GSS-API*) offers application programmers uniform access to security services atop a variety of underlying cryptographic mechanisms ... The* GSS-API *allows a caller application to ... apply security services such as confidentiality and integrity on a per-message basis. Examples of security mechanisms defined for* GSS-API *are the Simple Public-Key* GSS-API *Mechanism [*SPKM*] and the Kerberos Version 5* GSS-API *Mechanism [*KERBV5*].*'

The JGSS-API provides another approach to network security: it can be used as an alternative to JSSE in environments which support security mechanisms defined for GSS-API: typically, this means Kerberos.

Unlike JSSE, whose design consists of a façade over the Java Sockets classes, and which invisibly applies encryption and decryption to an authenticated data stream, the GSS-API is concerned entirely with the messages themselves, not with the communications technology: this is one reason why it is labelled 'generic'.[24]

When using the JGSS-API, a network connection is formed entirely with the java.net.Socket and java.net.ServerSocket classes. Authentication can be performed if required using the complementary JAAS (Java Authentication and Authorization Service) which is beyond the scope of this book. The JGSS-API is then used in three ways:

(a) To form a session or 'shared context' within which subsequent exchanges of data can be made secure.

(b) To *wrap* messages as 'tokens' for sending to the recipient: these may be encrypted, digitally signed, *etc. as required by the individual message.*

(c) To *unwrap* received tokens into messages.

(d) To end the session.

In the JGSS-API, an input stream can be wrapped and written directly to an output stream, or a byte array can be wrapped and returned as a token in another byte array; conversely, an input stream can be unwrapped and written directly to an output stream, or a received token byte array can be unwrapped as a message in a byte array. A message which was wrapped from a byte array can be unwrapped from an input stream and *vice versa.*[25]

When wrapping, message properties are supplied which specify *(i)* the required quality-of-protection (QOP) and *(ii)* whether or not encryption is required. QOP is defined as an integer whose precise meaning is defined by the underlying security provider (*e.g.* Kerberos). This information is recorded se-

---

24. Others being its language-neutrality and its independence of specific cryptographic technology.

25. Because byte arrays can be used as inputs and outputs, the JGSS-API can also be used with UDP.

curely in the resulting token. When a token is received and unwrapped into a message, it is decrypted if the token was encrypted; its signature is verified if the token was signed; *etc.* These decisions are based purely on the message-properties information contained (securely) within the token itself. The recipient does not need to know whether the token was originally decrypted, signed, *etc.*: the token protocol is self-describing and self-enforcing. The wrap and unwrap operations also support token expiry, sequencing, and detection of duplicates.

The JGSS-API therefore has the following interesting properties:

(a) Different levels of security can be applied to different messages by the sender.

(b) The level of security applied to a message can be varied arbitrarily at any time without affecting the recipient or the application protocol. For example, zero security can be used over trusted internal network link, and the highest level used over Internet links, depending on who the recipient is, its location, *etc.*

The JGSS-API is primarily implemented in the package org.ietf.jgss. For further information on the JGSS-API, see the online JDK documentation, following the links Guide to Features, Security and Signed Applets, Java JGSS-API.

CHAPTER 8

Scalable secure sockets

THIS CHAPTER DISCUSSES scalable secure sockets, showing how to obtain the security features of the previous chapter in a scalable architecture.

8.1 INTRODUCTION

8.1.1 The problem

Channel I/O and SSLSockets are largely strangers when they meet. You might think you can create a SocketChannel first, connect it, and then wrap its socket as an SSLSocket:

```
String          host; // initialization not shown …
int             port; // initialization not shown …
SocketChannel   channel= SocketChannel.open();
Socket          socket = channel.socket();
SocketAddress   address= new InetSocketAddress(host, port);
socket.connect(address);
SSLSocketFactory  sslFactory =
   (SSLSocketFactory)SSLSocketFactory.getDefault();
SSLSocket sslSocket=
   sslFactory.createSocket(socket, host, port, true);
```

Well, you *can*, but let's look into it further. At this point you have a SocketChannel and an SSLSocket. However, the input and output of the channel are connected to the lower-level I/O of the underlying Socket, not the higher-level I/O of the SSLSocket, which implements the s s l record protocol, so writing or reading the channel would bypass the record protocol, *i.e.* would violate the TLS/SSL specification: this will most likely cause the other end to fail with an

SSLProtocolException. To get around this, you must confine yourself to using the SSLSocket's input and output streams, possibly wrapped as further channels, making the original SocketChannel basically pointless.

Nor can you put the channel into non-blocking mode and expect to be able to select on it. The SSLSocket uses stream I/O in both the record protocol and the handshake protocol, but, as we saw in section 4.2.4, if you put the channel into non-blocking mode, stream I/O fails with an IllegalBlockingModeException.

This means that to use this scheme you would have to use blocking mode and streams for the actual I/O, and non-blocking mode when selecting. Having to use blocking I/O implies having to commit a thread, whereupon the scalability advantage of non-blocking I/O and selection is lost.

8.1.2 *The solution*

Instead of providing the obvious SSLSocketChannel, Sun have provided a lower-level construct called the SSLEngine in J D K 1.5. This 'engine' deals only with the data and leaves all I/O up to the caller, so it is capable of handling not only secure sessions via socket streams or channels but also via datagram sockets, files, pipes, or any other data stream that can be imagined.[1]

This means that scalable secure sockets can be implemented in Java using the javax.net.ssl.SSLEngine class introduced in J D K 1.5 (Java 5) in conjunction with the channel I/O features of the java.nio.channels package described in Chapter 5.

In this chapter we will examine the application of the SSLEngine to non-blocking SocketChannels in conjunction with Selectors.

8.2 The SSLEngine class

The SSLEngine class enables applications to deal in secure protocols such as s s l and t l s but is transport-independent. It does not deal with sockets or channels or streams: it deals only with ByteBuffers.

It is therefore possible to use the SSLEngine in conjunction with non-blocking I/O, a very important advantage for the server side of secure communications protocols.

Unfortunately, Sun's solution means that using s s l over socket channels is extremely complicated.

---

1. The demand was for an SSLSocketChannel. Why Sun didn't respond to it directly, or by providing *both* the SSLEngine *and* an SSLSocketChannel built using it, is a good question. Another good question is why they provided something that requires users to be able to write a state machine and to have a working knowledge of r f c 2246 to implement correctly.

8.2.1 Creating the SSLEngine

An SSLEngine is obtained from an *initialized* SSLContext (created as described in section 7.12.1) via the method:

```
class SSLContext
{
  SSLEngine  createSSLEngine();
  SSLEngine  createSSLEngine(String host, int port);
}
```

Providing the target host and port gives the SSLContext hints about session sharing, and is strongly recommended.

8.2.2 SSLEngine methods

The SSLEngine exports the following principal methods of interest:

```
class SSLEngine
{
  SSLEngineResult unwrap(ByteBuffer src, ByteBuffer dst)
     throws SSLException;
  SSLEngineResult unwrap(ByteBuffer[] src, ByteBuffer dst)
     throws SSLException;
  SSLEngineResult unwrap(ByteBuffer[] src, int offset,
    int length, ByteBuffer dst)
     throws SSLException;
  SSLEngineResult wrap(ByteBuffer src, ByteBuffer dst)
     throws SSLException;
  SSLEngineResult wrap(ByteBuffer src, ByteBuffer[] dst)
     throws SSLException;
  SSLEngineResult wrap(ByteBuffer src, ByteBuffer[] dst,
    int offset, int length)
     throws SSLException;
}
```

where the rather boringly named wrap and unwrap operations respectively *encode* data to be sent to the peer and *decode* data received from the peer.

8.2.3 Closure methods

The SSLEngine also exports these methods for use when closing a secure session:

```
class SSLEngine
{
  boolean  isInboundDone();
  boolean  isOutboundDone();
  void     closeInbound()   throws SSLException;
  void     closeOutbound()  throws SSLException;
}
```

These require comment.

The apparent naming confusion between 'close' and 'done' is there because isInboundDone can be true even if you haven't called closeInbound yourself: the condition can arise as a result of unwrapping an incoming TLS close_notify packet from the peer. (Such a packet could result from the peer calling closeOutbound and wrap and then writing the result to the network.)

Similarly, isOutboundDone is true if you have called closeOutbound, but also if you have unwrapped an incoming close_notify as described above. The engine automatically responds to this by returning the resulting NEED_WRAP condition described in section 8.2.4 below: if you respond correctly to this by calling SSLEngine.wrap, it will wrap an outgoing close_notify and set the isOutboundDone condition to true.

There are strict rules specified in RFC 2246 about closing TLS/SSL connections,[2] which must be obeyed if the inherent security in TLS/SSL is to be realized. As shown in Table 8.1, the application needs to have an understanding of RFC 2246 in order to implement closing of the connection correctly.

8.2.4 Using the SSLEngine class: Status and HandshakeStatus

As we would hope and expect, the SSLEngine takes care of all handshaking and establishment of secure sessions. However this still makes the engine rather difficult to use in practice. What appears to be a simple read or write—unwrap or wrap in the SSLEngine's terminology—may require several interspersed reads and writes to accomplish the session handshake before the application's read or write can complete, and these can occur at any point during the exchange of data with the peer (because either peer can request a new handshake at any time).

The SSLEngineResult returned by wrap and unwrap therefore contains *two* status indicators: an SSLEngineResult.Status item, which indicates the *success or failure of the operation just called,* and an SSLEngineResult.HandshakeStatus item which indicates *what the engine wants to do next.*

These are defined using the JDK 1.5 enum facility as follows:

---

2. RFC 2246 §7.2.1.

```
class SSLEngineResult
{
  enum Status
  {
    BUFFER_OVERFLOW,   // insufficient room in target buffer
    BUFFER_UNDERFLOW,  // no data in source buffer
    CLOSED,            // engine has been securely closed
    OK;                // operation completed successfully
  }
  enum HandshakeStatus
  {
    FINISHED,          // just finished handshaking
    NEED_TASK,         // application must run a delegated task
    NEED_UNWRAP,       // application must perform an unwrap
    NEED_WRAP,         // application must perform a wrap
    NOT_HANDSHAKING;   // no handshaking in progress
  }
  Status           getStatus();
  HandshakeStatus  getHandshakeStatus();
}
```

It is a mistake to consider these indicators in combination. The Status values need to be interpreted in the context of the operation just attempted, as shown in Table 8.1.

TABLE 8.1 SSLEngineResult.Status values

Operation	Status	Meaning
unwrap, wrap	OK	The operation completed successfully; the application can continue.
unwrap	CLOSED	Received an incoming TLS close_notify: the peer has closed its end of the connection. The application *must* continue processing the HandshakeStatus; the engine will want to wrap an outgoing close_notify.

TABLE 8.1 SSLEngineResult.Status values (continued)

Operation	Status	Meaning
wrap	CLOSED	If the engine was not already closed, the application has just closed this side of the engine (by calling SSLEngine.closeOutbound and wrap). The application must write the wrapped data (a TLS close_notify) to the socket. If the application was the initiator of the close it *may* then try to read and unwrap an incoming close_notify, but it only *must* do so if it was not the initiator of the close, which is the case described above for {unwrap,CLOSED}. However it must not receive or transmit any more data, and the SSLEngine will not permit it to do so.
unwrap	BUFFER_OVERFLOW	Target buffer overflow: the application needs to remove data from the target buffer of the unwrap operation and repeat the unwrap.
	BUFFER_UNDERFLOW	Nothing to unwrap: the application needs to obtain more data from the peer and repeat the unwrap.
wrap	BUFFER_OVERFLOW	Target buffer overflow: the application needs to send the target buffer of the wrap (encode) operation to the peer and repeat the wrap.
	BUFFER_UNDERFLOW	Nothing to wrap: no data was present in the source buffer.

The HandshakeStatus values are independent of the operation just attempted, but not of the Status value returned by it, so the operation just attempted must be retried if necessary as shown in Table 8.1 before the operation indicated by the HandshakeStatus can be carried out as shown in Table 8.2.

TABLE 8.2 SSLEngineResult.HandshakeStatus values

Value	Meaning
FINISHED	The SSLEngine has just finished handshaking.
NEED_TASK	The SSLEngine needs the results of one or more tasks which may block.
NEED_UNWRAP	The SSLEngine needs to receive and unwrap data from the remote peer.

TABLE 8.2 SSLEngineResult.HandshakeStatus values (continued)

Value	Meaning
NEED_WRAP	The SSLEngine needs to wrap and send data to the remote peer.
NOT_HANDSHAKING	The SSLEngine is not currently handshaking.

The handshake status can also be obtained from the SSLEngine:

```
class SSLEngine
{
  SSLEngineResult.HandshakeStatus getHandshakeStatus();
}
```

The application must provide four ByteBuffers: two application buffers for plaintext (one for sent and one for received data), and two packet buffers for encrypted data (one for sent and one for received data), as follows:

(a) An application send buffer, of arbitrary size, used to hold application data waiting to be encoded and sent to the peer.

(b) A packet send buffer, whose size must be at least equal to the value returned by SSLSession.getPacketBufferSize, used to hold encoded data for sending to the peer (after being encoded from the application send buffer).

(c) A packet receive buffer, whose size must be at least equal to the value returned by SSLSession.getPacketBufferSize, used to receive encoded data from the peer (for decoding into the application receive buffer).

(d) An application receive buffer, whose size must be at least equal to the value returned by SSLSession.getApplicationBufferSize, used to hold data decoded after receipt from the peer.

8.2.5 Summary

All this really makes the SSLEngine rather a luxury for the client side of an application. However the advantages of non-blocking I/O for the server side of an application are so irresistible that it is well worth exploring how to best make use of the engine.

8.3 DESIGNING AN SSLEngineManager CLASS

We will design and implement an SSLEngineManager class that is a bit like a Channel in that it has methods for reading, writing, and closing, and is designed to be operated in non-blocking mode. It delegates all its I/O to a SocketChannel, manages all the ByteBuffers described above, and delegates all SSL processing to an SSLEngine. Its principal methods will be as follows:

```
class SSLEngineManager
{
    // Constructor
    SSLEngineManager(SocketChannel channel, SSLEngine engine);

    int  read() throws IOException;
    int  write() throws IOException;
    void close() throws IOException;

    ByteBuffer getAppRecvBuffer();
    ByteBuffer getAppSendBuffer();

    SSLEngine  getEngine();
}
```

8.3.1 Constructor: design

The constructor will take two arguments:

(a) A SocketChannel, assumed to be connected and non-blocking, resulting either from SocketChannel.open or ServerSocketChannel.accept depending on whether the application is a client or a server, and

(b) An initialized SSLEngine, assumed to be in client or server mode as required by the application and to have had any other required initialization already performed such as requiring client authentication, selection of protocols and cipher suites, *etc.*

The constructor will create the four ByteBuffers described above at the appropriate sizes and make the application send and receive buffers available via the accessor methods shown above.

8.3.2 read method: design

The read method will assume *(i)* that there is space in the application receive buffer, and *(ii)* that the application has waited for OP_READ before calling it. It will take no arguments and may throw an IOException. It will behave correctly if no data is available, or if an end-of-stream indication is received, either in the form of a TLS close_notify packet which indicates an orderly TLS end of stream or a physical EOF which indicates a possible truncation attack, where in each case the 'correct' behaviour is defined by RFC 2246. The method will behave appropriately if the secure channel is already closed. The method will deal with handshakes arising at any stage of the session.

8.3.3 write method: design

The write method will assume that there is data in the application send buffer; however, in accordance with the philosophy of OP_WRITE suggested in section 5.3, it does *not* assume that the application has waited for OP_WRITE; instead, it will just try the write and return the count of bytes written, possibly zero, leaving it up to the application to deal with short writes. The method takes no argments and may throw an IOException. The method will behave appropriately if the secure channel is already closed. The method will deal with handshakes arising at any stage of the session.

8.3.4 close method: design

The close method will implement the closure requirements of RFC 2246 in terms of the TLS/SSL protocols and will also physically close the channel.

8.3.5 Internal methods: design

Obviously the SSLEngineManager will require methods to process handshakes (NEED_WRAP and NEED_UNWRAP) and delegated tasks (NEED_TASK):

```
class SSLEngineManager
{
    private boolean   processHandshake();
    protected boolean runDelegatedTasks();
}
```

The processHandshake method will only be called internally so it will be private. For convenience it will return a boolean indicating whether it needs to be called again, typically via:

```
while (processHandshake())
    ;
```

The runDelegatedTasks method will be provided as a protected method with a simple implementation, allowing derived classes to over-ride it with more sophisticated implementations.

8.4 IMPLEMENTING THE SSLEngineManager CLASS

In this section we will explore the implementation of the class described above.

8.4.1 *Simplifying assumptions*

The following assumptions and principles will be observed to simplify the implementation of this class.

1. All ByteBuffers will be assumed to be always ready for a read (or put) operation, as they are on creation. When a write (or get) operation is required it will be preceded by a flip operation and followed by a compact operation, to return it to the initial state. In this way the state of all buffers will be known and consistent.

2. Buffer underflows and overflows in the read and write methods will be reported via the java.nio exceptions BufferUnderflowException and BufferOverflowException, rather than as zero return values. This will encourage application authors to plan for these conditions in advance.

3. The class will be implemented as a state machine driven by the current SSLEngineResult. In particular it will make no assumptions about the sequence of wraps and unwraps required to peform a handshake, or about when handshakes may occur. It will therefore cope correctly with multiple handshakes arising at any time during the session and initiated from either peer. The class will cope both with complete handshakes establishing a new session and with handshakes which just change the session key.

The general sequence of operation of the state machine is as follows:

(a) Perform the unwrap or wrap indicated by the method (read or write);

(b) Check the SSLEngineResult.Status arising from that operation, throwing an exception if appropriate;

(c) Perform any indicated handshaking (NEED_WRAP or NEED_UNWRAP);

(d) Check the SSLEngineResult.Status arising from the handshake operation;

(e) Repeat steps (c) and (d) if no error has arisen and handshaking is still in progress.

8.4.2 *Import statements*

The following import statements are assumed throughout.

```
import java.io.*;
import java.nio.*;
import java.nio.channels.*;
import java.net.*;
import java.security.*;
```

```
import java.util.*;
import javax.net.*;
import javax.net.ssl.*;
```

EXAMPLE 8.1 SSLEngineManager imports

8.4.3 Declaration: implementation

The class declaration and member variables are as follows:

```
/**
 * SSLEngineManager - manager for an SSLEngine.
 * Copyright © Esmond Pitt, 2005. All rights reserved.
 */
class SSLEngineManager
{
    private SocketChannel    channel;
    private SSLEngine        engine;
    private ByteBuffer       appSendBuffer;
    private ByteBuffer       netSendBuffer;
    private ByteBuffer       appRecvBuffer;
    private ByteBuffer       netRecvBuffer;
    private SSLEngineResult  engineResult = null;
```

These declaration statements declare the socket channel, the SSL engine, the four buffers, and the current engine result (maintained as an instance variable).

8.4.4 Constructor: implementation

The implementation of the constructor is as follows:

```
SSLEngineManager(SocketChannel channel, SSLEngine engine)
{
    this.channel = channel;
    this.engine = engine;
    SSLSession session = engine.getSession();
    int netBufferSize = session.getPacketBufferSize();
    int appBufferSize = session.getApplicationBufferSize()
    this.appSendBuffer = ByteBuffer.allocate(appBufferSize);
    this.netSendBuffer = ByteBuffer.allocate(netBufferSize);
    this.appRecvBuffer = ByteBuffer.allocate(appBufferSize);
```

```
    this.netRecvBuffer = ByteBuffer.allocate(netBufferSize);
  }
}
```

EXAMPLE 8.2 SSLEngineManager declarations and constructor

This implementation merely ensures that all the buffers are the minimum required sizes. An obvious improvement would be to allow the application to specify larger sizes, or arrays of ByteBuffers, via additional constructors. It might be thought that a further obvious improvement would be to check that the channel is connected, but this will be detected soon enough by the I/O methods anyway so it is not really necessary.

The trivial implementations of the accessor methods for the application send and receive buffers and the SSLEngine are not shown.

8.4.5 read method: implementation

The implementation of the read method is as follows:

```java
public int read() throws IOException, SSLException
{
  if (engine.isInboundDone())
    // Kind test to return another EOF:
    // SocketChannels react badly
    // if you try to read at EOF more than once.
    return -1;

  int pos = appRecvBuffer.position();

  // Read from the channel
  int count = channel.read(netRecvBuffer);

  // Unwrap the data just read
  netRecvBuffer.flip();
  engineResult =
    engine.unwrap(netRecvBuffer,appRecvBuffer);
  netRecvBuffer.compact();

  // Process the engineResult.Status
  switch (engineResult.getStatus())
  {
  case BUFFER_UNDERFLOW:
    return 0;// nothing was read, nothing was produced

  case BUFFER_OVERFLOW:
    // no room in appRecvBuffer: application must clear it
    throw new BufferOverflowException();
```

```
    case CLOSED:
      channel.socket().shutdownInput();// no more input
      // outbound close_notify will be sent by engine
      break;
    case OK:
      break;
  }
  // process any handshaking now required
  while (processHandshake())
      ;
  if (count == -1)
  {
    engine.closeInbound();
    // throws SSLException if close_notify not received.
  }
  if (engine.isInboundDone())
  {
    return -1;
  }
  // return count of application data read
  count = appRecvBuffer.position()-pos;
  return count;
}
```

EXAMPLE 8.3 SSLEngineManager.read method

This implementation is straightforward, relying principally on correct implementation of the processHandshake method to be shown in section 8.4.8.

The handling of closure requires comment. RFC 2246 §7.2.1 states:

Either party may initiate a close by sending a close_notify alert. Any data received after a closure alert is ignored.

Each party is required to send a close_notify alert before closing the write side of the connection. It is required that the other party respond with a close_notify alert of its own and close down the connection immediately, discarding any pending writes. It is not required for the initiator of the close to wait for the responding close_notify alert before closing the read side of the connection.

The SSLEngine takes care of some of this. When the SSLEngineResult.Status becomes CLOSED after a read/unwrap sequence, the application *must* process the resulting NEED_WRAP handshake status, and write the outbound closure message which results from this wrap. The engine will not unwrap any more data once the close_notify has been received, signalled by isInboundDone returning true. In the implementation above, this is signalled to the caller by returning -1 if isInboundDone is true, *i.e.* if closeInbound has been called by any of these steps. As a safety measure, the input side of the socket is shut down as well.

Note that the raw read count returned from the network read cannot be returned to the application: instead, the count of application data actually produced by unwrapping is returned. One of the many reasons for this is that there may be no application data at all, just a lot of handshake data, which doesn't produce any application data when unwrapped. Another reason is that the byte-counts of raw data and encrypted data are not the same, because of TLS/SSL protocol overheads such as padding to block boundaries, message authentication codes, digital signatures.

8.4.6 *write method: implementation*

The write method is implemented for convenience with a separate flush method which can also be called by processHandshake.

```
public int write() throws IOException, SSLException
{
  int pos = appSendBuffer.position();

  netSendBuffer.clear();
  // Wrap the data to be written
  appSendBuffer.flip();
  engineResult = engine.wrap(appSendBuffer,netSendBuffer);
  appSendBuffer.compact();

  // Process the engineResult.Status
  switch (engineResult.getStatus())
  {
  case BUFFER_UNDERFLOW:
    throw new BufferUnderflowException();

  case BUFFER_OVERFLOW:
    // this cannot occur if there is a flush after every
    // wrap, as there is here.
    throw new BufferOverflowException();

  case CLOSED:
    throw new SSLException("SSLEngine is CLOSED");

  case OK:
    break;
  }
  // Process handshakes
  while (processHandshake())
    ;
```

```
// Flush any pending data to the network
flush();

// return count of application bytes written.
return pos-appSendBuffer.position();
}
```

EXAMPLE 8.4 SSLEngineManager.write method

Again this implementation is straightforward, relying on a correct implementation of processHandshake.

Note that this method relies on SSLEngine.wrap to tell it whether the engine is already closed and the write therefore illegal.

Again the raw byte count written to the network is of no interest; we are interested only in how much application data has been consumed by the write method.

A more sophisticated implementation of this method might not actually call the flush method at all, leaving this to the read and close methods, or leaving it up to the application to call flush explicitly, or perhaps waiting for a BUFFER_OVERFLOW condition to arise before physically writing to the network.[3] This strategy would theoretically save a lot of small handshake packets being written to the network during a handshake. However the present JDK 1.5 implementation of SSLEngine requires *empty* target buffers for the wrap and unwrap methods, returning BUFFER_OVERFLOW otherwise, so the actual effect of such an improvement at present would be nil. Sun's implementation can be expected to become more intelligent in subsequent JDK versions, when this strategy should be reconsidered.

The flush method is as follows:

```
public int flush() throws IOException
{
  netSendBuffer.flip();
  int count = channel.write(netSendBuffer);
  netSendBuffer.compact();
  return count;
}
```

EXAMPLE 8.5 SSLEngineManager.flush method

8.4.7 close method: implementation

The implementation of the close method follows.

---

3. As in an early prototype of this SSLEngineManager.

```
/**
 * Close the session and the channel.
 * @exception IOException on any I/O error.
 * @exception SSLException on any SSL error.
 */
public void close() throws IOException, SSLException
{
  try
  {
    // Flush any pending output data
    flush();

    if (!engine.isOutboundDone())
    {
      engine.closeOutbound();
      while (processHandshake())
        ;

      /*
       * RFC 2246 #7.2.1: if we are initiating this
       * close, we may send the close_notify without
       * waiting for an incoming close_notify.
       * If we weren't the initiator we would have already
       * received the inbound close_notify in read(),
       * and therefore already have done closeOutbound(),
       * so, we are initiating the close,
       * so we can skip the closeInbound().
       */
    }
    else
    if (!engine.isInboundDone())
    {
      // throws SSLException if close_notify not received.
      engine.closeInbound();
      processHandshake();
    }
  }
  finally
  {
    // Close the channel.
    channel.close();
  }
}
```

EXAMPLE 8.6 SSLEngineManager.close method

Once again the implementation is straightforward and relies on a correct implementation of processHandshake.

Note that we have taken advantage of the permission given by RFC 2246 quoted above not to wait for the incoming close_notify if we are initiating the close. This strategy avoids having to do network reads in the close method, which would otherwise raise a host of design issues such as timeouts, retries, application interestOps modifications *etc.*, while still conforming to the RFC and thus maintaining adequate security over the connection.

Note also that if SSLEngine.closeInbound is called, it will throw an exception if the incoming close_notify has not been received.

Finally, note the finally block to ensure that the channel is physically closed regardless of any exceptions that may be thrown.

8.4.8 processHandshake method: implementation

The implementation of the processHandshake method follows. This method returns true if it needs to be called again.

```
/**
 * Process handshake status.
 * @return true iff handshaking can continue.
 */

private boolean processHandshake() throws IOException
{
  int count;

  // process the handshake status
  switch (engine.getHandshakeStatus())
  {

  case NEED_TASK:
    runDelegatedTasks();
    return false;// can't continue during tasks

  case NEED_UNWRAP:
    // Don't read if inbound is already closed
    count = engine.isInboundDone()
            ? -1
            : channel.read(netRecvBuffer);
    netRecvBuffer.flip();
    engineResult =
      engine.unwrap(netRecvBuffer,appRecvBuffer);
    netRecvBuffer.compact();
    break;
```

```
case NEED_WRAP:
  appSendBuffer.flip();
  engineResult =
    engine.wrap(appSendBuffer,netSendBuffer);
  appSendBuffer.compact();
  if (engineResult.getStatus() ==
    SSLEngineResult.Status.CLOSED)
  {
    // RFC 2246 #7.2.1 requires us to respond to an
    // incoming close_notify with an outgoing
    // close_notify. The engine takes care of this, so we
    // are now trying to send a close_notify, which can
    // only happen if we have just received a
    // close_notify.
    // Try to flush the close_notify.
    try
    {
      count = flush();
    }
    catch (SocketException exc)
    {
      // tried but failed to send close_notify back:
      // this can happen if the peer has sent its
      // close_notify and then closed the socket,
      // which is permitted by RFC 2246.
//    exc.printStackTrace();
    }
  }
  else
  {
    // flush without the try/catch,
    // letting any exceptions propagate.
    count = flush();
  }
  break;
case FINISHED:
case NOT_HANDSHAKING:
  // handshaking can cease.
  return false;
}
// Check the result of the preceding wrap or unwrap.
switch (engineResult.getStatus())
{
case BUFFER_UNDERFLOW:// fall through
```

```
    case BUFFER_OVERFLOW:
      // handshaking cannot continue.
      return false;
    case CLOSED:
      if (engine.isOutboundDone())
      {
        channel.socket().shutdownOutput();// stop sending
      }
      return false;
    case OK:
      // handshaking can continue.
      break;
    }
    return true;
}
```

EXAMPLE 8.7 SSLEngineManager.processHandshake method

Again this is straightforward once the requirement is understood: a simple state machine with a continuation indicator. The remarks about delayed writing in section 8.4.6 apply equally to this method. The state machine is driven by the HandshakeStatus returned by the engine, not the one embedded in our engineResult member. This is for simplicity; however one side-effect is that the FINISHED state is never seen by the state machine.[4]

To overcome this, the state machine could be driven by the handshake status returned by engineResult.getHandshakeStatus() rather than the handshake status returned by engine.getHandshakeStatus(), so as not to miss the FINISHED state, but the implementation of runDelegatedTask (discussed in section 8.4.9) must then update the engineResult with the current handshake status after the delegated tasks have been executed:

```
engineResult = new SSLEngineResult
               (
                 engineResult.getStatus(),
                 engine.getHandshakeStatus(),
                 engineResult.bytesProduced(),
                 engineResult.bytesConsumed()
               );
```

EXAMPLE 8.8 Updating the engineResult

---

4. FINISHED is only ever returned as part of an SSLEngineStatus by the SSLEngine.wrap/unwrap methods, and is never stored for return by SSLEngine.getHandshakeStatus, this being a simple way to ensure it is only returned once.

because running a delegated task is of course *intended* to alter the handshake status, and the state machine must be able to see this change. Otherwise it will loop forever in the NEED_TASK case.

8.4.9 *runDelegatedTasks method: implementation*

There are at least three possible implementations of the runDelegatedTasks method, and an industrial design of this class would probably allow different implementations to be plugged in either via a setter method or via over-riding in a derived class.

Trivially all that is required is the following:

```
protected void   runDelegatedTasks()
{
    // run delegated tasks
    Runnable task;
    while ((task = engine.getDelegatedTask()) != null)
    {
      task.run();
    }
}
```

EXAMPLE 8.9 SSLEngineManager.runDelegatedTasks method—inline

This implementation has the severe disadvantage of causing the SSLEngineManager to block, which is entirely contrary to its design intent.

Another possible implementation would use a new thread per invocation:

```
private int  threadNumber = 1;

protected void   runDelegatedTasks()
{
  Thread delegatedTaskThread
    = new Thread
        ("SSLEngine.TaskThread-"+(threadNumber++))
  {
    public void  run()
    {
      // run delegated tasks
      Runnable task;
      while ((task = engine.getDelegatedTask()) != null)
      {
        task.run();
      }
    }
  }
```

```
    };
    delegatedTaskThread.start();
}
```

EXAMPLE 8.10 SSLEngineManager.runDelegatedTasks method—threaded

Further possible implementations of runDelegatedTasks include:

(a) A single separate thread which continually processes a queue of Runnables
     to be executed, which are placed on the queue by runDelegatedTasks;

(b) An implementation which despatches tasks into a thread-pool.

Any implementation such as Example 8.10 which uses a separate thread or
threads needs to find a way to signal to the application when the
SSLEngineManager has tasks waiting to be executed, during which it cannot sensibly be called for reading or writing, and afterwards to signal to the application
when it is now ready for these methods to be called. At the least, some interaction
is required with the engineResult as described in section 8.4.8, and with the
NEED_TASK case in the processHandshake method of section 8.4.8, to prevent
the SSLEngineManager from hard-looping while the tasks are running.

The solution of this problem is left as an exercise for the reader. There are
many techniques that could be applied: semaphores, wait/notify, callbacks, *etc.*

One attractive possibility may be to supply the SelectionKey for the channel to
the SSLEngineManager constructor (instead of the SocketChannel, which can be
recovered from the SelectionKey), and have the SSLEngineManager manipulate
the key's interestOps by setting them to zero while tasks are running and restor-
ing them when all tasks are complete.

8.5 USING THE SSLEngineManager CLASS

The SSLEngineManager class presented above has been extensively tested for use
by both clients and servers.

8.5.1 Echo server

The following simple echo server shows how to use the SSLEngineManager class
described above in a secure server.

```
// SSLNIOEchoServer.
public class SSLNIOEchoServer
{
    SSLContext context;
    ServerSocketChannel ssc;
    Selector    sel;
```

```
public SSLNIOEchoServer() throws Exception
{
  // Create the SSLContext
  this.context = SSLContext.getInstance("TLS");
  // Initialize KMF ...
  KeyManagerFactory kmf =
    KeyManagerFactory.getInstance("SunX509");
  KeyStore        ks = KeyStore.getInstance("JKS");
  char[]password =
    System.getProperty("javax.net.ssl.keyStorePassword")
    .toCharArray();
  ks.load
    (new FileInputStream
      (System.getProperty
        ("javax.net.ssl.keyStore")),password);
  kmf.init(ks,password);
  context.init(kmf.getKeyManagers(),null,null);
```

At this point the SSL context has been established to a point where SSL engines can be created.

```
  // Start the server
  this.ssc = ServerSocketChannel.open();
  ssc.configureBlocking(false);
  ssc.socket().bind
    (new InetSocketAddress((InetAddress)null,0),50);
  System.out.println("Server: listening at "+ssc);
  this.sel = Selector.open();
  ssc.register(sel,SelectionKey.OP_ACCEPT);
}
```

At this point the server socket channel has been established to a point where connections can be accepted. Now follows the familiar selector loop.

```
public void run()
{
  // Selector loop
  int count;

  while (sel.keys().size() > 0)
  {
    try
    {
      count = sel.select(30*1000);
      if (count < 0)
```

```
      {
        System.out.println("Server: select timeout");
        continue;
      }
    }
    catch (IOException exc)
    {
      exc.printStackTrace();
      sel.close();
      ssc.close();
      return;
    }

    System.out.println("Server: select count="+count);
    Set selKeys = sel.selectedKeys();
    Iterator it = selKeys.iterator();

    // process ready keys
    while (it.hasNext())
    {
      SelectionKey sk = (SelectionKey)it.next();
      it.remove();
      if (!sk.isValid())
        continue;
      try
      {
        if (sk.isAcceptable())
          handleAccept(sk);
        if (sk.isReadable())
          handleRead(sk);
        if (sk.isWritable())
          handleWrite(sk);
      }
      catch (IOException exc)
      {
        exc.printStackTrace();
        sk.channel().close();
      }
    }
  }
} // run()
```

The implementation of the handler for OP_ACCEPT follows:

```java
// Process OP_ACCEPT
void handleAccept(SelectionKey sk) throws IOException
{
  ServerSocketChannel ssc =
    (ServerSocketChannel)sk.channel();
  SocketChannel     sc = ssc.accept();
  if (sc != null)
  {
    System.out.println("Server: accepted "+sc);
    sc.configureBlocking(false);

    // Create an SSL engine for this connection
    SSLEngine  engine =
      context
      .createSSLEngine
        ("localhost",sc.socket().getPort());

    // This is the server end
    engine.setUseClientMode(false);

    // Create engine manager for the channel & engine
    SSLEngineManager  mgr =
      new SSLEngineManager(sc,engine);

    // Register for OP_READ with mgr as attachment
    sc.register(sel,SelectionKey.OP_READ,mgr);
  }
}
```

The handler for OP_READ follows.

```java
// process OP_READ
void handleRead(SelectionKey sk) throws IOException
{
  SSLEngineManager  mgr =
        (SSLEngineManager)sk.attachment();
  SSLEngine  engine = mgr.getEngine();
  ByteBuffer request = mgr.getAppRecvBuffer();
  System.out.println("Server: reading");
  count = mgr.read();
  System.out.println
    ("Server: read count="+count+" request="+request);
  if (count < 0)
  {
    // client has closed
    mgr.close();
    // finished with this key
    sk.cancel();
```

```
      // finished with this test actually
      ssc.close();
   }

   else
   if (request.position() > 0)
   {
      // client request
      System.out.println
        ("Server: read "
        +new String(
          request.array(),0,request.position()));
      ByteBuffer reply = mgr.getAppSendBuffer();
      request.flip();
      reply.put(request);
      request.compact();
      handleWrite(sk);
}
```

The handler for OP_WRITE follows.

```
  // Process OP_WRITE
  void handleWrite(SelectionKey sk) throws IOException
  {
    SSLEngineManager  mgr =
      (SSLEngineManager)sk.attachment();
    ByteBuffer reply = mgr.getAppSendBuffer();
    System.out.println("Server: writing "+reply);
    int count = 0;

    while (reply.position() > 0)
    {
      reply.flip();
      count = mgr.write();
      reply.compact();
      if (count == 0)
        break;
    }
    if (reply.position() > 0)
      // short write:
      // Register for OP_WRITE and come back here when ready
      sk.interestOps
        (sk.interestOps() | SelectionKey.OP_WRITE);
    }
    else
    {
```

```
    // Write succeeded, don't need OP_WRITE any more
    sk.interestOps
      (sk.interestOps() & ~SelectionKey.OP_WRITE);
  }
}
```

The main program follows.

```
  // Main program
  public static void main(String[] args) throws Exception
  {
// System.setProperty("javax.net.debug","ssl");

    // TODO adjust these values to suit your local system.
    // These values are for the JDK SSL samples 'testkeys'.
    System.setProperty
      ("javax.net.ssl.keyStore","testkeys");
    System.setProperty
      ("javax.net.ssl.keyStorePassword","passphrase");

    new SSLNIOEchoServer().run();

    System.out.println("Exiting.");
  }
}
```

EXAMPLE 8.11 SSLNIOEchoServer class

8.5.2 *Test client*

The following test echo client exercises the SSLNIOEchoServer class shown above. Note that it requests a new handshake before every read or write, and before closing, which will cause a short cipher-key handshake, and requests a new session before the second write, which will cause a full handshake. This is a reasonably severe test of the SSLEngineManager's state machine implementation.

```
class SSLEchoClient extends Thread
{
  SSLSocket  socket;

  SSLEchoClient(SSLContext context, String host, int port)
    throws IOException
  {
    this.socket = (SSLSocket)context
      .getSocketFactory()
      .createSocket(host, port);
  }
```

```
public void run()
{
  try
  {
    int   count;
    byte[]buffer = new byte[8192];
    // send request
    socket.getOutputStream().write("hello".getBytes());
    // handshake before read
    socket.startHandshake();
    // read reply
    count = socket.getInputStream().read(buffer);
    System.out.println("client: (1) got "
      +new String(buffer,0,count)+":"+count);
    // get a new session & do a full handshake
    socket.getSession().invalidate();
    socket.startHandshake();
    // send another request
    socket.getOutputStream().write
      ("hello again after new handshake".getBytes());
    // Do a partial handshake before reading the reply
    socket.startHandshake();
    // read reply
    count = socket.getInputStream().read(buffer);
    System.out.println("client: (2) got "
      +new String(buffer,0,count)+":"+count);
  }
  catch (IOException exc)
  {
    exc.printStackTrace();
  }
  finally
  {
    try
    {
      socket.close();
      System.out.println("client: socket closed");
    }
    catch (IOException exc)
    {
      // ignored
    }
```

```
        }
      }
    }
```

EXAMPLE 8.12 SSLEchoClient class

8.6 EXERCISES

This is not really an exercise book, but the questions thrown up by the SSLEngineManager are so interesting that I couldn't resist.

The SSLEngineManager class can be elaborated in many ways which are left as exercises for the reader.

1. Add a startHandshake method to the SSLEngineManager.

2. Add shutdownInput and shutdownOutput methods to the SSLEngineManager, taking care to obey the requirements of RFC 2246 §7.2.1 quoted above.

3. The present implementation makes no attempt at thread-safety, on the assumption that it will be only used by a single thread. Enhance it to be safe for use by multiple threads.

4. Implement the suggestion in section 8.4.6 about delaying calls to the flush method.

5. Redesign and reimplement the class so it will handle *arrays* of ByteBuffers as read targets and write sources.

6. Elaborate some of the variations of the runDelegatedTasks method which are described in section 8.4.9.

7. Rewrite the simple echo client above using SocketChannels and the the SSLEngineManager class described above.

8. Implement the suggestion in section 8.4.9 about using the interestOps of the SelectionKey to defer scheduling of read and write calls while tasks are in progress.

9. Examine the design and implementation issues concerning whether the manager class can be implemented as an SSLSocketChannel that can be registered with a Selector, and selected for readability and writability just like a plain SocketChannel. Examine the question whether such a class should extend SocketChannel or AbstractSelectableChannel.[5] Examine the question of how to allow the application to choose despatching methods for delegated tasks.

10. When you have read Chapter 10, implement an SSLEngineManager-like class for DatagramSocketChannels. Initially, assume no packet losses.

When you have read section 9.15, add the reliable datagram protocol of Example 9.8 to the manager.

---

5. Sun's stated reason for not providing an SSLSocketChannel family of classes reads 'There were a lot of very difficult questions about what a SSLSocketChannel should be, including its class hierarchy and how it should interoperate with Selectors and other types of SocketChannels. Each proposal brought up more quesitons than answers. It was noted than any new API abstraction extended to work with SSL/TLS would requirethe same significant analysis and oculd result in large and complex APIS.' (JSSE Reference Guide.) Having implemented an integrated SSLSocketChannel family of classes in an afternoon, I am unable to agree.

Part IV

U D P — User Datagram Protocol

CHAPTER 9

Unicast U D P

THIS CHAPTER INTRODUCES UDP, the User Datagram Protocol, and its realization in Java DatagramSockets and DatagramPackets. In this chapter we are
only concerned with point-to-point or 'unicast' U D P in blocking mode. U D P
channel I/O and non-blocking mode are discussed in Chapter 10. Multicasting
(MulticastSockets) and broadcasting are discussed in Chapter 11.

9.1 OVERVIEW

In this section we briefly review the basics of unicast U D P and how it is programmed in Java.

U D P is specified in R F C 768 as amended.[1]

9.1.1 *Sockets in* U D P

As we saw in section 2.2.5, a socket is an abstraction representing a communications endpoint, and is associated with an I P address and a port number on the
local host. There are significant differences between U D P sockets and T C P sockets:

(a) U D P sockets do not implement reliable data streams. They implement unreliable datagrams, as discussed in section 9.1.2.

(b) U D P only has 'active' sockets, in contrast to T C P, which has 'active' and 'passive' sockets.

(c) U D P has no explicit 'accept' step as in T C P.[2]

---

1. Postel, J., R F C 768, *User Datagram Protocol*, August 1980.

(d) U D P sockets are not explicitly connected together or disconnected by network operations.

(e) U D P sockets are represented in Java as objects of type DatagramSocket.

U D P sockets and T C P sockets occupy different 'name-spaces': a T C P socket and a U D P socket are always distinct, even if they have the same address and port number. U D P sockets and T C P sockets cannot be interconnected.

9.1.2 Datagrams

A 'datagram' is a single transmission which may be delivered zero or more times. Its sequencing with respect to other datagrams between the same two endpoints is not guaranteed. In other words it may be delivered out of order, or not at all, or multiple times.

A datagram is sent in a single I P packet. Unlike T C P streams, datagrams are subject to size constraints:

(a) The I P V 4 protocol limits them to 65507 bytes, and most implementations limit them to 8 K B, although in some implementations this can be raised by increasing the socket send and receive buffer sizes, as described in section 9.11.

(b) I P V 4 routers are entitled to fragment any I P packet, including T C P segments and U D P datagrams. Unlike a T C P segment, however, a U D P datagram once fragmented is never reassembled, so it is effectively discarded. Practical exploitations of I P V 4 U D P often restrict messages to 512 bytes—a single I P packet—to avoid fragmentation problems.[3]

(c) I P V 6 has 'jumbograms' at the I P level; this allows U D P datagrams up to $2^{32} - 1$ bytes: see R F C 2675. However, the R F C goes on to say that 'Jumbograms are relevant only to I P V 6 nodes that may be attached to links with a link M T U greater than 65,575 octets, and need not be implemented or understood by I P V 6 nodes that do not support attachment to links with such

---

2. As discussed in section 9.3.7, to avoid certain Java and kernel overheads, a sender may 'connect' to the remote address and port prior to doing a number of sends. This is a *local* operation, not a network operation: the remote peer is unaware of this operation and of any corresponding disconnect operation.

3. Some more liberal maximum sizes you might consider are *(i)* 1472, which matches the nominal 1500-byte M T U for Ethernet, after allowing for I P and U D P headers, *(ii)* 1464, which matches a very common M T U, or *(iii)* 1400, which allows room for virtual private network (V P N) tunnelling overheads. If your application is only intended for a L A N, you can safely consider using the larger U D P packet sizes. Otherwise you need to consider the *product* of *(i)* the number of I P packets produced after fragmentation and *(ii)* the packet-loss rate of the W A N.

large M T U S'. In other words, jumbograms can only be expected to be communicable among hosts which are all connected to such links.

If a datagram is delivered at all, it arrives intact, *i.e.* free of transmission errors, dropouts, and internal sequencing errors among its bytes. However if a received datagram is larger than the space available to Java, the excess data is silently ignored.

9.1.3 *Benefits of U D P*

(a) As the protocol is connectionless, there is no network overhead for connection or disconnection. In contrast, we have seen in section 3.2.2 that T C P requires a three-way packet exchange to set up a connection, and a four-way packet exchange to disconnect it.

(b) The architecture of U D P servers is much simpler than the architecture of T C P servers, as there is no connection socket to accept and close.

(c) Similarly, the architecture of U D P clients is somewhat simpler than that of T C P clients, there being no connection to create or terminate.

9.1.4 *Limitations of U D P*

(a) There is no support for reassembly of fragmented datagrams.

(b) The payload is very limited in practice. Datagram payloads above 512 bytes are apt to be fragmented by routers and therefore effectively lost.

(c) There is no support for pacing transmissions according to prevailing network conditions.

(d) There is no support for packet sequencing.

(e) There is no detection of packet loss and retransmission.

Some of these limitations are more apparent than real. The datagram model is highly suited to applications where:

(a) Transactions are request-reply

(b) Payloads are small

(c) Servers are stateless

(d) Transactions are 'idempotent', *i.e.* can be repeated without affecting the overall result of the computation.[4]

The datagram model is much closer than the T C P stream model to the underlying reality of the network: packets being exchanged, resequenced, and lost. The datagram model is also much closer than the T C P stream model to the 'overlying' realities of many applications. In essence, datagrams naturally provide an 'at least zero' delivery guarantee. This makes the client's view of a sent request pretty simple: either the transaction has been received and acknowledged, or it has to be retransmitted.

Datagrams can be made to give an 'exactly once' delivery model with a very small amount of extra programming at both ends:

(a) At the client, transaction requests are sequenced, sent via a datagram, and a reply with the same sequence number is awaited. If the reply doesn't arrive, the request is simply repeated until a reply is received or a maximum retry count or transaction timeout is exceeded.[5] If the 'wrong' reply arrives it is ignored.

(b) At the server, if a request arrives in duplicate, the original reply is simply retransmitted without re-executing the semantics of the request; if an out-of-order request is received, indicating a missing prior request, it is ignored.

Clearly this is pretty easy to program, and rather obliterates the apparent limitations of unreliable delivery and sequencing.

By contrast, T C P can be made to give an 'at most once' model when very carefully programmed as in Java R M I, and can only be made to give an 'exactly once' model by essentially adopting the above datagram approach layered over T C P's streams: this may seem perverse, and is certainly both more complicated to program, having to deal with connections, and far less efficient on the network.

> Variations on the protocol outined above are possible: the client might want to do something more intelligent with a reply sequence number which is too high; ditto the server with an out-of-sequence request. Both conditions indicate an application protocol error. This quickly becomes an exercise in protocol design, a non-trivial discipline in its own right.

In summary, U D P supports unreliable, unconnected, limited-size datagram communications in a peer-to-peer architecture. Each peer creates a datagram socket. To receive data, a U D P socket must be bound to a port. To send data, a datagram packet is formed and sent via a datagram socket to a remote I P address and port number.

---

4. Some arithmetic examples may make this clear. Adding zero, multiplying by one, or raising to the zero[th] power are all idempotent: more interestingly, so is the modulus operation. Crediting a sum to a bank account is *not* idempotent, but any operation can be made idempotent by permanently associating it with a unique sequence number and arranging not to apply repeated transactions.

5. The intervals between retries should be made larger than would be required by any network-sensitive transmission pacing. See also section 3.12, section 9.15, and Example 9.7.

Although U D P is a peer-to-peer protocol, in many practical applications we can still distinguish between requesting peers as 'clients' which send a request and wait for a response, and responding peers as 'servers' which wait for a request and send a response.

9.1.5 *Import statements*

The following Java import statements are assumed in the examples throughout this chapter.

```
import java.io.*;
import java.net.*;
import java.util.*;
```

9.2 SIMPLE U D P SERVERS AND CLIENTS

In Java, a U D P socket is represented by an object of type java.net.DatagramSocket; a U D P datagram is represented by an object of type java.net.DatagramPacket.

9.2.1 *Simple U D P servers*

The simplest possible U D P server is shown in Example 9.1.

```
public class UDPServer implements Runnable
{
  DatagramSocket   socket;
  public UDPServer(int port) throws IOException
  {
    this.socket = new DatagramSocket(port);
  }
  public void  run()
  {
    for (;;)
    {
      try
      {
        byte[] buffer      = new byte[8192];
        DatagramPacket packet= new DatagramPacket
          (buffer, buffer.length);
        socket.receive(packet);
        new ConnectionHandler(socket, packet).run();
      }
```

```
      catch (IOException e)
      {
        // …
      }
    } // for (;;)
  } // run()
} // class
```

EXAMPLE 9.1 Simple U D P server

The connection-handling class for this and subsequent servers is shown in Example 9.2.

```
class ConnectionHandler implements Runnable
{
  DatagramSocket socket;
  DatagramPacket packet;

  ConnectionHandler(DatagramSocket socket,
    DatagramPacket packet)
  {
    this.socket = socket;
    this.packet = packet;
  }

  public void run()
  {
    handlePacket(socket, packet);
  }

  public void handlePacket(DatagramSocket socket,
                  DatagramPacket packet)
  {
    try
    {
      byte[] buffer = packet.getData();
      int    offset = packet.getOffset();
      int    length = packet.getLength();
      // conversation not shown …
      // sets reply into buffer/offset/length
      packet.setData(buffer, offset, length);
      // write reply to the output
      socket.send(packet);
    }
```

```
    catch (IOException e) { /* ... */ }
  } // handlePacket()
} // class
```

The single-threaded design of Example 9.1 is not usually adequate, as it processes clients sequentially, not concurrently—a new client blocks while the previous client is being serviced. To handle clients concurrently, the server must use a different thread per accepted connection. The simplest form of such a UDP server, using the same connection-handling class, is sketched in Example 9.3.

```
public class ConcurrentUDPServer extends UDPServer
{
  public ConcurrentUDPServer(int port) throws IOException
  {
    super(port);
  }
  public void run()
  {
    for (;;)
    {
      try
      {
        byte[]          buffer= new byte[8192];
        DatagramPacket packet = new DatagramPacket
          (buffer, buffer.length);
        socket.receive(packet);
        new Thread
          (new ConnectionHandler(socket, packet)).start();
      }
      catch (IOException e)
      {
        // …
      }
    } / for (;;)
  } // run()
} // class
```

EXAMPLE 9.3 Simple UDP server—multithreaded

A connection-handling class which simply echoes its input to its output—very useful for testing—is shown in Example 9.4.

```
class EchoConnectionHandler implements Runnable
{
  DatagramSocket   socket;
  DatagramPacket   packet;

  ConnectionHandler
    (DatagramSocket socket, DatagramPacket packet)
  {
    this.socket = socket;
    this.packet = packet;
  }

  public void  run()
  {
    handlePacket(socket, packet);
  }

  public void  handlePacket(DatagramSocket socket,
                    DatagramPacket packet)
  {
    try
    {
      byte[] buffer = packet.getData();
      int    offset = packet.getOffset();
      int    length = packet.getLength();
      // The reply is the same as the request,
      // which is already in buffer/offset/length
      packet.setData(buffer, offset, length);
      // write reply to the output
      socket.send(packet);
    }

    catch (IOException e)
    {
      // …
    }
  } // handlePacket()
} // class
```

EXAMPLE 9.4 U D P server connection handler—echo service

9.2.2 Simple U D P clients

The client's DatagramSocket is usually bound to a system-chosen port. A simple U D P client for the preceding U D P server is shown in Example 9.5.

```
public class UDPClient implements Runnable
{
  DatagramSocket  socket;     // socket for communications
  InetAddress     address;    // remote host
  int             port;       // remote port
  public UDPClient(InetAddress address, int port)
    throws IOException
  {
    this.socket = new DatagramSocket();// ephemeral port
    this.address = address;
    this.port = port;
  }
  /**
   * Send the data in {buffer, offset, length}
   * and overwrite it with the reply.
   * @return the actual reply length.
   * @exception IOException on any error
   */
  public int sendReceive(byte[] buffer, int offset,
      int length)
    throws IOException
  {
    try
    {
      // Create packet
      DatagramPacket packet = new DatagramPacket
        (buffer, offset, length, address, port);
      socket.send(packet);
      socket.receive(packet);
      return packet.getLength();
    }
    catch (IOException e)
    {
      // …
    }
  } // sendReceive()
} // class
```

EXAMPLE 9.5 Simple U D P client

9.2.3 *The DatagramPacket class*

As we saw in section 9.1.2, a U D P datagram is a single transmission unit, and it is convenient to represent it in Java as a single object. This object is a DatagramPacket. U D P isn't a streaming protocol, so the streams-based programming techniques used for T C P do not apply. Unlike T C P sockets, which support the familiar InputStreams and OutputStreams, U D P sockets in Java support input and output via methods which send and receive entire DatagramPackets.

9.2.4 *DatagramPacket constructors*

A DatagramPacket is constructed by one of the methods:

```
class DatagramPacket
{
  DatagramPacket(byte[] data, int length);
  DatagramPacket(byte[] data, int length,
    InetAddress address, int port);
  DatagramPacket(byte[] data, int offset, int length);
  DatagramPacket(byte[] data, int offset, int length,
      InetAddress address, int port);
  DatagramPacket(byte[] data, int length,
    SocketAddress socketAddress);
  DatagramPacket(byte[] data, int offset, int length,
    SocketAddress socketAddress);
}
```

where *length* and *offset* are non-negative, and the following invariant applies:[6]

$$0 \leq \text{length} + \text{offset} \leq \text{data.length} \qquad (\text{EQ 9.1})$$

Note that, unlike the T C P protocol, it is possible to both send and receive zero-length datagrams in U D P. This could be useful in an application protocol, *e.g.* for 'I'm alive' messages or pings.

The *data, offset, length, address,* and *port* attributes can all be set separately after construction by corresponding set methods, and they can all be interrogated with corresponding get methods.

These attributes are all described separately below.

9.2.5 *DatagramPacket data*

The data in a DatagramPacket is specified as a byte array, an offset, and a length. These can all be set on construction, and can subsequently be set and interrogated by the methods:

---

6. This invariant always applies in Java when dealing with byte arrays, offsets, and lengths, and it is enforced by any constructors or methods which specify them: an IllegalArgumentException is thrown if the invariant is violated.

```
class DatagramPacket
{
  byte[] getData();
  void   setData(byte[] data);
  void   setData(byte[] data, int length);
  void   setData(byte[] data, int offset, int length);

  int    getLength();
  void   setLength(int length);

  int    getOffset();
  void   setOffset(int offset);
}
```

The default values for *data*, *offset*, and *length* are null, zero, and zero respectively. When setting any of these attributes, Equation 9.1 is enforced.

When *sending* a datagram, it is up to the application to format its data into the byte array. One way to do so is via either a DataOutputStream or an ObjectOutputStream, coupled to a ByteArrayOutputStream:

```
DatagramPacket  packet = new DatagramPacket();
ByteArrayOutputStream
                baos  = new ByteArrayOutputStream();
DataOutputStream     dos = new DataOutputStream(baos);
dos.writeInt(...);     // or as per application protocol
dos.flush();
packet.setData(baos.toByteArray(), baos.size());
```

When *receiving* a datagram, Java places the received data into the byte array of the DatagramPacket starting at the current value of the offset attribute and ending one before the current length attribute of the DatagramPacket. The application must have pre-allocated the byte array, and ensured that it is adequate for the data expected, as well as setting appropriate values for offset and length: the byte array, offset, and length must always satisfy Equation 9.1. Usually applications will set *offset* to zero and *length* to the length of the byte array prior to receiving a DatagramPacket.

Java adjusts the *length* attribute of the DatagramPacket to the length of the received data if it is less than the original length; however, as we saw in section 9.1.2, excess data is silently truncated, in which case *length* is undisturbed: in other words, no indication (such as an excessive length) is received that the data was truncated.

This means that the length attribute of a datagram which is re-used for multiple receive operations must be reset before the second and subsequence receives; otherwise it continually shrinks to the size of the smallest datagram received so far. It also means that the application can't distinguish between a datagram which was exactly the maximum length and a datagram which was too big and got truncated. The usual technique for handling this problem is to allocate space for the largest expected datagram plus one byte. If a datagram of this extra length is received, it was unexpectedly large, *i.e.* at least one byte too long.

It is up to the application to format the byte array into its own data. One way to do so is via either a DataInputStream or an ObjectInputStream, coupled to a ByteArrayInputStream:

```
DatagramPacket          packet;
// initialization & receive not shown …
ByteArrayInputStream bais = new ByteArrayInputStream
  (packet.getData(), packet.getOffset(),
    packet.getLength());
DataInputStream        dis = new DataInputStream(bais);
int i = dis.readInt();// or as per application protocol
```

It should be clear that this technique is the reverse of the ByteArrayOutputStream technique given earlier in this section.

9.2.6 *DatagramPacket address and port*

A DatagramPacket is associated with an I P address and port: these represent the remote U D P socket where an inbound datagram came from, or an outbound datagram is being sent to. They can be set on construction or via the methods:

```
class DatagramPacket
{
  SocketAddress  getSocketAddress();
  void           setSocketAddress(SocketAddress address);
  InetAddress    getAddress();
  void           setAddress(InetAddress address);
  int            getPort();
  void           setPort(int port);
}
```

remembering that a J D K 1.4 SocketAddress represents an {InetAddress, port} pair.

When a datagram is *received*, Java sets its {*address, port*} to the remote source of the datagram, so that you know where it came from.

When *sending* a datagram, its {*address, port*} must be already set to the target where the datagram is to be sent. If the datagram initiates the conversation, the application must set {*address, port*} itself. However, to reply to a datagram just received, instead of constructing a new DatagramPacket and setting its {*address, port*}, it is simpler to re-use the received datagram for the reply: place the reply data into the datagram with the DatagramPacket.setData method, and leave the {*address, port*} undisturbed. This technique saves on created objects, and avoids error-prone copying of {*address, port*} information between request and reply.

9.3 DATAGRAM SOCKET INITIALIZATION

9.3.1 *Constructors*

Objects of type DatagramSocket are created with one of these constructors:

```
class DatagramSocket
{
  DatagramSocket()             throws IOException;
  DatagramSocket(int port)  throws IOException;
  DatagramSocket(int port, InetAddress localAddress)
                               throws IOException;
  DatagramSocket(SocketAddress localSocketAddress)
                               throws IOException;
}
```

In most of these cases the socket is constructed already 'bound', meaning that it is already associated with a local I P address and port. A bound socket can be used immediately for sending and receiving. However, if the constructor which takes a SocketAddress is called with a null, the socket is constructed 'unbound', *i.e.* not yet associated with a local I P address or port. An unbound socket can be used immediately for sending, but before receiving it must first be 'bound' with the DatagramSocket.bind method described in section 9.3.5.

First we look at the parameters for constructing bound sockets; we then look at the method for binding unbound sockets.

9.3.2 *Port*

U D P receivers usually specify the local port on which they receive, by supplying a non-zero port number to the constructor or the bind method. If the port number is omitted or zero, an *ephemeral*—system-allocated—port number is used, whose value can be obtained by calling the method:

```
class DatagramSocket
{
  int     getLocalPort();
}
```

Ephemeral ports are generally used by U D P clients, unless they need to specify a particular port to satisfy local networking constraints such as firewall policies. Ephemeral ports are *not* generally used by U D P servers, as otherwise some external means is required of communicating the actual port number to clients; otherwise they won't know how to send to the receiver: typically this function is assumed by a naming service such as an L D A P directory service. In Sun R P C it was assumed by the R P C *portmapper* service.

9.3.3 Local address

The *local address* of a datagram socket is the I P address at which it receives. By default, U D P sockets receive at all local I P addresses. They can be made to receive at a *single* local I P address, by supplying either a non-null InetAddress, or an InetSocketAddress with a non-null InetAddress, to a DatagramSocket constructor.

If the InetAddress is omitted or null (the 'wildcard' address), the socket is bound to all local addresses, meaning that it receives from any address.

Specifying a local I P address only makes sense if the local host is multi-homed, *i.e.* has more than one I P address, usually because it has more than one physical network interface. In such a circumstance, a U D P receiver may only want to make itself available via one of these I P addresses rather than all of them. See the discussion of multi-homing in section 9.12 for more detail.

The local I P address to which a datagram socket is bound is returned by the methods:

```
class DatagramSocket
{
  InetAddress     getInetAddress();
  SocketAddress getLocalSocketAddress();
}
```

These methods return null if the socket is not yet bound.

9.3.4 Reusing the local address

Before binding the datagram socket as described in section 9.3.4, you may wish to set the 'reuse local address' option. This really means reusing the local port.

The reuse-address methods were added in J D K 1.4:

```
class DatagramSocket
{
  void      setReuseAddress(boolean reuse)
                            throws SocketException;
  boolean  getReuseAddress() throws SocketException;
}
```

You *must* use this setting if you want to receive at the same port on multiple I P addresses by binding multiple DatagramSockets to the same port number and different local I P addresses, either within the same J V M or in multiple J V M s on the same host.

> Changing this setting after a datagram socket is bound, or constructed other than with a null SocketAddress, has no effect. Note that these methods set and get a boolean state, not some sort of address as their names may suggest.

9.3.5 Bind operation

A DatagramSocket constructed with a null SocketAddress in the constructor introduced in J D K 1.4 must be bound before datagrams can be received (although it need not be bound for datagrams to be sent). Binding of datagram sockets is supported by the J D K 1.4 methods:

```
class DatagramSocket
{
  void      bind(SocketAddress localSocketAddress)
    throws IOException;
  boolean  isBound();
}
```

where localSocketAddress is usually an InetSocketAddress constructed with a port number as described in section 9.3.2 and an InetAddress as described in section 9.3.3. The socket is bound to either an ephemeral or a specified local port, at either a specified local I P address or all of them, according to the value of the localSocketAddress parameter as shown in Table 9.1.

TABLE 9.1 U D P bind parameters

SocketAddress	InetAddress	port	Bound to
null	-	-	Ephemeral port, all local I P addresses
InetSocketAddress	null	zero	Ephemeral port, all local I P addresses
InetSocketAddress	null	non-zero	Specified port, all local I P addresses
InetSocketAddress	non-null	zero	Ephemeral port, specified local I P address
InetSocketAddress	non-null	non-zero	Specified port and local I P address

As discussed in section 9.3.2, a server would normally specify a specific port number: a client might or might not, depending mostly on whether it needs to use a fixed port number for firewall-traversal purposes. The bind method *must* be called before performing channel datagram input, discussed in section 10.2. For multi-homed hosts see also the discussion in section 9.12.

A DatagramSocket cannot be re-bound. The isBound method returns true if the socket is already bound.

9.3.6 Setting buffer sizes

Before using a datagram socket, its send and receive buffer sizes should be adjusted as described in section 9.11.

9.3.7 Connect operation

A DatagramSocket can be connected to a remote U D P socket. Unlike the T C P connect operation, a U D P 'connect' is only a local operation: it has no effect on the network, and therefore no effect on the remote end; it merely conditions the local end so that data can only be received from or sent to the specified address. If the {*address, port*} attributes of an *incoming* DatagramPacket disagree with the settings specified to the connect method, the datagram is silently discarded; if those of an *outgoing* DatagramPacket disagree with the settings specified to the connect method, DatagramSocket.send throws an IllegalArgumentException.

Connecting of datagram sockets is supported by the methods:

```
class DatagramSocket
{
  void      connect(InetAddress address, int port);
  void      connect(SocketAddress socketAddress)
               throws SocketException;
  boolean   isConnected();
}
```

where either:

(a) address and port specify a remote U D P socket {*address, port*} as described in section 9.2.6, or

(b) socketAddress is (usually) an InetSocketAddress constructed with a remote U D P socket {*address, port*} as described in section 9.2.6.

As no network protocol is involved, there is no guarantee that the remote U D P port exists, even though the connect method may have completed successfully. Therefore a subsequent send or receive operation on a connected DatagramSocket may throw a PortUnreachableException. Worse, the send or receive may simply fail silently without an exception being thrown. The actual be-haviour which occurs depends on the platform and j d k version.

Connecting a datagram socket saves some Java overheads: it allows the con-nection permission to the target to be checked once at connect time, rather than on each transmission to or reception from the target. If the required SocketPermission for the 'connect' action is not granted, a SecurityException is thrown: this is a run-time error and so is not checked by the compiler.

In the Berkeley Sockets API, connecting a datagram socket also eliminates some kernel overheads. Prior to j d k 1.4, Java didn't call the underlying *connect*() API, it just mim-icked its actions at the Java level, so the kernel overheads weren't eliminated, and PortUnreachableException wasn't thrown by I/O operations on a connected DatagramSocket.

The isConnected method tells whether the *local* socket has been connected: it tells you nothing about the other end, including whether or not it even exists.

A DatagramSocket cannot be closed and then connected or re-connected, but it can be disconnected as described in section 9.5 and then re-connected.

If you don't have j d k 1.4 and its DatagramSocket.isConnected method, you can use the methods:

```
class DatagramSocket
{
  InetAddress  getInetAddress();
  int          getPort();
}
```

for the same purpose. These methods return the remote address or port to which the socket is connected, or null or -1 (as appropriate) if the socket is not currently connected.

9.4 Datagram I/O

Datagram I/O is performed with the methods:

```
class DatagramSocket
{
  void  send(DatagramPacket packet)     throws IOException:
  void  receive(DatagramPacket packet) throws IOException:
}
```

9.4.1 *Datagram output*

Once you have formatted the output data into a byte array and constructed a
DatagramPacket from it as shown in section 9.2.5, and set the target address in
the datagram as discussed in section 9.2.6, sending the datagram to a destination is simply a matter of calling the DatagramSocket.send method as shown below:

```
// initializations not shown
InetAddress        address;
DatagramPacket     packet;
int                port;
byte[]             buffer; // see section 9.2.5
DatagramSocket     socket = new DatagramSocket();
packet.setData(buffer, length);

// pre-JDK 1.4 …
packet.setAddress(address);
packet.setPort(port);
socket.send(packet);
```

From J D K 1.4, the setAddress and setPort calls above can be replaced with a single call to setSocketAddress:

```
// From JDK 1.4 …
packet.setSocketAddress
  (new InetSocketAddress(address, port));
```

The DatagramSocket.send method is not synchronized: this is one reason why
the concurrent U D P server shown in Example 9.3 doesn't need a second
DatagramSocket to send a reply for an incoming packet. Any internal sequential-
ization needed is taken care of by the underlying U D P implementation.

Exception handling for datagram sockets is discussed in section 9.8.

9.4.2 *Datagram input*

Receiving datagrams is even simpler than sending, as shown below:

```
int port; // initialization not shown
DatagramSocket socket = new DatagramSocket(port);
// declare array at required length+1
byte[]         buffer = new byte[8192+1];
DatagramPacket packet = new DatagramPacket
  (buffer, buffer.length);
socket.receive(packet);
```

If no datagram is pending, the receive method blocks until a datagram is received. At this point, the packet.getData method yields the data received, packet.getOffset gives its offset, and packet.getLength gives its total length, so we can proceed as follows:

```
ByteArrayInputStream bais = new ByteArrayInputStream
  (packet.getData(), packet.getOffset(),
    packet.getLength());
// etc as in section 9.2.5
```

In the case above we didn't specify an offset when creating the packet, so we might use the simpler form:

```
new ByteArrayInputStream
  (packet.getData(), packet.getLength());
// ...
```

although really defensive programming should not assume a zero offset like this.

If we want to reply to this datagram, we saw in section 9.2.6 that a received datagram already contains the sender's address and port, so all we have to do is set the reply data and call DatagramSocket.send as described in section 9.4.1.

The DatagramSocket.receive method is not synchronized.

The receive method of the default datagram socket implementation class (discussed in section 9.6) is synchronized. Concurrent receives on the same datagram socket from multiple threads are sequentialized by Java.

9.5 TERMINATION

There is no explicit disconnection protocol in U D P, so when a conversation with a particular peer has ended no specific action is required. Connected datagram sockets can be disconnected and re-used in either unconnected or connected mode if required. Datagram sockets must be closed after use.

9.5.1 *Disconnect*

If a datagram socket has been connected, it can be disconnected with the method:

```
class DatagramSocket
{
  void disconnect();
}
```

This method does nothing if the socket wasn't connected.

If a datagram socket is to be used in the connected mode, it would normally be connected at the beginning of a conversation and disconnected at the end of the conversation.

9.5.2 *Close*

When you have finished with a DatagramSocket you must close it:

```
class DatagramSocket
{
  void     close()  throws IOException;
  boolean  isClosed();
}
```

The isClosed method tells whether the *local* socket has been closed. It doesn't tell you anything about the connection, for the very good reason that in U D P there *is* no connection in the network sense.

After being closed, the socket is no longer usable for any purpose.

9.6 Socket factories

As we saw in section 3.8.1, java.net socket factories are used by Java to provide itself with socket implementations.

The java.net.DatagramSocket class is really a facade. It defines the Java sockets A P I, but delegates all its actions to socket-implementation objects which do all the real work. Datagram socket implementations extend the abstract java.net.DatagramSocketImpl class:

```
class DatagramSocketImpl
{
  // ...
}
```

The factory which supplies objects of type DatagramSocketImpl implements the java.net.DatagramSocketImplFactory interface:

```
interface DatagramSocketImplFactory
{
  DatagramSocketImpl  createDatagramSocketImpl();
}
```

A default socket factory is always installed, which delivers implementation objects of the package-protected java.net.PlainDatagramSocketImpl class. This class has native methods which interface with the local C-language sockets A P I, *e.g.* the Berkeley Sockets A P I or W I N S O C K.

The socket factory can be set:

```
class DatagramSocket
{
  static void  setDatagramSocketImplFactory
                (DatagramSocketImplFactory factory);
}
```

The setSocketFactory method can only be called once in the lifetime of a J V M. It requires the RuntimePermission 'setFactory' to be granted, otherwise a SecurityException is thrown.

Applications have little or no use for this facility.

9.7 PERMISSIONS

If a Java 2 security manager is installed, various java.net.SocketPermissions are required for datagram socket operations. These are shown in Table 9.2.

TABLE 9.2 Permissions in U D P

Action	Comments
accept	Required in the receive and connect methods of DatagramSocket. The target *host* and *port* specify the remote U D P socket.
connect	Required in the send and connect methods of DatagramSocket, and when obtaining InetAddress objects. The target *host* and *port* and *port* specify the remote U D P socket.
listen	Required when constructing a DatagramSocket, and in its bind method. The target *host* and *port* and *port* specify the *local* U D P socket. Most loosely specified as "localhost:1024-".
resolve	This permission is implied by the 'connect' action, so there is little need to specify it explicitly. The target *host* and *port* and *port* specify the remote U D P socket.

9.8 EXCEPTIONS

The significant Java exceptions that can arise during datagram socket operations are shown in Table 9.3.

TABLE 9.3 Exceptions in U D P

Exception	Thrown by	Meaning
java.net. BindException	DatagramSocket constructors and bind method	The requested local address or port cannot be assigned, *e.g.* it is already in use and the 'reuse address' option is not set.
java.lang. IllegalArgumentException	Several constructors and methods of DatagramPacket; several methods of DatagramSocket and InetSocketAddress	Equation 9.1 is violated, or arguments are null or out of range. This is a RuntimeException, and therefore not shown in method signatures or checked by the compiler.
java.nio. IllegalBlockingModeException	send and receive methods of DatagramSocket	The socket has an associated channel which is in non-blocking mode; from J D K 1.4.
java.io. InterruptedIOException	receive method of DatagramSocket	A timeout has occured; prior to J D K 1.4.
java.io. IOException	send method of DatagramSocket	A general I/O error has occurred.
		Exceptions derived from this exception include IllegalBlockingModeException, InterruptedIOException, SocketException and UnknownHostException.
java.net. PortUnreachableException	send and receive methods of DatagramSocket	The socket is connected to a currently unreachable destination; from J D K 1.4.
java.lang. SecurityException	several methods of DatagramSocket	A required SocketPermission is not granted as shown in Table 9.2. This is a RuntimeException, , and therefore not shown in method signatures or checked by the compiler.

TABLE 9.3 Exceptions in U D P (continued)

Exception	Thrown by	Meaning
java.net. SocketException	many DatagramSocket methods, especially receive	An underlying U D P error has occured, or the socket is closed by another thread other than via the close method of DatagramChannel.
		Many exceptions are derived from this exception, including BindException.
java.net. SocketTimeoutException	receive method of DatagramSocket	A timeout has occured; from J D K 1.4.
		Extends InterruptedIOException for backwards compatibility with pre-J D K 1.4 programs.
java.net. UnknownHostException	Factory methods of InetAddress, or implicit use of these when using String hostnames	The I P address of the named host cannot be determined.

9.9 Socket options

Several socket options are available which control advanced features of U D P sockets. In Java, datagram socket options can be set and interrogated via methods in java.net.DatagramSocket.

Datagram socket options are presented below more or less in order of their relative importance. The later in the chapter an option appears, the less you need to be concerned with it.

9.10 Timeout

As we have seen in section 3.12 (and will see again in section 13.2.5–section 13.2.6), it cannot be assumed that an application can wait forever for a remote service, nor that the service will always be rendered in a timely manner, nor that the service or the intervening network infrastructure will only fail in detectable ways. Any network program which reads with infinite timeout is sooner or later going to experience an infinite delay.

For all these reasons, prudent network programming almost always uses a finite receive timeout at clients. The receive timeout is set and interrogated with the methods:

```
class DatagramSocket
{
    void  setSoTimeout(int timeout)   throws SocketException;
    int   getSoTimeout()              throws SocketException;
}
```

where timeout is specified in milliseconds, and must be either positive, indicating a finite timeout, or zero, indicating an infinite timeout. By default, the read timeout is infinite.

If the timeout has been set to a finite value prior to a blocking receive operation on the socket, the receive will block for up to the timeout period if data is not available, and will then throw an InterruptedIOException or, as shown in Table 9.3, the J D K 1.4 SocketTimeoutException which is derived from it. If the timeout is infinite, the receive will block forever if data is not available and no error occurs.

The remarks in section 3.12 about timeout durations for T C P apply equally well to U D P.

U D P servers which are waiting for a client request need not use timeouts, as unlike T C P servers they don't have connections to expire. A U D P server timeout can be used to poll a number of DatagramSockets in a single thread, although the Selector class described in section 5.3.1 provides a better way to do this.

9.11 BUFFERS

U D P allocates a send buffer and a receive buffer to each socket. These buffers exist in the address space of the kernel or the U D P protocol stack (if different), not in the J V M or process address space. The default size of these buffers is determined by the underlying platform's implementation of U D P, not by Java. In current U D P implementations, the send and receive buffer sizes are at least 8Kb, and often 32K B or more by default, and can be set as high as 256M B or more in some implementations. The target system's characteristics must be investigated before deciding whether, and how, to modify socket buffer sizes.

The send and receive buffer sizes are set and interrogated by the methods:

```
class DatagramSocket
{
    void  setReceiveBufferSize(int size)
                                throws SocketException;
    int   getReceiveBufferSize() throws SocketException;
```

```
int   getSendBufferSize()      throws SocketException;
void  setSendBufferSize(int size)
                               throws SocketException;
}
```

where size is specified in bytes. Values supplied to these methods act only as a hint to the underlying platform, and may be adjusted in either direction to fit into the allowable range, or rounded up or down to appropriate boundaries. Values returned by these methods may not match the values you sent, and may not match the actual values being used by the underlying platform.

You can perform these operations at any time before the socket is closed.

9.11.1 *How big should a datagram socket buffer be?*

The size of the *receive* buffer is generally used by the underlying U D P transport to determine the maximum size of the datagram that the socket can receive. Therefore, at a minimum, the receive buffer should be at least as big as the largest expected datagram plus one byte as suggested in section 9.2.5. Increasing the receive buffer beyond this size may allow the implementation to buffer multiple packets when they arrive faster than they are being received by the DatagramSocket.receive method. In other words the receive buffer should be a multiple of the largest datagram expected to be received plus one byte, where the multiplier determines the length of the input queue, say 40 or 50.

The size of the *send* buffer is generally used by the underlying U D P transport to determine the maximum datagram size that can be sent on the socket. Therefore, at a minimum, the send buffer should be at least as big as the largest datagram to be sent. Increasing the send buffer further may allow the implementation to queue multiple datagrams for transmission when the send rate is high. In other words the send buffer should be a multiple of the size of the largest datagram expected to be sent, where the multiplier determines the length of the output queue, and must be at least one.

Unlike T C P, there may be little point in allowing a U D P application to get significantly ahead of the network when sending datagrams. Because datagram delivery is not guaranteed, the application protocol generally requires the last datagram to be acknowledged before the next datagram can be sent.

9.12 MULTI-HOMING

We saw in section 3.14 that a multi-homed host is a host which has more than one I P address, typically because it has more than one physical network interface. The J D K 1.4 NetworkInterface class can return all the network interfaces for a host and all the I P addresses supported by a given network interface.

Multi-homing has non-trivial consequences for U D P servers, and trivial consequences for clients.

9.12.1 *Multi-homing—U D P servers*

A U D P server normally listens at all available local I P addresses, and such a server need not usually be concerned with the fact that it may be running in a multi-homed host. There are a few situations in which a U D P server may need to be aware of multi-homing:

(a)   If the server is intended to service only one subnet, it should bind itself to the appropriate local I P address. This in turn may require use of the DatagramSocket.setReuseAddress method discussed in section 9.3.4.

(b)   Clients often match up I P addresses in request and reply packets to associate replies with corresponding requests. This particularly occurs in clients which deal asynchronously with multiple services. In such cases, the source I P address in the reply packet from the server needs to match the I P address which the client sent the datagram to. In the Berkely Sockets A P I this can be accomplished by sending the reply from a socket bound to the target I P address of the received datagram. Java doesn't provide access to the target I P address of an inbound datagram,[7] so a server which deals with such clients needs to set up one datagram socket bound to each interface; should receive requests from each socket; and should send each reply via the same socket that the corresponding request was received from.

(c)   In directory services when registering service descriptors, the server must advertise itself via an I P address which all clients can access. Typically the client doesn't have access to all the I P addresses of the server, but can only access it on one of them. The best way to assure that advertised service addresses are most usable is to advertise the 'most public' I P address or hostname in each case.

9.12.2 *Multi-homing—U D P clients*

A U D P client normally pays no attention to its local I P addresses, as we have seen in section 9.3.5. If for some reason it really cares about which network interface it uses to send, it should specify the local I P address when constructed or bound, as discussed in section 9.3.3.

---

7. Presumably because some platforms don't support the IP_RECVDSTADDR option in the C-language socket *recv()* API.

9.13 TRAFFIC CLASS

The 'traffic class' associated with a datagram socket can be set and interrogated with the methods:

```
class DatagramSocket
{
  void setTrafficClass(int tc)   throws SocketException;
  int  getTrafficClass()         throws SocketException;
}
```

IP traffic classes are discussed in section 3.19.

9.14 PUTTING IT ALL TOGETHER

A revision to the constructor of the simple UDP server of Example 9.1 with the improvements we have seen above is shown in Example 9.6.

```
public class UDPServer implements Runnable
{
  public static final int   MAX_DATAGRAM_BYTES = 512;
  public static final int   MAX_SEND_QUEUE = 4;
  public static final int   MAX_RECV_QUEUE = 40;
  DatagramSocket   socket;
  DatagramPacket   packet = null;

  public UDPServer(int port) throws IOException
  {
    this.socket = new DatagramSocket(port);
    // outgoing queue of about 4 datagrams
    socket.setSendBufferSize
      (MAX_DATAGRAM_BYTES*MAX_SEND_QUEUE);
    // incoming queue of about 40 datagrams, with pad byte
    socket.setReceiveBufferSize
      ((MAX_DATAGRAM_BYTES+1)*MAX_RECV_QUEUE);
  }

  // run method is as before
} // class
```

EXAMPLE 9.6 Simple UDP server—revised

A revision of the UDP client of Example 9.5, with the improvements we have seen above, and exhibiting rudimentary error-recovery, is shown in Example 9.7.

```java
public class UDPClient
{
  public static final int   MAX_DATAGRAM_BYTES = 512;
  public static final int   MAX_SEND_QUEUE = 4;
  public static final int   MAX_RECV_QUEUE = 4;
  public static final int   MAX_RETRIES = 4;
  public static final int   TIMEOUT = 2*1000;
  DatagramSocket            socket;
  DatagramPacket            packet;

  public UDPClient(InetAddress address, int port)
    throws IOException
  {
    this.socket = new DatagramSocket();// system-chosen port
    this.packet = new DatagramPacket
      (null, 0, address, port);
    socket.setSendBufferSize
      (MAX_DATAGRAM_BYTES*MAX_SEND_QUEUE);
    socket.setReceiveBufferSize
      (MAX_DATAGRAM_BYTES*MAX_RECV_QUEUE);
  }

  // Retry as necessary at increasing intervals:
  // throw InterruptedIOException if no reply

  public int sendReceive(byte[] buffer, int offset,
      int length)
      throws IOException
  {
    packet.setData(buffer, offset, length);
    IOException exception = null;
    int timeout = TIMEOUT;
    for (int i = 0; i < MAX_RETRIES; i++)
    {
      socket.send(packet);
      try
      {
        socket.setSoTimeout(timeout);
        socket.receive(packet);
        return packet.getLength();// return actual length
      }
      // catch InterruptedIOException rather than
      // SocketTimeoutException, so as to support all JDKs

      catch (InterruptedIOException iioexc)
      {
        exception = iioexc;
```

```
        timeout *= 2;          // exponential backoff
    }
  }
  throw exception;
} // sendReceive()
} // class
```

EXAMPLE 9.7 Complete U D P client

9.15 RELIABLE U D P

To send datagrams over lossy network segments with significant latency (*e.g.* the Internet, especially when xDSL network segments are present), we need something stronger than the examples of section 9.14.

As we saw in section 9.1.4, U D P does not guarantee the arrival or the correct sequence of datagrams. We have also seen that a simple combination of a sequence-numbering scheme with timeouts and retransmissions can be used to overcome this limitation:

(a) All datagrams are sequence-numbered

(b) The sender uses acknowledgement timeouts and retransmits requests whose acknowledgements have not arrived in time.

Most existing U D P applications such as the Domain Name Service exhibit both these features.

9.15.1 Sequence numbering

Sequence-numbering is simple. The client places a unique sequence number in each request datagram; the server must use the same sequence number in its reply. This lets the client associate an acknowledgment with a request, and allows the server to have some policy about out-of-sequence datagrams.

9.15.2 Adaptive timeout and retransmission

Timeout and retransmission is not so simple. The naïve approach is to use a fixed application-determined timeout, but this takes no account of the nature of the actual network, nor of its current state. The network might be anything between a 1G bps Ethernet LAN or a 9.6K bps dial-up modem; it might be lightly or heavily loaded at any particular time, which can change rapidly; it may be misbehaving badly due to some transient hardware condition such as a failing router.

It would be better to 'learn' how well the network is performing rather than sticking doggedly to some preconception. We should adapt the behaviour of our application to the current network load in two critical ways. First, we should transmit datagrams at a rate appropriate to the current network conditions, so that we get the best possible performance out of a lightly loaded network while not flooding a heavily loaded network with data it can't handle. Second, when we are re-transmitting dropped packets, we must aim at reducing the congestion on the network rather than making it worse.

9.15.3 Implementation in T C P

These techniques already exist in the T C P protocol, as a result of many years of design and experimentation, and can be applied to any network application. Specifically, the T C P protocol:

(a) Maintains a statistical estimate of the current round-trip time for a datagram to get from sender to receive and back again: this aims at sending packets into the network as fast as they can be received, but no faster, *i.e.* avoiding 'filling' the network

(b) Uses an 'exponential backoff' when computing retry timeouts, so that timeouts increase exponentially when repeated failures occur: this tends to empty the network of packets, increasing the likelihood that the next re-transmission will get through.

9.15.4 Implementation for U D P in Java

These techniques can easily be adapted to U D P datagrams in Java. The Java code following implements a ReliableDatagramSocket class along the lines indicated, which:

(a) Automatically prepends a unique sequence number to all outgoing transmissions and retrieves it from incoming transmissions, invisibly to the caller

(b) Introduces methods to get the incoming sequence number and set the outgoing sequence number, for use by servers when replying

(c) Introduces a sendReceive method for use by clients, which takes two arguments: an outgoing datagram and an incoming reply datagram, and which transmits the outgoing datagram and waits for the reply, adaptively timing-out and re-transmitting as necessary until a maximum retry count is reached, in which case it throws an InterruptedIOException as shown in Table 9.3.

The round-trip timer is now part of the standard for T C P (R F C 1122), and the ideas underlying it first appeared in Van Jacobson, *Congestion Avoidance and Control*, Computer Communications Review, vol. 18. no. 4, pp. 314–329, Proceedings of the ACM SIGCOMM '88 Workshop, August, 1988. The ReliableDatagramSocket class presented here in Java ultimately derives from a discussion and C code in W. Richard Stevens,

Unix Network Programming, 2nd edition, Vol I, Prentice Hall, 1998, §20.5, which explains how and why the round-trip timer statistics are maintained.

```java
/*
 * ReliableDatagramSocket.java.
 * Copyright © Esmond Pitt, 1997, 2005. All rights reserved.
 * Permission to use is granted provided this copyright
 * and permission notice is preserved.
 */
import java.io.*;
import java.net.*;
import java.text.*;
import java.util.*;
// All times are expressed in seconds.
// ReliabilityConstants interface, just defines constants.
interface ReliabilityConstants
{
  // Timeout minima/maxima
  public static final int  MIN_RETRANSMIT_TIMEOUT = 1;
  public static final int  MAX_RETRANSMIT_TIMEOUT = 64;
  // Maximum retransmissions per datagram, suggest 3 or 4.
  public static final int  MAX_RETRANSMISSIONS = 4;
}
```

The RoundTripTimer class manages current and smoothed round-trip timers and the related timeouts:

```java
// RoundTripTimer class.
class RoundTripTimer implements ReliabilityConstants
{
  float   roundTripTime = 0.0f;// most recent RTT
  float   smoothedTripTime = 0.0f;// smoothed RTT
  float   deviation = 0.75f;  // smoothed mean deviation
  short   retransmissions = 0;// retransmit count: 0, 1, 2, …
  // current retransmit timeout
  float   currentTimeout =
    minmax(calculateRetransmitTimeout());

  /** @return the re-transmission timeout. */
  private int calculateRetransmitTimeout()
  {
    return (int)(smoothedTripTime+4.0*deviation);
  }
```

```java
/** @return the bounded retransmission timeout. */
private float minmax(float rto)
{
  return Math.min
    (Math.max(rto, MIN_RETRANSMIT_TIMEOUT),
     MAX_RETRANSMIT_TIMEOUT);
}

/** Called before each new packet is transmitted. */
void newPacket()
{
  retransmissions = 0;
}

/**
 * @return the timeout for the packet.
 */
float currentTimeout()
{
  return currentTimeout;
}

/**
 * Called straight after a successful receive.
 * Calculates the round-trip time, then updates the
 * smoothed round-trip time and the variance (deviation).
 * @param ms time in ms since starting the transmission.
 */
void stoppedAt(long ms)
{
  // Calculate the round-trip time for this packet.
  roundTripTime = ms/1000;
  // Update our estimators of round-trip time
  // and its mean deviation.
  double delta = roundTripTime - smoothedTripTime;
  smoothedTripTime += delta/8.0;
  deviation += (Math.abs(delta)-deviation)/4.0;
  // Recalculate the current timeout.
  currentTimeout = minmax(calculateRetransmitTimeout());
}
```

```
/**
 * Called after a timeout has occurred.
 * @return true if it's time to give up,
 * false if we can retransmit.
 */

boolean  isTimeout()
{
  currentTimeout *= 2;  // next retransmit timeout
  retransmissions++;
  return retransmissions > MAX_RETRANSMISSIONS;
}
} // RoundTripTimer class
```

The ReliableDatagramSocket class exports a sendReceive method like the ones
we have already seen.

```
// ReliableDatagramSocket class

public class ReliableDatagramSocket
  extends     DatagramSocket
  implements ReliabilityConstants
{
  RoundTripTimer  roundTripTimer = new RoundTripTimer();
  private boolean reinit = false;
  private long    sendSequenceNo = 0; // send sequence #
  private long    recvSequenceNo = 0; // recv sequence #

  /* anonymous initialization for all constructors */
  {
    init();
  }

  /**
   * Construct a ReliableDatagramSocket
   * @param port Local port: reeive on any interface/address
   * @exception SocketException can't create the socket
   */

  public ReliableDatagramSocket(int port)
    throws SocketException
  {
    super(port);
  }
```

```java
/**
 * Construct a ReliableDatagramSocket
 * @param port Local port
 * @param localAddr local interface address to use
 * @exception SocketException can't create the socket
 */
public ReliableDatagramSocket
  (int port, InetAddress localAddr) throws SocketException
{
  super(port, localAddr);
}
/**
 * Construct a ReliableDatagramSocket, JDK >= 1.4.
 * @param localAddr local socket address to use
 * @exception SocketException can't create the socket
 */
public ReliableDatagramSocket(SocketAddress localAddr)
  throws SocketException
{
  super(localAddr);
}
/**
 * Overrides DatagramSocket.connect():
 * Does the connect, then (re-)initializes
 * the statistics for the connection.
 * @param dest Destination address
 * @param port Destination port
 */
public void connect(InetAddress dest, int port)
{
  super.connect(dest, port);
  init();
}
```

```
/**
 * Overrides JDK 1.4 DatagramSocket.connect().
 * Does the connect, then (re-)initializes
 * the statistics for the connection.
 * @param dest Destination address
 */
public void connect(SocketAddress dest)
{
  super.connect(dest);
  init();
}
/** Initialize */
private void init()
{
  this.roundTripTimer = new RoundTripTimer();
}
/**
 * Send and receive reliably,
 * retrying adaptively with exponential backoff
 * until the response is received or timeout occurs.
 * @param sendPacket outgoing request datagram
 * @param recvPacket incoming reply datagram
 * @exception IOException on any error
 * @exception InterruptedIOException on timeout
 */
public synchronized void sendReceive
  (DatagramPacket sendPacket, DatagramPacket recvPacket)
    throws IOException, InterruptedIOException
{
  // re-initialize after timeout
  if (reinit)
  {
    init();
    reinit = false;
  }

  roundTripTimer.newPacket();
  long start = System.currentTimeMillis();
  long sequenceNumber = getSendSequenceNo();
  // Loop until final timeout or some unexpected exception
  for (;;)
  {
    // keep using the same sequenceNumber while retrying
```

```java
setSendSequenceNo(sequenceNumber);
send(sendPacket);// may throw
int   timeout =
  (int)(roundTripTimer.currentTimeout()*1000.0+0.5);
long soTimeoutStart = System.currentTimeMillis();

try
{
  for (;;)
  {
    // Adjust socket timeout for time already elapsed
    int soTimeout = timeout-(int)
      (System.currentTimeMillis()-soTimeoutStart);
    setSoTimeout(soTimeout);
    receive(recvPacket);
    long recvSequenceNumber = getRecvSequenceNo();
    if (recvSequenceNumber == sequenceNumber)
    {
      // Got the correct reply:
      // stop timer, calculate new RTT values
      long ms = System.currentTimeMillis()-start;
      roundTripTimer.stoppedAt(ms);
      return;
    }
  }
}
catch (InterruptedIOException exc)
{
  // timeout: retry?
  if (roundTripTimer.isTimeout())
  {
    reinit = true;
    // rethrow InterruptedIOException to caller
    throw exc;
  }
  // else continue
}
// may throw other SocketException or IOException
} // end re-transmit loop
} // sendReceive()
```

```java
/**
 * @return the last received sequence number;
 * used by servers to obtain the reply sequenceNumber.
 */
public long getRecvSequenceNo()
{
  return recvSequenceNo;
}
/** @return the last sent sequence number */
private long getSendSequenceNo()
{
  return sendSequenceNo;
}
/**
 * Set the next send sequence number.
 * Used by servers to set the reply
 * sequenceNumber from the received packet:
 *
 * socket.setSendSequenceNo(socket.getRecvSequenceNo());
 *
 * @param sendSequenceNo Next sequence number to send.
 */
public void setSendSequenceNo(long sendSequenceNo)
{
  this.sendSequenceNo = sendSequenceNo;
}
/**
 * override for DatagramSocket.receive:
 * handles the sequence number.
 * @param packet DatagramPacket
 * @exception IOException I/O error
 */
public void receive(DatagramPacket packet)
  throws IOException
{
  super.receive(packet);

  // read sequence number and remove it from the packet
  ByteArrayInputStream bais = new ByteArrayInputStream
    (packet.getData(), packet.getOffset(),
      packet.getLength());
  DataInputStream dis = new DataInputStream(bais);
  recvSequenceNo = dis.readLong();
```

```
    byte[] buffer = new byte[dis.available()];
    dis.read(buffer);
    packet.setData(buffer,0,buffer.length);
}

/**
 * override for DatagramSocket.send:
 * handles the sequence number.
 * @param packet DatagramPacket
 * @exception IOException I/O error
 */
public void send(DatagramPacket packet)
  throws IOException
{
  ByteArrayOutputStreambaos = new ByteArrayOutputStream();
  DataOutputStreamdos = new DataOutputStream(baos);

  // Write the sequence number, then the user data.
  dos.writeLong(sendSequenceNo++);
  dos.write
    (packet.getData(), packet.getOffset(),
      packet.getLength());
  dos.flush();

  // Construct a new packet with this new data and send it.
  byte[]data = baos.toByteArray();
  packet = new DatagramPacket
    (data, baos.size(), packet.getAddress(),
      packet.getPort());
  super.send(packet);
}

} // end of ReliableDatagramSocket class
```

9.15.5 *Notes*

Strictly speaking, ReliableDatagramSocket should maintain a RoundTripTimer object for each destination, rather than one per socket.[8] The implementation above is reasonable as long as each client only communicates with one server, or even with one server per ReliableDatagramSocket (*e.g.* if the socket is logically

---

8. Although even this implementation is an improvement over Stevens', which just maintains one static set of statistics for all sockets. If the application communicates with multiple servers, each send/receive operation starts out with possibly irrelevant historical statistics, as Stevens agreed. — W.R. Stevens, private communication with the author, 1999.

connected), and not wildly unreasonable if it communicates with multiple servers along similar network paths.

A server for this protocol must obey two simple protocol rules:

(a) Each reply packet must have the same sequence number as the correspond-
     ing request packet: this is achieved by calling

        `socket.setSendSequenceNo(socket.getRecvSequenceNo());`

     before each transmission.

(b) If the underlying service is not idempotent, the server must keep track of
     sequence numbers and replies *per client*, and retransmit the same reply
     without re-excuting the service if it receives a duplicate request.

The latter raises some questions of protocol design and application policy. The
following are 'left as exercises for the reader':

(a) Is it safe to discard a reply once a higher-numbered request has been re-
     ceived from a client?

     The answer to this is probably 'yes', unless the client has strange behaviour.
     The client shouldn't use a new sequence number until it has an acknowl-
     edgement of the old sequence number. This can occur in the above imple-
     mentation of ReliableDatagramSocket if a packet is sent after a previous
     send has timed out, but perhaps you shouldn't be doing this, or if you do
     perhaps the control of outgoing sequence numbers needs to be revised.

(b) If so, what if anything should be done if a duplicate request is received
     whose reply has already been discarded?

     This should only arise because the network has redelivered the request. If
     so, the duplicate request can be completely ignored. The client shouldn't
     have re-sent it: having used a new sequence number, it has no business to
     reuse an old sequence number. This can only occur in the implementation
     of ReliableDatagramSocket above after 2^{64} iterations, which is unlikely to be
     reached in practice.

(c) What should be done if a higher sequence number than expected is re-
     ceived?

     In a protocol with negative acknowledgements you would send a N A C K for
     the next expected sequence number; otherwise the answer to this is proba-
     bly 'debug the client's strange behaviour'. This can't occur in the implemen-
     tation of ReliableDatagramSocket above.

Protocols with negative acknowledgements are also known as 'N A C K-based' protocols. These are further discussed in section 9.15.6.

Code for a reliable U D P echo server observing this protocol is shown in
Example 9.8.

```java
public class ReliableEchoServer implements Runnable
{
  ReliableDatagramSocket
                 socket;
  byte[]         buffer = new byte[1024];
  DatagramPacket recvPacket =
    new DatagramPacket(buffer, buffer.length);

  ReliableEchoServer(int port) throws IOException
  {
    this.socket = new ReliableDatagramSocket(port);
  }
  public void run()
  {
    for (;;)
    {
      try
      {
        // Restore the receive length to the maximum
        recvPacket.setLength(buffer.length);
        socket.receive(recvPacket);
        // Reply must have same seqno as request
        long seqno = socket.getRecvSequenceNo();
        socket.setSendSequenceNo(seqno);
        // Echo the request back as the response
        socket.send(recvPacket);
      }
      catch (IOException exc)
      {
        exc.printStackTrace();
      }
    } // for (;;)
  } // run()
} // class
```

EXAMPLE 9.8 Reliable U D P server

9.15.6 N A C K -*based protocols*

The reliable datagram socket above implements an 'A C K -based' protocol, in which a positive acknowledgment (A C K) indicates one or more packet(s) received. The opposite of this is called a negative acknowledgement-based or 'N A C K -based' protocol, in which a *negative* acknowledgement (N A C K) indicates packet(s) *not* received. Some protocols, including T C P, have both A C K and N A C K features.

Pure N A C K-based protocols are sometimes used when streaming data down a highly reliable network path. Under these circumstances, if the data is well paced and the packet-loss rate is low, these protocols can be considerably more efficient than A C K-based protocols, as a N A C K only has to be issued when a packet is lost, which may be quite rare.

To implement such a protocol over U D P, sequence numbering is again required. Sent datagrams and N A C K s both contain sequence numbers, where the sequence number of a N A C K indicates a datagram not received. The sender transmits sequenced datagrams at a controlled rate, while asynchronously looking for N A C K replies. Each N A C K causes a retransmission of the datagram with the sequence number advised in the N A C K, implying some sort of cache or backing-up mechanism in the sender. The receiver receives datagrams and processes them until it receives one out of sequence:

(a) If the sequence number is lower than expected, it is a duplicate which has already been received and can be ignored.

(b) If it is higher than expected, the datagrams between the last received sequence number and the current one have not been received, indicating a 'hole' in the received data: this is advised to the sender by issuing N A C K s for the missing numbers (or a single N A C K containing all the missing numbers if the protocol allows it).

Several classic issues arise in the design of N A C K-based protocols:[9]

(a) How does the receiver know when and whether message *N* was sent?

(b) If message *N* was lost or corrupt and a N A C K is sent, what happens if the N A C K is itself lost?

(c) If the data receiver does not *retransmit* its N A C K (in response to still not receiving message *N*), how can the data sender know to retransmit?

Timeouts are often used to resolve these issues. An end-of-sequence indication in the application protocol is also required to resolve (a).

9.15.7 Erasure codes

N A C K-based protocols can be used in conjunction with 'erasure codes', which add redundancy to the data stream in order to reduce the need for N A C K s and retransmissions. Indeed, erasure codes of sufficient strength can be used *instead* of N A C K-based protocols.

Erasure codes are a special case of 'forward error correction' (F E C), a technique often used in hardware to provide correction of arbitrary errors or omis-

---

9. Vernon Schryver, *re: Adding reliability to U D P*, news:comp.protocols.tcp-ip, 3 March 2002.

sions. The 8-to-14 Reed-Solomon encoding used on an audio C D is an F E C technique. F E C in full generality deals with arbitrary bit errors in unknown places, whereas, as their name implies, erasure codes only deal with missing data in known places ('erasures'). Erasure codes are computationally much simpler than full F E C, and their function is well matched to the general U D P problem that datagrams arrive either intact or not at all.

One well-known type of erasure code is used by R A I D [10] hard disk technology. Consider four blocks of data which we will label A, B, C, and D (*e.g.* four sequenced datagrams of 512 bytes each). We can construct a fifth 'checksum' block E by a sequence of exclusive-OR operations on A ... D:

$$E = A \char`\^ B \char`\^ C \char`\^ D \qquad\qquad (\text{EQ } 9.2)$$

where E_i, the ith byte of E, is formed by exclusive-ORing together A_i ... D_i, the ith bytes of A ... D. We choose the exclusive-OR operator because it has the interesting and useful mathematical property that its inverse function is itself, *i.e.*:

$$A = B \char`\^ C \quad\Rightarrow\quad B = A \char`\^ C \qquad\qquad (\text{EQ } 9.3)$$

(and similarly C = A ^ B). Applying this to Equation 9.2 , we then have:

$$A = B \char`\^ C \char`\^ D \char`\^ E \qquad\qquad (\text{EQ } 9.4)$$

and similarly for B, C, and D. In other words, any of the five blocks is the exclusive-OR of the other four. Therefore, of these five blocks of data, we only need any four: we can take advantage of Equation 9.3 to reconstruct the missing one. In other words if we transmit these five blocks, the receiver can tolerate the loss of any one of them. If the network fails to deliver E, there is no real loss as it is just the checksum block, but if it fails to deliver say B, it can be reconstructed from the other four.

Being able to reconstruct a missing block avoids having to send a N A C K for it to request the sender to retransmit it. Obviously this is achieved at the expense of the extra data transmission. Note that there is nothing magic about using four blocks to compute the checksum block. We can use any number N from zero upwards, depending on the packet-loss rate we are anticipating. At N = 0 we have normal non-redundant transmission; at N = 1 we effectively transmit each datagram twice, corresponding to disk mirroring, with an overhead of 100%; at N = 2 we have overhead of 50%; at N = 4 we have overhead of 25%; and so on. The choice of N corresponds to an expected packet-loss rate of $1/N$ (assuming we *never* want to send a N A C K). The overhead for any value of N > 0 as a percentage

---

10. R A I D: redundant arrays of inexpensive disks.

is given by $100/N$. Higher values of N require more memory at sender and receiver. In general we would choose small values of N such that:

$$N < 1/\text{packet-loss rate} \qquad\qquad (\text{EQ } 9.5)$$

where the packet-loss rate is expressed as a fraction (lost packets divided by total packets). Single-digit values of N are generally practical.

Obviously, this particular erasure code cannot deal with the loss of more than one packet of a sequence of N (*e.g.* more than one of A, B, C, D, and E for $N = 5$), any more than R A I D can cope with the loss of more than one disk. In this case a more elaborate erasure code would be required, or a N A C K protocol could take over responsibility for repairing the data stream.

CHAPTER 10

Scalable U D P

THIS CHAPTER DISCUSSES the use of J D K 1.4 scalable I/O with U D P datagrams.

10.1 CHANNELS FOR U D P

Scalable I/O over U D P is performed with the DatagramChannel class we encountered in passing in section 4.2.1.

10.1.1 *Import statements*

The following Java import statements are assumed in the examples throughout this chapter.

```
import java.io.*;
import java.net.*;
import java.nio.*;
import java.nio.channels.*;
import java.util.*;
```

10.1.2 *Creating a DatagramChannel*

The DatagramChannel class exports much the same opening and closing methods we have already encountered for SocketChannel:

```
class DatagramChannel
{
  static DatagramChannel open()    throws IOException
```

```
boolean                 isOpen();
void                    close()   throws IOException;
}
```

Opening a DatagramChannel returns a channel which is in blocking mode and ready for use. Its socket can be bound if required as discussed in section 9.3.5. The channel must be closed when it is finished with. *Caveat:* see the remarks about closing registered channels in section 5.2.5, which apply equally to DatagramChannel.

10.1.3 *Connect operation*

A DatagramChannel can be connected and disconnected directly, as well as via its DatagramSocket:

```
class DatagramChannel
{
  DatagramChannel connect(SocketAddress target)
                                 throws IOException;
  DatagramChannel disconnect()   throws IOException;
  boolean         isConnected();
}
```

These methods operate identically to the corresponding methods of DatagramSocket. Unlike the connection methods of SocketChannel, the connect method is *not* a non-blocking version of the U D P socket connection operation: DatagramChannel.connect and DatagramSocket.connect are semantically identical.

The isConnected method tells whether the *local* socket has been connected.

As we saw in section 9.3.7, connecting a datagram socket is a purely local operation with no network implications, *i.e.* with nothing to block on.

10.2 DatagramChannel I/O

DatagramChannel exports the read and write operations we have already seen in section 4.2.2, as required by the interfaces which it implements:

```
class DatagramChannel
{
  int read(ByteBuffer)              throws IOException;
  int read(ByteBuffer[] buffers) throws IOException;
  int read(ByteBuffer[] buffers, int offset, int length)
                                 throws IOException;
```

```
int write(ByteBuffer)                  throws IOException;
int write(ByteBuffer[] buffers)throws IOException;
int write(ByteBuffer[] buffers, int offset, int length)
                                throws IOException;
}
```

Now, this A P I is completely different from the DatagramPacket-oriented A P I exported by the DatagramSocket class described in section 9.4.1 and section 9.4.2. Specifically, there is nowhere to specify the destination address of an outgoing datagram, or to receive the source address of an incoming one. For this reason, the read and write methods are subject to an important semantic restriction in DatagramChannel: they can only be used if the associated socket is *connected* as defined in section 9.3.7. In this state the source or target address of a received or sent datagram can only be the target address to which the socket is connected, so the read/write A P I above is adequate.

To handle *unconnected* datagram sockets, DatagramChannel provides two new methods:

```
class DatagramChannel
{
  SocketAddress  receive(ByteBuffer buffer)
      throws IOException;
  int         send
    (ByteBuffer buffer, SocketAddress target)
      throws IOException;
}
```

These correspond to the DatagramSocket.receive and DatagramSocket.send methods respectively. The *target* parameter of DatagramChannel.send is the remote target for the transmission. The return value of DatagramChannel.receive is a SocketAddress, as seen in section 2.2, representing the remote source of the transmission.

10.2.1 *Blocking* U D P *I/O*

As we saw in section 10.1, a DatagramChannel is created in blocking mode. In this mode:

(a) A read operation blocks until an incoming datagram has been received into the socket receive buffer if none is already present.

(b) A write operation blocks until space is available to queue the outgoing datagram in the socket send-buffer, i.e. until enough datagrams previously queued have been transmitted to the network: this delay, if it occurs, is usually very short, as datagrams are transmitted at the maximum rate.

10.2.2 *Non-blocking* U D P *I/O*

A DatagramChannel can be put into non-blocking mode:

```
class DatagramChannel
{
  SelectableChannel configureBlocking(boolean block)
    throws IOException;
  boolean           isBlocking();
}
```

In *non-blocking* mode, the write and send methods may return zero, indicating that the socket send-buffer was full and no transfer could be performed; similarly, the read and receive methods may return zero or null respectively, indicating that no datagram was available.

A simple non-blocking U D P I/O sequence is illustrated in Example 10.1.

```
ByteBuffer       buffer = ByteBuffer.allocate(8192);
DatagramChannel  channel= DatagramChannel.open();
channel.configureBlocking(false);
SocketAddress address
  = new InetSocketAddress("localhost", 7);
buffer.put(…);
buffer.flip();
while (channel.send(buffer, address) == 0)
  ; // do something useful …
buffer.clear();
while ((address = channel.receive(buffer)) == null)
  ; // do something useful …
```

EXAMPLE 10.1 Simple non-blocking U D P client I/O

As the comments say, the program should be doing useful work or sleeping instead of spinning mindlessly while the I/O transfers return zero.

10.3 MULTIPLEXING

10.3.1 *Selectable I/O operations in* U D P

Selectable I/O operations in U D P all apply to DatagramChannel objects. The meanings of their 'ready' states are shown in Table 10.1.

TABLE 10.1 Selectable I/O operations in UDP

Operation	Meaning
OP_READ	Data is present in the socket receive-buffer or an exception is pending.
OP_WRITE	Space exists in the socket send-buffer or an exception is pending. In UDP, OP_WRITE is almost always ready except for the moments during which space is unavailable in the socket send-buffer. It is best only to register for OP_WRITE once this buffer-full condition has been detected, i.e. when a channel write returns less than the requested write length, and to deregister for OP_WRITE once it has cleared, *i.e.* a channel write has fully succeeded.

10.3.2 *Multiplexed I/O*

A DatagramChannel can be registered with a selector and the Selector.select method called to await readability or writability of the channel, as discussed in section 10.3.1:

```
DatagramChannelchannel = DatagramChannel.open();
// bind to port 1100
channel.bind(new InetSocketAddress(1100));
Selector        selector = Selector.open();
// register for OP_READ
channel.register(selector, SelectionKey.OP_READ);
// Select
selector.select();
```

10.3.3 *Example*

A simple multiplexing UDP echo server is shown in Example 10.2.

```
public class NIOUDPEchoServer implements Runnable
{
  static final int        TIMEOUT = 5000;// 5s
  private ByteBuffer      buffer =
    ByteBuffer.allocate(8192);
  private DatagramChannel channel;
  private List<Datagram> outputQueue =
    new LinkedList<Datagram>();
  // Create new NIOUDPEchoServer
  public NIOUDPEchoServer(int port) throws IOException
  {
    this.channel = DatagramChannel.open();
```

```java
    channel.socket().bind(new InetSocketAddress(port));
    channel.configureBlocking(false);
}

// Runnable. run method
public void run()
{
  try
  {
    Selector selector = Selector.open();
    channel.register(selector, SelectionKey.OP_READ);
    // loop while there are any registered channels
    while (!selector.keys().isEmpty())
    {
      int keysAdded = selector.select(TIMEOUT);
      // Standard post-select processing ...
      Set selectedKeys = selector.selectedKeys();
      synchronized (selectedKeys)
      {
        Iterator it = selectedKeys.iterator();
        while (it.hasNext())
        {
          SelectionKey key = (SelectionKey)it.next();
          it.remove();
          if (!key.isValid())
            continue;
          if (key.isReadable())
            handleReadable(key);
          if (key.isWritable())
            handleWritable(key);
        } // while
      } // synchronized
    } // while
  } // try
  catch (IOException e)
  {
    // ...
  }
} // run()

// handle readable key
void handleReadable(SelectionKey key)
{
  DatagramChannel channel =
    (DatagramChannel)key.channel();
```

```
    try
    {
      buffer.clear();
      SocketAddress address = channel.receive(buffer);
      if (address == null)
        return;          // no data
      buffer.flip();
      channel.send(buffer, address);
      int count = buffer.remaining();
      if (count > 0)
      {
        // Write failure: queue the write request
        // as a DatagramPacket, as this nicely holds
        // the data and reply address
        byte[] bytes = new byte[count];
        buffer.get(bytes);
        outputQueue.add
          (new DatagramPacket(bytes, count, address));
        // Register for OP_WRITE
        key.interestOps
          (SelectionKey.OP_READ|SelectionKey.OP_WRITE);
      }
    }
    catch (IOException e)
    {
      // …
    }
  } // handleReadable()

  // handle writable key
  void handleWritable(SelectionKey key)
  {
    DatagramChannel channel =
      (DatagramChannel)key.channel();
    try
    {
      while (!outputQueue.isEmpty())
      {
        DatagramPacket packet = outputQueue.get(0);
        buffer.clear();
        buffer.put(packet.getData());
        buffer.flip();
        channel.send(buffer, packet.getSocketAddress());
        if (buffer.hasRemaining()) // write failed, retry
          return;
```

```
      outputQueue.remove(0);
    }
    // All writes succeeded & queue empty, so
    // deregister for OP_WRITE
    key.interestOps(SelectionKey.OP_READ);
  }
  catch (IOException e)
  {
    // ...
  }
} // handleWritable()
} // end of NIOUDPEchoServer
```

EXAMPLE 10.2 Simple multiplexing U D P echo server

This server never blocks in an I/O operation, only in Selector.select. As we saw in section 9.2.1, it's quite a bit simpler than a T C P server, not having to manage client connections. In multiplexed I/O this means that it doesn't have to manage the SelectionKey.isAcceptable state, or handle another socket for the connection. It does have to manage an output queue containing both data and target addresses. Fortunately the java.net.DatagramPacket class containing exactly these data items is already to hand.

CHAPTER II

Multicast U D P

IN THIS CHAPTER we introduce U D P multicasting and broadcasting, and how they are realized in the Java DatagramSocket, MulticastSocket, and DatagramPacket classes. We have already discussed point-to-point or 'unicast' U D P in Chapter 9 (streams and blocking mode) and Chapter 10 (channel I/O and non-blocking mode).

II.I INTRODUCTION

Up to now we have dealt only with *unicast* transmissions, which are sent to and received by a single I P address. In essence, unicasting is an addressing technique. There are other addressing techniques:

(a) A *multicast* address identifies a dynamic group which can be joined and left: transmissions are received by all group members, subject to routing policies.

(b) A *broadcast* address identifies a static group representing all I P addresses in a net or subnet: transmissions to the address are received by all group members, subject to addressing limits and routing policies.

(c) I P V 6 also plans support for 'anycast' addresses. An *anycast* address identifies a dynamic group which can be joined and left: transmissions to the address are received by *any one* of the group members.[1]

These techniques are available or planned as shown in Table II.I.

---

[1]. R F C 1546 suggests that an anycast transmission is received by 'at least one, and preferably only one'; R F C 2373 specifies that an anycast transmission is received by the nearest group member in the routing topology.

TABLE 11.1 Hierarchy of address types[a]

Type	IPV4	IPV6	TCP	UDP	Sent to	Received by
Unicast	Yes	Yes	Yes	Yes	one	one
Anycast	No	Yes	Planned	Yes	a set	any one in set
Multicast	Optional	Yes	No	Yes	a set	all in set
Broadcast	Yes	No	No	Yes	all	all

a. after Stevens, W.R., *Unix Network Programming*, 2nd edition, Vol I, fig. 18.1.

11.1.1 *Motivation*

As we saw in Chapter 9, a U D P datagram is normally sent to a known unicast address. This action sends a single copy of the datagram to that address, and it is received only by that address. Normally this is exactly what we want: normally, there is only one peer that we want to send the datagram to.

If we want to send the same data to more than one peer via unicasting, we must do multiple sends—we must send out the datagram multiple times. This requirement might arise for example in a multi-player game, a software distribution application, a video-conferencing system, a multi-media viewing system, a system to distribute market quotations, *etc.* Applications like these are only viable if there is a cheaper technique for distributing datagrams than sending out one per recipient. Can we get the network to do the distribution for us, so that we only have to send each datagram out once?

The answer is 'yes'. In addition to unicasting, I P provides *broadcast* and *multicast*. These are supported as special kinds of I P address. Datagrams sent to either a broadcast or a multicast address are propagated as necessary by the network, and need be sent only once—subject to any restrictions imposed by intermediate routers, and bearing in mind that UDP datagrams only get 'best-effort' delivery, not guaranteed delivery.

Broadcasting and multicasting are also useful when clients need to look for services. Instead of sending out unicast requests by cycling through a range of addresses where the service might be, the client can send out a single broadcast or multicast request. Instances of the service are listening for such broadcasts or multicasts, and each instance responds by sending its unicast address back to the client: this completes the service-location process. The Jini Lookup and Discovery Service uses this technique. 'Anycast', when implemented, will be even more useful for this purpose.

Broadcasting and multicasting are *similar* in that they propagate a single datagram so as to reach all addressees. Logically speaking, broadcasting to everybody is a special case of multicasting to a set of recipients. Broadcasting are *different* in that broadcasting is indiscriminate, propagating datagrams even where no-one is listening, whereas multicasting is intelligent, only propagating where multicast listeners are known to exist. Broadcasting and multicasting also differ in the mechanisms used: broadcasting relies simply on normal U D P operations using special broadcast addresses, whereas multicasting uses new operations and Java APIs as well as special multicast addresses.

11.1.2 Broadcast addresses

A *broadcast address* is a special 'logical' address which indicates all nodes on a network. No single node actually has a broadcast address as its I P address.

I P V 4 defines two major kinds of broadcast address. Remember that I P addresses are composed of a network part, the subnet ID, and a host part, where the network and subnet IDs can be masked off by the netmask. The two kinds of broadcast address and their semantics are as follows:

(a) The *limited* broadcast address is 'all ones', or 255.255.255.255 (ff.ff.ff.ff): the network ID, the subnet ID, and the host ID are all ones. Datagrams addressed to this address will be delivered to and received by all hosts connected to the connected physical network. The limited broadcast address is intended only for use during host startup, when the local host may not know its own subnet mask or I P address yet.

(b) *Directed* broadcast addresses are those whose host ID is all ones, and whose network and subnet IDs indicate the target networks.[2] Datagrams addressed to such addresses will be delivered to all hosts connected to the connected physical network, and received by all hosts on that network whose network and subnet IDs match those of the broadcast address.

This can be further subdivided. What we have just described is really 'subnet-directed' broadcasting; there are also all-subnets-directed broadcasting and net-directed broadcasting, which we will not discuss here, as they are considered harmful, essentially obsolete, and unlikely to be supported by the routers concerned.

Sending a limited or directed broadcast is simply a matter of sending a datagram to the appropriate broadcast address. Receiving limited or directed broadcasts is simply a matter of binding a datagram socket to the wildcard address and executing a receive operation. Broadcasting in Java is discussed in detail in section 11.5.

I P V 6 does not define *any* broadcast addresses: their function is superseded by multicast addresses.[3]

---

2. Historically, a host ID of all zeroes was also capable of being interpreted as a broadcast address in certain circumstances which are now obsolete.

3. Hinden, R. & Deering, S., R F C 2373: I P Version 6 Addressing Architecture, §2.0.

11.1.3 *Multicast addresses*

A *multicast address* is a 'logical' IP address which identifies a *multicast group*, which in turn is a set of zero or more hosts which have joined the group. Transmissions sent to a multicast address are delivered to all current members of the group. A host must join a multicast group to *receive* multicasts, but it is not necessary to join a group to *send* multicasts to it. Special API operations are provided for joining and leaving multicast groups.

IPV4 defines multicast addresses as all IPV4 addresses which start with 1110 in the most significant four bits, i.e. 224.0.0.0 to 239.255.255.255 (e0.0.0.0 to ef.ff.ff.ff). Addresses in the range 224.0.0.0 to 224.0.0.255 are reserved for low-level multicasting support operations.

IPV6 defines multicast addresses as all IPV6 addresses which start with ff in the high-order byte, *i.e.* from ff00::0 to ffff:ffff:ffff:ffff:ffff:ffff:ffff:ffff. Some sub-ranges of this range are reserved.

11.1.4 *Scopes*

The *scope* of a multicast is the distance it will propagate before being discarded. The following are some common scope names and their meanings:

(a) *node-local*—not propagated beyond the local node (i.e. never output by a network interface)

(b) *link-local*—not propagated beyond a router

(c) *site-local*—not propagated beyond the site, as defined by the site's network administrators

(d) *organization-local*—not propagated beyond the organization, as defined by the organization's network administrators

(e) *region-local*—not propagated beyond the region, however defined

(f) *continent-local*—not propagated beyond the continent, however defined

(g) *global*—propagated everywhere.

(This list is a mixture of IPV4 and IPV6 scopes.)

There are two forms of scoping: TTL-based or 'dynamic' scoping discussed in section 11.1.5, and address-based or 'administrative' scoping discussed in section 11.1.6. TTL-based scoping is the older technique: it remains accepted and recommended, but administrative scoping is preferred where possible.

11.1.5 *TTL-based scopes*

TTL-based scopes are only available in IPV4.

Every IP packet is associated with a 'time-to-live' or TTL. In TCP the TTL is not within the application's control,so it is of no interest to us. However, in IPV4 multicasting, the TTL is used to control the 'scope' of the multicast, i.e. how 'far' the multicast datagram can propagate.

The default time-to-live for a multicast datagram is one: this means that the datagram is not forwarded out of the current subnet. A value of zero indicates that the datagram shouldn't be forwarded out of the current host (*e.g.* if multiple processes within the host are having a closed multicast conversation); values of two or greater indicate successively larger scopes, as shown in Table 11.2.

TABLE 11.2 IPV4 TTL-based dynamic scopes

TTL	Scope
0	node-local
1	link-local
< 32	site-local
< 64	region-local
< 128	continent-local
< 255	global

11.1.6 Address-based scopes

Multicast addresses are divided into administrative scopes. These have two purposes: they specify how far a multicast datagram will travel, and they specify the range within which the address is expected to be unique.

In IPV4, the address range 239.0.0.0 to 239.255.255.255 is defined as the administratively scoped multicast address space. The IPV4 administrative scopes and their corresponding address ranges are defined in RFC 2365 and shown in Table 11.3.[4]

In IPV6, the 4-bit 'scope' field in the second-highest byte of the multicast address explicitly defines the multicast scope. For example, an IPV6 address beginning with ff01 is node-local, with ff02 is link-local, and so on. This is the true meaning of the InetAddress methods such as isMCLinkLocal shown in Table 2.3.

A mapping between IPV6 scopes and IPV4 administrative scopes is defined in RFC 2365. This information plus the IPV4 TTL corresponding to each scope is shown in Table 11.3.[5] Note that this mapping is not one-to-one: several IPV4 TTL values are unmapped, and 'site-local' has different semantics in IPV4 and IPV6.

---

4. Meyer, D., RFC 2365: *Administratively Scoped IP Multicast.*

5. After Stevens, W.R., *Unix Network Programming,* 2nd edition, Vol I, fig. 19.2, with corrections to match RFC 2365.

TABLE 11.3 Administrative and dynamic scopes

IPV6 scope	IPV4 prefix	IPV4 TTL	Scope name
1		0	node-local
2	224.0.0.0/24	1	link-local
3	239.255.0.0/16	< 32	unassigned
5			site-local
8	239.192.0.0/14		organization-local
14	224.0.1.0 to 238.255.255.255	< 255	global

11.1.7 Multicast operations—join and leave

In addition to the usual sending and receiving operations, multicast introduces the operations of *joining* and *leaving* a multicast group. These operations have several effects:

(a) They form or break an association between the socket's bind-address and the multicast address.

(b) They condition the host to receive or ignore messages addressed to the group.

(c) They condition the nearest router to receive or ignore messages addresses to the multicast group, subject to multicasting being supported in that router.

(d) The router in turn propagates this conditioning to adjacent routers, and so on recursively, subject to multicasting being supported in those routers.

These actions are carried out only for the first 'join' and the last 'leave' of a group, as follows:

(a) When an application in a host *joins* a multicast group, if this causes the number of members of the group in the current host to increase from zero to one, the host tells the nearest router (via an IGMP[6] message) that the host is now interested in receiving multicasts addressed to the specified multicast group. Subject to the same zero-to-one rule and the router's own policy, the router then informs adjacent routers that it wants to receive those multicasts, and so on recursively.

(b) Similarly, when an application *leaves* a multicast group, if this causes the number of members of the group in the current host to fall from one to zero, the host tells the nearest router (via an IGMP message) that the host is no

---

6. Internet Group Management Protocol.

longer interested in receiving multicasts addressed to the specified multi-cast group. Subject to the same one-to-zero rule and the router's own policy, the router then informs adjacent routers that it no longer wants to receive those multicasts, and so on recursively.

In this way the entire routing tree eventually comes to know, for each adjacent router, which (if any) multicast addresses it wants to receive multicasts for, at a minor cost in I G M P messages—and a cost which scales well to large groups.

When an application closes a socket which has joined but not left one or more multicast groups, leave-group processing for each such group occurs automatically as part of the close process.

11.2 BENEFITS

Multicasting has a number of benefits over unicasting the same information to the same recipients. Most obviously, there is a substantial saving in network bandwidth and therefore in network usage costs: if the cost to unicast a given amount of data to N recipients is $1, the cost to multicast the same data to the same recipients is $\$1/N$. There is also a saving in time to propagate the data to the N recipients, as the total transmission is completed in $1/N$ the time compared to unicasting it. This has the secondary advantage of reducing the load on the server.

Another benefit of multicasting is that, ignoring packet loss and retransmission issues, all recipients receive the data at much the same time. This has useful applications in time-sensitive applications such as distributing stock-market quotations (stock tickers).

As compared to unicasting, multicasting becomes more and more economic the more recipients there are. To put this another way, multicasting is a solution which scales far better than unicasting.

When the number of recipients is very large, huge-scale applications such as movie shows over the Internet become technically and economically viable: these could never be feasible via unicast. In this sense, Internet multicasting is comparable in importance to the introduction of broadcast radio and television.

These economic drivers behind multicast *appear* to be irresistible in the long term, although at the time of writing there is considerable bandwidth overcapacity in much of the Internet, which suggests that widespread adoption of multicast is not imminent.

11.3 LIMITATIONS

Multicasting in general, including broadcasting as a special case, has three significant limitations.

1. It is a UDP mechanism and therefore does not offer inherent reliability: it needs a reliability layer of the kind discussed in section 11.10 and following.

2. It requires co-operation from routers, as discussed in more detail in section 11.3.1 and section 11.3.3.

3. The question of multicast security is *extremely* complex.[7]

11.3.1 Broadcasting and routers

Routers and broadcasts generally do not mix. Routers *never* forward limited-broadcast datagrams. Routers *may* forward directed-broadcast datagrams to other networks, where they *may* be received by the router into those networks. A router which receives a directed broadcast will deliver it to the locally connected physical network, where it will be received by all hosts on that network whose network ID matches the network ID of the address.

However, as RFC 2644 states: 'While directed broadcasts have uses, their use on the Internet backbone appears to be comprised entirely of malicious attacks on other networks.'[8] The use of directed broadcasts on the Internet is therefore discouraged, and probably limited by router policies: according to the Router Requirements RFCs,[9] Internet routers may receive and forward directed broadcasts, but they must also have an option to disable both receiving and forwarding, and both must be off by default.

11.3.2 Broadcast considered harmful

The main problem with broadcasting—as opposed to multicasting proper—is the unwanted load incurred by hosts which aren't listening. The broadcast datagram is still received by the network interface and propagated upwards through the various layers of the protocol stack: the device driver, the IP layer, and the UDP layer, to the point where UDP discovers that the target port is not in use. Multicasting proper, as opposed to broadcasting, does not share this problem, as irrelevant multicasts are discarded at the lowest possible level—usually the network interface or device driver—without disturbing the UDP layer at all.

From all these hints, and from the complete absence of broadcasting in IPV6, you should conclude that UDP broadcasting is to be avoided if possible. It certainly should not be considered for any deployment requiring broadcasting through routers. Use multicasting if possible.

---

7. So complex that I cannot even begin to discuss it here. For a thorough survey see Hardjono and Dondeti, *Multicast and Group Security*, Artech House, 2003.

8. Senie, D., RFC 2644: Changing the Default for Directed Broadcasts in Routers.

9. Baker, F., RFC 1812: Requirements for IP Version 4 Routers, §4.2.2.11 (d), updated by RFC 2644.

11.3.3 *Multicasting and routers*

Multicasting is supported by a given router if and only if specifically enabled by its administrator. Currently few ISPs support multicast propagation through their routers. This is largely a chicken-and-egg problem: presently there are few multicast applications on the Internet and therefore small demand for multicast support, which in turn is discouraging the development and deployment of the applications. This may change over time as multicast applications are developed.

11.3.4 *Multicasting and group membership*

One of the peculiarities of multicasting is that it provides no built-in way of determining how many group members currently exist. There isn't even a way of determining whether *any* group members exist. Thus, a group member cannot tell whether there are any other group members out there. Neither can a transmitting application tell whether anybody out there is listening. These characteristsics are important when designing application protocols.

Unless the application protocol provides it, there is no way for a transmitting application to know how many receivers there currently are: therefore, if responses are expected, there is no way to determine whether all expected responses have been received. The transmitter can't even know whether or not there is currently any point in transmitting anything.

A solution to this limitation may or may not be required: if it is, the application protocol must provide an explicit sign-on/sign-off negotiation.

11.4 APPLICATIONS OF MULTICAST

We have already seen some major applications of multicast. Here is a more complete list:

(a)   Software distribution

(b)   Time services

(c)   Naming services like DNS

(d)   Stock-market tickers, race results, and the like

(e)   Database replication

(f)   Video and audio streaming: video conferencing, movie shows, etc

(g)   Multi-player gaming

(h)   Distributed resource allocation

(i)   Service discovery.

In most multicast applications, the *client* is a member of a multicast group. The server most probably is not, unless it wants to listen to its own output for some reason. However when multicast is used for service discovery, generally both client and server join the multicast group, as seen in the Jini Lookup and Discovery Service protocol.

11.5 Broadcasting in Java

The following subsections describe the techniques used for Java broadcasting. section 11.5.1 describes how to send a broadcast; section 11.5.2 describes how to receive broadcasts; section 11.5.3 discusses broadcast 'loopback'; and section 11.5.4 discusses broadcasting to and from multi-homed hosts.

11.5.1 Sending broadcasts

Sending a broadcast in Java is identical to sending a normal UDP datagram to a broadcast address. Java code to send a datagram via a DatagramSocket to all nodes on the current physical network at UDP port 8888 is shown in Example 11.1.[10]

```
int    port = 8888;
byte[] data = …;// initialization not shown
// send to all nodes on the current physical network
// via the limited broadcast address
InetAddress address
  = InetAddress.getByName("255.255.255.255");
DatagramPacket packet =
  new DatagramPacket(data, data.length, address, port);
DatagramSocket socket = new DatagramSocket();
socket.send(packet);
```

EXAMPLE 11.1 Broadcast to current physical network

To send a datagram to a directed-broadcast address, just change the address as demonstrated in Example 11.2. This example sends to all nodes in the 192.168.1.* network: change to suit your own network. The example assumes that the routers will co-operate: as discussed in section 11.3.1, this assumption is probably invalid.

---

10. See section 11.5.4 for a discussion of broadcasting from multi-homed hosts.

```
// send to all nodes in 192.168.*.*
// via a directed broadcast address
InetAddress address =
   InetAddress.getByName("192.168.1.255");
```

EXAMPLE 11.2 Directed broadcast

11.5.2 *Receiving broadcasts*

Receiving broadcasts in Java is identical to receiving normal U D P datagrams. It makes no difference whether the broadcast was sent to a limited or a directed broadcast address. The receiving socket should be bound to the wildcard address.[11] This is the default: it can also be explicitly specified as the null InetAddress when constructing or binding a datagram socket. Some platforms may support broadcast reception by sockets bound to a specific address.

Java code to receive the datagram which was broadcast to port 8888 by the previous send examples is shown in Example 11.3.

```
int             port = 8888;
DatagramSocket  socket = new DatagramSocket(port);
byte[]          data = new byte[8192+1];
DatagramPacket  packet
  = new DatagramPacket(data, data.length);
socket.receive(packet);
```

EXAMPLE 11.3 Receive broadcast datagrams

From J D K 1.4 the receiving socket can be initialized equivalently as shown in Example 11.4.

```
DatagramSocket  socket = new DatagramSocket(null);
socket.bind(new InetSocketAddress(8888));
```

EXAMPLE 11.4 Alternate DatagramSocket initialization— J D K 1.4

Note that the following J D K 1.4 sequence does *not* work:

```
DatagramSocket  socket = new DatagramSocket();
socket.bind(new InetSocketAddress(8888));
```

because DatagramSocket's default constructor binds it to an ephemeral local port (see section 9.3.2): a DatagramSocket cannot be rebound, so the bind will fail.

---

11. It *must* be bound to the wildcard address if the host is multi-homed: see section 11.5.4.

11.5.3 Broadcast loopback

When an application is both sending and receiving broadcasts to and from the same port, the application will receive its own transmissions. This 'local loopback' cannot be disabled. If the application isn't interested in processsing its own transmissions, it must check the source of received datagrams via the DatagramPacket.getAddress or DatagramPacket.getSocketAddress methods, and ignore those which it sent itself.

11.5.4 Broadcast and multi-homing

Receiving a broadcast in a multi-homed host only requires that the receiving socket is bound to the wildcard address: this is the default, and it is usually required for receiving broadcasts anyway. Similarly, sending a directed broadcast from a multi-homed host presents no difficulty, because the system routes a directed broadcast to the target subnet via the appropriate interface.

However, sending a limited broadcast from multi-homed host generally doesn't work. A limited broadcast should be sent to all connected subnets, i.e. via all network interfaces. However, as the relevant R F C 'takes no stand' on whether the system must send a limited broadcast via one or all network interfaces, an application cannot rely on either behaviour.[12] The only reliable solution is to send a directed broadcast to each interface, addressed in each case to the appropriate broadcast address. This cannot be programmed automatically in Java, which provides no access to the netmask, which is needed to compute the corresponding broadcast address: the subnet broadcast address snba is given by

$$\text{snba} = \text{address} \mid (\text{netmask} \wedge \text{0xffffffff}) \qquad (\text{EQ 11.1})$$

An approximate solution which simply assumes a netmask of 0xffffff00 (class D) for all local interfaces is shown in Example 11.5.

As shown, this solution will also broadcast to 127.0.0.255, which is only an internal loopback, and therefore pointless; this broadcast address, or the interface address 127.0.0.1, should be filtered out. This and any other adjustments (e.g. for different netmasks) are left as an exercise for the reader. If you can't use the NetworkInterface feature of J D K 1.4, you'll have to arrange for the application to know all its I P addresses via some external configuration, or some J N I horror. As a last resort, you could also assume a netmask of wider scope, e.g. 0xfffff000, if you are really prepared to trust your routers to suppress these broadcasts before they escape too widely: every bit you clear in the netmask doubles the host address space.

Please don't use this technique: read on and use a multicast solution.

---

12. Braden, R., R F C 1122, *Requirements for Internet Hosts—Communication Layers*, §3.3.6.

```
DatagramSocket   socket = new DatagramSocket();
DatagramPacket   packet;// initialization not shown
Enumeration      interfaces =
  NetworkInterface.getNetworkInterfaces();
while (interfaces.hasMoreElements())
{
  NetworkInterface  networkInterf =
    (NetworkInterface)interfaces.nextElement();
  Enumeration    addresses
    = networkInterf.getInetAddresses();
  while (addresses.hasMoreElements())
  {
    InetAddress inetAddress
      = (InetAddress)addresses.nextElement();
    byte[]      addr = inetAddress.getAddress();
    int netmask = 0xffffff00;// (assumes class D subnet)
    // form subnet broadcast address
    int broadcastAddr = netmask ^ 0xffffffff;
    for (int i = 3; i >= 0; i--)
        addr[i] |= (byte)(broadcastAddr >>> (3-i)*8);
    InetAddress bcAddr = InetAddress.getByAddress(addr);
    packet.setAddress(bcAddr);
    // assuming data, length, & port are already set
    socket.send(packet);
  }
}
```

EXAMPLE 11.5 Broadcast from multi-homed host

11.6 MULTICASTING IN JAVA

The following subsections describe the techniques used for multicasting in Java.

In section 11.6.1 we will see how to send multicasts; in section 11.6.2 we will see how to control the time-to-live (TTL) of a sent multicast; section 11.6.3 introduces multicast receiving operations; section 11.6.4 describes initialization of multicast sockets; section 11.6.5 describes joining and leaving multicast groups; section 11.6.6 describes the actual reception process; section 11.6.7 discusses multicast 'loopback' and how to control it; and section 11.6.8 discusses multicasting to and from multi-homed hosts.

11.6.1 Sending multicasts

Sending a multicast in Java is identical to sending a normal U D P datagram to a
multicast address. Java code to send a datagram to a multicast address at U D P
port 8888 is shown in Example 11.6.

```
int    port = 8888;
byte[] data;     // initialization not shown
// multicast address to send to
InetAddress  address
  = InetAddress.getByName("239.1.14.126");
DatagramPacket  packet =
  new DatagramPacket(data, data.length, address, port);
DatagramSocket  socket = new DatagramSocket();
socket.send(packet);
```

EXAMPLE 11.6 Sending a multicast

Note that multicast data can be sent with a DatagramSocket. Of course, by inheritance you *can* send with a MulticastSocket, although there is no need to do so
unless you want to *receive* multicasts with the same socket, or if you want to use
the advanced sending facilities described in section 11.6.2 and section 11.6.8. As
we will see in section 11.6.4, the constructors for MulticastSocket correspond
precisely to those of DatagramSocket, and the inherited bind and send methods
are identical by inheritance.

11.6.2 Multicast time-to-live

MulticastSocket allows you to multicast a datagram with a non-standard time-to-
live. Just call its setTimeToLive method, or use its overload of the send method
which takes a time-to-live parameter:

```
class MulticastSocket extends DatagramSocket
{
  int   getTimeToLive()          throws IOException;
  void  setTimeToLive(int ttl)   throws IOException;
  void  send(DatagramPacket packet, byte ttl)
                                 throws IOException;
}
```

as shown in Example 11.7. This feature is used to implement T T L -based dynamic
scoping as described in section 11.1.5. You can also use these methods to send
datagrams with non-standard T T L values to *non*-multicast addresses, if you know
what you are doing.

```
MulticastSocket socket = new MulticastSocket();
int             ttl = 4;
socket.setTimeToLive(ttl);
// or
socket.send(packet, (byte)ttl);
```

EXAMPLE 11.7 Setting a non-standard time-to-live

The get/setTimeToLive methods were introduced in JDK 1.2. JDK 1.1 provided methods entitled getTTL and setTTL, now deprecated, which took and returned a byte value in the range -128 to +127. TTL values are defined in the range 0 to 255, which is easier to handle as an integer. Use the get/setTimeToLive methods or the send overload which takes a TTL parameter.

11.6.3 Receiving operations

Receiving a multicast in Java requires use of a MulticastSocket object: it cannot be done with a DatagramSocket. This in turn requires three distinct operations:

(a)   Initializing a MulticastSocket

(b)   Joining a multicast group

(c)   Receiving a datagram.

These are discussed individually below.

11.6.4 Initializing a MulticastSocket

A MulticastSocket is initialized via one of the constructors:

```
class MulticastSocket extends DatagramSocket
{
  MulticastSocket()            throws IOException;
  MulticastSocket(int port)    throws IOException;
  MulticastSocket
    (SocketAddress address)    throws IOException;
}
```

If a null SocketAddress is supplied, the socket is constructed unbound and must be bound before receiving. This is done with the method:

```
class MulticastSocket extends DatagramSocket
{
  void bind(SocketAddress address) throws IOException;
}
```

where address is an InetSocketAddress specifying the I P address and the port to be bound, *i.e.* the address and port at which the socket will receive. The I P address can be omitted or null, indicating the wildcard address; the port can be zero, indicating a system-chosen 'ephemeral' port.

In multicasting, it is most likely that you will bind to the wildcard address, indicating that you want to receive multicasts from anywhere; conversely, it is not very likely that you'll bind to an ephemeral port, as you will be joining a multicast group whose port number has most probably already been defined, as discussed in section 11.6.5.

Unlike a DatagramSocket, a MulticastSocket can be bound to the same address and port as an existing MulticastSocket in the same host (in other words, it uses the setReuseAddress feature). This allows multiple threads within a J V M to receive multicasts independently, from the same group or different groups.

11.6.5 Joining and leaving

Next you must join the multicast group(s) you will be listening to. This is done with the methods:

```
class MulticastSocket extends DatagramSocket
{
  void joinGroup(InetAddress mcastAddr) throws IOException;
  void joinGroup(SocketAddress mcastAddr,
    NetworkInterface intf)                throws IOException;

  void leaveGroup(InetAddress mcastAddr)
                                          throws IOException;
  void leaveGroup(SocketAddress mcastAddr,
    NetworkInterface intf)                throws IOException;
}
```

The intf parameter to the joinGroup and leaveGroup methods specifies the network interface to be used for sending any I G M P messages generated by the method.[13]

If this parameter is omitted, joinGroup and leaveGroup implicitly use the getInterface result to specify the interface for I G M P messages. If you're sure you're in a single-homed host, you can omit this parameter. See section 11.6.8 for a discussion of multi-homing issues.

> It would be a rare system in which the interface specified to joinGroup was different to the interface specified to leaveGroup.

---

13. The J D K 1.4.0 documentation incorrectly states that the intf parameter to joinGroup specifies the local interface for receiving multicast packets. The latter function is performed by the bind address. See section 11.6.8 for further discussion.

A given MulticastSocket may join more than one group. Each join must specify either:

(a) A multicast group which is not currently joined by this socket, or

(b) A multicast group which is currently joined by this socket but is now joined via a different interface from the previous joins for that group and socket.

If neither of these conditions is satisifed, or the specified address is not a multicast address, an IOException is thrown.

Host operationing systems may limit the number of groups a socket can join, *e.g.* to 20 for Berkely-derived implementations.

A socket cannot leave a group of which it is not already a member. If an interface is specified when leaving a group, the socket must have joined the group on the same interface. If either of these conditions is violated, or the specified address is not a multicast address, an IOException is thrown.

11.6.6 Receiving multicasts

Receiving multicasts in Java is identical to receiving normal U D P datagrams or broadcasts as shown in section 11.5.2. The receiving socket may be bound to the wildcard address (the default binding), or it can be bound to an explicit I P address (not recommended—see section 11.5.4).

Java code to join a multicast group and receive a datagram which was sent to the group on port 8888 is shown in Example 11.8.

```
int     port = 8888;
MulticastSocket socket = new MulticastSocket(port);
// multicast address to receive from
InetAddress mcastAddr =
  InetAddress.getByName("239.1.14.126");
socket.joinGroup(mcastAddr);
byte[]          data = new byte[8193];
DatagramPacket  packet =
  new DatagramPacket(data, data.length);
socket.receive(packet);
```

EXAMPLE 11.8 Join and receive multicast datagrams

An equivalent initialization of the receiving socket using J D K 1.4 features is shown in Example 11.9.

Note that the following J D K 1.4 sequence does *not* work:

```
MulticastSocket socket = new MulticastSocket();
socket.bind(new InetSocketAddress(8888));
```

```
MulticastSocket socket = new MulticastSocket(null);
socket.bind(new InetSocketAddress(port));
```

EXAMPLE 11.9 Alternative MulticastSocket initialization— J D K 1.4

because, as discussed for DatagramSocket in section 9.3.2, the default constructor for MulticastSocket binds it to an anonymous local port. As the socket is already bound, binding the socket to an explicit port will fail.

11.6.7 Multicast loopback

By default, when an application is both sending and receiving multicasts to and
from the same group, port, and interface, the application will receive its own
transmissions. This 'local loopback' can be disabled on some systems via the
methods:

```
class MulticastSocket
{
  boolean   getLoopbackMode() throws SocketException;
  void      setLoopbackMode(boolean loopback)
                            throws SocketException;
}
```

The loopback value supplied to the setLoopbackMode method only acts as a hint,
as the underlying system may not process the request. The actual state of loopback is returned by the getLoopbackMode method.

The meaning of the value of loopback is counter-intuitive: if true, it means that
loopback is *disabled*.[14]

11.6.8 Multicast and multi-homing

There are three simple rules to be followed for applications which will execute in
multi-homed hosts, or where you don't know in advance whether the host will be
multi-homed or not:

(a)   Multicast datagrams should be sent via each available interface in turn.

(b)   Multicast receiving sockets should be bound to the wildcard address.

(c)   Join and leave operations should be performed via each available interface
      in turn.

---

14. In J D K 1.4.0 this seems to have confused the developers too, as it was implemented back-to-
front (i.e. behaves intuitively). This was fixed in 1.4.1. See Bug Parade, bug ID 4686717.

These three rules are sufficient to make multi-homed multicasting work. The reasons for these rules are discussed in the rest of this section.

Multicast is complex in multi-homed hosts, for two fundamental reasons. First, the system does *not* send multicasts via all local network interfaces: it uses a single sending interface—the interface specified by the user for the operation (join, leave, or send) if any, otherwise the interface dictated by the unicast routing tables. Second, the underlying system design conceivably allows a multicasting application to use four different network interfaces for four different purposes simultaneously: joining, leaving, receiving, and sending.

The latter aspect of multicasting causes a lot of confusion.[15] Like the underlying Berkely Sockets A P I, the Java multicasting A P I uses local network interfaces or addresses for three different purposes:

(a) Binding the socket

(b) Controlling the interface used for sending

(c) Controlling the interface used for joining and leaving groups.

It is important to understand these different purposes when programming for multi-homed hosts. The various address/interface items and their purposes are summarized in Table 11.4.

TABLE 11.4 Addresses and interfaces in multicasting

Item	Methods	Description
Bind address	Constructors of MulticastSocket, bind	Determines the I P address via which datagrams can be received: defaults to the wildcard address.[a]
Send interface	setInterface, setNetworkInterface	Determines the network interface via which multicasts are sent: defaults to a system-chosen interface in a platform-specific way.
Join & leave interface	joinGroup, leaveGroup	Determines the network interface via which I G M P join and leave requests are sent: defaults to the interface returned by getInterface if omitted.

a. If bound to a specific rather than the wildcard address, it also determines the interface via which the socket sends unicast and broadcast datagrams, but *not* multicast datagrams.

Setting the sending interface is *only* important in multi-homed hosts (in single-homed hosts there is only one choice). What you set it to depends on where

15. Notably among Sun's Jini developers, the Java A P I documenters, and certain authors on Java networking.

the members of the target multicast group are: if you are sending to a public group on the Internet, use the most public interface; if you are sending to a private group within your own organization, use whichever interface is appropriate (*e.g.* possibly the most private). If members of the group can be in only one such place, you must either:

(a) Ensure that the host knows the correct unicast route to the multicast group,[16] or

(b) Send via the appropriate interface (i.e. do the routing explicitly yourself).

If members of the group are in more than one such place, or if you don't know in advance, you *must* send via each appropriate interface in turn, so that the multicast will get to all the right places. Generally speaking this requires sending via every interface in turn, as shown in Example 11.10.

```
MulticastSocket socket;  // initialization not shown
DatagramPacket  packet;  // initialization not shown
Enumeration intfs =
  NetworkInterface.getNetworkInterfaces();
while (intfs.hasMoreElements())
{
  NetworkInterface intf =
    (NetworkInterface)intfs.nextElement();
  socket.setNetworkInterface(intf);
  socket.send(packet);
}
```

EXAMPLE 11.10 Sending multicasts via all interfaces

S E N D I N G . The network interface via which multicasts are *sent* can be managed by the methods:

```
class MulticastSocket extends DatagramSocket
{
  InetAddress         getInterface()  throws IOException;
  void                setInterface(InetAddress address)
                                      throws IOException;
```

---

16. *i.e.* by ensuring the appropriate route exists, by executing appropriate *route* commands or whatever it takes to configure routes on your system.

```
NetworkInterface  getNetworkInterface()
                              throws IOException;
void              setNetworkInterface
                    (NetworkInterface intf)
                              throws IOException;
}
```

If not explicitly set, a *single* sending interface is used by the system, chosen according to the unicast routing tables. The sending interface cannot be set to null. The current sending interface can be retrieved with the getInterface or getNetworkInterface methods: these never return null.

BINDING. You should almost always bind a multicast socket in a multi-homed host to the wildcard address. Otherwise it will only receive multicasts via the interface it is bound to, and it won't receive multicasts from any other subnet. This is usually undesirable.

JOINING & LEAVING. In a multi-homed host, you should issue joinGroup and leaveGroup once for *each* network interface, as shown in Example 11.11: this is a multi-homed version of Example 11.8. As we saw above, the system only uses one

```
int             port = 8888;
MulticastSocket socket = new MulticastSocket(port);
SocketAddress   mcastAddr;     // initialization not shown
Enumeration     intfs
  = NetworkInterface.getNetworkInterfaces();
while (intfs.hasMoreElements())
{
  NetworkInterface  intf =
    (NetworkInterface)intfs.nextElement();
  socket.joinGroup(mcastAddr, intf);
}
byte[]          data = new byte[8193];
DatagramPacket  packet
  = new DatagramPacket(data,data.length);
socket.receive(packet);
```

EXAMPLE 11.11 Multi-homed join and receive

route to a multicast address, and IGMP uses multicasts itself. Therefore, for each group join or leave, the system only sends a single IGMP request via a network interface of its choosing, and so in effect you have only joined or left the group as far as the subnet connected to that interface is concerned.[17]

The system operation underlying the setInterface method really controls outgoing multicasts, whereas joinGroup and leaveGroup control incoming multicasts. Prior to J D K 1.4, the setInterface method was overloaded to have an effect on incoming multicasts: this unfortunate and confusing necessity stemmed from the absence of a NetworkInterface class. The overloads introduced in J D K 1.4 for joinGroup and leaveGroup with a NetworkInterface parameter should be used in multi-homed hosts where possible.

In retrospect, not much was gained by giving the programmer three extra opportunities to specify network interfaces in the multicasting part of the Berkeley Sockets A P I . The design is at a lower level than that for unicasting and broadcasting. Providing so many places to specify a network interface only provided several unneccesary degrees of freedom and several possible sources of error. Multicasting could have been implemented more completely in the kernel without any major loss of function. The programmer could have been entirely unconcerned with network interfaces except at bind time; asocket bound to the wildcard address could have sent all multicasts (including I G M P requests) via all network interfaces; a socket bound to a specific interface could have sent only via that interface. No doubt the similar, unresolved controversy over multi-homed broadcasting influenced the design. Anyway it is about twenty years too late to mention this, which I only do to note that multi-homed multicasting leaves much more up to the programmer than T C P or U D P unicasting or U D P broadcasting.

11.7 MULTICASTING AND CHANNEL I/O

Because broadcasting just uses DatagramSockets, you can send and receive broadcasts using the U D P channel I/O techniques of Chapter 10.

Similarly, you can use channel I/O when sending multicasts, provided they are sent from a DatagramSocket as described in section 11.6.1, rather than a MulticastSocket. This means that you won't have access to the time-to-live or sending-interface features.

Support for multicast socket channels was not provided in J D K 1.4: a java.nio.channels.MulticastSocketChannel class was reportedly planned for J D K 1.5 but did not appear. When this feature becaomes available it will be possible to use channel I/O to send and receiving multicasts in a way similar to that already seen in Chapter 10.

---

17. Prior to Jini 1.2, this problem existed in Sun's implementations of the Jini Lookup and Discovery Service and the *reggie* Registrar service.

11.8 Broadcast and multicast permissions

The Java permissions required for broadcasting when a security manager is installed are identical to those required for normal U D P operations as described in Table 9.2.

The Java permissions required for multicasting when a security manager is installed are summarized in Table 11.5.

TABLE 11.5 Multicast SocketPermissions

Action	Target	Description
listen	address:port	Required when constructing or binding a MulticastSocket to *address:port*
accept, connect	address	Required when joining or leaving a multicast group at *address*
accept, connect	address	Required when sending to *address* if it is a multicast address
connect	address:port	Required when sending to *address* if it is not a multicast address
accept	address	Required when receiving a datagram from *address*

In both the broadcast and multicast cases, if a permission is required and not granted, a java.lang.SecurityException is thrown. This is a runtime exception and is not checked by the compiler.

11.9 Multicast address allocation

So far we haven't considered how multicast group addresses are allocated. There are two general approaches: static and dynamic. These approaches correspond to the two approaches to port allocation: *(i)* you can statically bind a socket to a fixed port, or *(ii)* you can allow the system to dynamically allocate an ephemeral port.

Static allocation of multicast group addresses requires some central authority to assign addresses to multicast groups permanently. The I A N A (Internet Assigned Numbers Authority) performs this function for groups whose scope is the entire Internet. For example, R F C 1700 reserves 224.0.0.0/24 for various multicast routing protocols, 224.0.1.0/24 for various well-known services such as time protocols, and so on. For multicast groups whose administrative scope is an organization or site, the relevant network administrator could fulfil the same function.

Static allocation policies do not scale to large numbers of services, and exhaust the address space prematurely. This is the motivation for dynamic allocation policies, which allow addresses to be allocated on demand and released when not in use. Dynamic allocation requires an allocation service and an allocation protocol.

RFC 2730 defines MADCAP —multicast address dynamic client allocation protocol.[18] MADCAP provides basic operations for negotiating the dynamic allocation and release of multicast addresses, as well as a sub-protocol based on multicast discovery for locating an address allocation server. The details of the protocol are fairly complex but it is based around a leasing concept similar to DHCP's and Jini's: a client locates a server, requests allocation of one or more addresses for a stated period of time, and is returned the required number of addresses in association with a lease. The client must renew or release the lease before it expires. When a lease expires or is released, its associated addresses become available for reallocation.

The server end of MADCAP is implemented by Multicast Address Allocation Servers (MAAS), which are supported by two related protocols. The Multicast Address Allocation Protocol (Multicast AAP) is used by MAAS servers to co-ordinate address allocations within a domain in order to ensure that they do not collide. The Multicast Address Set Claim (MASC) protocol is used by routers to claim address sets that satisfy the needs of MAAS servers within their allocation domain. Child domains listen to multicast address ranges acquired by their parents and select sub-ranges that will be used for their proper needs. When a MASC router discovers that there are not enough multicast address available, it claims a larger address set.

The client end of the protocol would be supported by a MADCAP client library along the lines of the API specified in RFC 2771.[19] Implementations of MADCAP in Java are not yet available at the time of writing.

As an example of an object-oriented API, it is not too hard to imagine concealing the MADCAP protocol behind a Jini discovery/lease façade and managing it with a Jini LeaseRenewalManager or LeaseRenewalService.

11.10 RELIABLE MULTICAST

As we keep noting, UDP is an unreliable medium,[20] offering only 'best-effort' delivery: therefore, raw UDP multicast is also unreliable. The Internet Engineering Task Force (IETF) is running a working group on on reliable multicast transport protocols, whose initial efforts concern *(i)* shareable building blocks for reliable multicast (RM) protocols and *(ii)* RM protocols for the 'one-to-many transport of large amounts of data'.[21]

---

18. Hanna *et al.*, RFC 2730, *MADCAP—Multicast address dynamic client allocation protocol,* December 1999.

19. Finlayson, R., RFC 2771, *An Abstract API for multicast address allocation,* February 2000.

20. It is sometimes claimed that the 'U' in UDP stands for 'unreliable': actually it stands for 'user', but the confusion is understandable.

21. http://www.ietf.org/html.charters/rmt-charter.html.

R F C 2887, *The Reliable Multicast Design Space for Bulk Data Transfer,* August 2000, lists a number of application requirements that significantly affect design or choice of reliable multicast protocols:

(a) Does the application need to know that everyone received the data?

(b) Does the application need to constrain differences between receivers?

(c) Does the application need to scale to large numbers of receivers?

(d) Does the application need to be totally reliable?

(e) Does the application need ordered data?

(f) Does the application need to provide low-delay delivery?

(g) Does the application need to provide time-bounded delivery?

(h) Does the application need many interacting senders?

(i) Is the application data flow intermittent?

(j) Does the application need to work in the public Internet?

(k) Does the application need to work without a return path (*e.g.* satellite)?

(l) Does the application need to provide secure delivery?

Because of the extent and diversity of this list, it is unlikely that a single protocol can be designed to meet the requirements of all such applications. The working group therefore expects to initially standardize three such protocols: a N A C K - based protocol (see section 11.10.2); a tree-based A C K protocol (see section 11.10.1); and an 'asynchronous layered coding' protocol using erasure codes (see section 11.10.3).

Several higher-level reliable multicast protocols have been developed, and research is continuing in this very interesting area.

11.10.1 *Tree-based protocols*

The tree-based protocols rely on multicast group members organizing themselves statically or dynamically into receiving trees such that the originating sender is the root of the tree. Any receiver which finds itself at an interior node of the tree acts as a 'group leader', *i.e.* assumes some responsibility for retransmitting lost datagrams to the subtree below it. In other words it must maintain some sort of cache, trying to satisfy incoming retransmission requests from its cache, only requesting a retransmission itself when the request cannot be satisified from its own cache. T R A M , the Tree-based Reliable Multicast Protocol implements such a scheme. The adaptive tree-building schemes found in such protocols are often very ingenious, but one might suspect that such solutions are excessively complex and not sufficiently scalable.

11.10.2 N A C K -*based protocols*

A C K -based protocols retransmit data which hasn't been acknowledged within some timeout period. As we saw in section 9.15.6, N A C K -based protocols rely on the receivers sending negative acknowledgements (N A C K s) to inform the sender that one or more packets need to be retransmitted. N A C K -based protocols are attractive for multicasting because, provided the network isn't losing too many packets, the bandwidth required for negative feedback is considerably less than for positive feedback, and probably scale much better as well. The reliable multicast working group has drafted N O R M , a family of N A C K -Oriented Reliable Multicast Protocol.[22] L R M P , the Lightweight Reliable Multicast Protocol, was an earlier such scheme.[23]

11.10.3 *Asynchronous layered coding protocols*

The tree-based and N A C K -based protocols described above use a combination of feedback and retransmission to overcome the inherent unreliability of U D P . The sender can use the feedback to tune its sending rate, satisfying the requirement for congestion control.

A more promising approach for multicasting of bulk data doesn't have a feedback channel at all, and uses continuous transmission of the data in the form of high-order erasure codes (see section 9.15.7). This is sometimes called 'open loop'. Under erasure codes, k blocks of source data are encoded at the sender to produce n blocks of encoded data; these are transmitted. The encoding can be done in such a way that receiving any k distinct encoded blocks is sufficient to reconstruct the entire source data. This is called an (n,k) linear erasure code, and it allows the receiver to tolerate loss of up to $n-k$ of a group of n encoded blocks, so, naively, it can tolerate a packet loss rate of $(n-k)/n$. Complete retransmission of the source data n times can be classified as an $(n,1)$ code; the X O R technique of section 9.15.7 used in R A I D -5 can be classifed as a $(k+1,k)$ code. Given a well-chosen erasure code function, the overhead in space and time can be surprisingly small.

Without a feedback channel, a different kind of mechanism for congestion control is needed. The mechanism chosen by the working group is 'asynchronous layering', whereby data is multicast simultaneously to multiple groups at different rates (*e.g.* 33.6Kbps, 56Kbps, 128Kbps, and 256kbps), and the receiver subscribes to whichever group can provide the best throughput without excessive packet loss; this can be determined dynamically. The highest rate at the transmitter can be determined statically, *e.g.* by the bandwidth of the uplink to the sender's I S P . Alternatively, it can be allowed to sort itself out dynamically. By the properties of multicast, if there are no members of any multicast group (*e.g.* in this case the maximum-rate group) beyond any specific router, no transmis-

---

22. http://www.ietf.org/internet-drafts/draft-ietf-rmt-pi-norm-04.txt.
23. See http://webcanal.inria.fr/lrmp/draft-liao-lrmp-00.txt.

sions into the group will occur beyond that router. If there are no members of the group at all, *i.e.* the group is being fed faster than can be read by any receiver, multicasts to the group won't get beyond the router nearest the transmitter, so the cost of sending at any unused rate is only borne locally within the sender's L A N or even perhaps only within the sending host.

The working group has proposed a protocol called A L C —Asynchronous Layered Coding protocol—in R F C 3450, buliding on the separate 'Layered Coding Transport (LCT)', 'multiple rate congestion control', and 'Forward Error Correction (FEC)' building blocks specified in R F C 3451–3.[24] Among other features, these specifications support an open-ended set of linear erasure codes which are negotiated separately, rather like the way that s s l supports an open-ended set of cryptographic techniques.

> At this point, many a reader may be 'gagging' for a Java code example, but Java code to demonstrate A L C would be both prohibitively lengthy and commercially valuable.[25] I expect a Java framework for A L C with pluggable erasure code implementations to appear at some stage, along the lines of the Java Reliable Multicast Service described in the next section.

11.10.4 *The Java Reliable Multicast Service*

The Java Reliable Multicast Service (J R M S) is not a product but a research project from Sun Microsystems Laboratories.[26] J R M S provides APIs for address allocation, service advertising, and reliable multicast: as in many Java class libraries, these constitute a framework behind which multiple implementations can be provided. J R M S supports the experimental protocols T R A M and L R M P described above.

---

24. See http://www.ietf.org/rfc/rfc3450.txt &ff.

25. A commercial implementation of a linear erasure code system is described in the White Paper for the 'Digital Fountain' product which is available online at the Digital Fountain website http://www.digitalfountain.com/getDocument.htm/technology/DF_MetaContentWhitePaper_v4.pdf.

26. Sun Microsystems Laboratories Inc, Technical Report T R-98-66, abstract and full report available online via http://www.experimentalstuff.com/sun/research/techrep/1998/abstract-68.html. The J R M S documentation and s D K are available via http://www.experimentalstuff.com/Technologies/JRMS/index.html. The J R M S mailing list had been inactive for some years at the time of writing.

Part V

In Practice

CHAPTER 12

Server and client models

WE HAVE ALREADY seen a couple of simple models for TCP servers in Chapter 3. This chapter discusses advanced models for TCP servers and clients. We will use blocking stream I/O (introduced in Chapter 3) as well as channel I/O (introduced in Chapter 5) in both blocking and non-blocking modes.

The discussion is focussed on the performance-related factors of thread usage, connection usage, queueing techniques, blocking *versus* non-blocking mode, and multiplexing. We will see how these factors can be varied both independently and in conjunction, and look at the design- and performance-related effects of doing so.

This chapter is really about server and client design as a numerical exercise.[1] It is not about design patterns, and it is not presented in the design-patterns style. However, much of the chapter is *related* to existing design patterns, especially the Reactor, Proactor, and Leader-Follower server patterns presented by Schmidt *et al* (although they do not present any client-side patterns),[2] and I have used the standard design-patterns terminology of Adapters, Factories, Facades, etc where appropriate.

I present several short and simple pieces of Java or pseudo-Java code. These are not presented as the best or only solutions, but to provoke thought and understanding in the reader. For the same reason I have not provided anything like an 'ideal' implementation or framework for servers or clients. I don't believe there is any such thing.

---

1. It is really an application of elementary queueing theory, which is discussed at an introductory level in Tanner, M. *Practical Queueing Analysis*, McGraw-Hill, 1995, Gunther, N. *The Practical Performance Analyst*, McGraw-Hill, 1998, or Martine, R. *Basic Traffic Analysis*, Prentice-Hall, 1993.
2. Schmidt *et al.*, *Pattern-Oriented Software Architecture, Vol 2: Patterns for Concurrent and Networked Objects*, Wiley 2000. See also Doug Lea's invaluable Java redaction of the Reactor and associated patterns for Java NIO at http://gee.cs.oswego.edu/dl/cpjslides/nio.pdf.

12.1 IMPORT STATEMENTS

The following Java import statements are required for examples in this chapter, and are not shown in individual code examples:

```
import java.io.*;
import java.net.*;
import java.nio.*;          // channel I/O examples only
import java.nio.channels.*;// channel I/O examples only
import java.util.*;
```

12.2 SERVERS

Apart from the design of the actual service being implemented, the principal issues to be considered when designing TCP servers are:

(a)   The number of clients required to be handled simultaneously.

(b)   The length of time required to service each client

Whenever (a) is greater than one, as it usually is, and (b) is non-trivial, as it usually is, we immediately encounter the need to use Java threads so as not to hold up other clients while we service the first one. We therefore need to consider:

(a)   The creation of processing threads.

(b)   The operations performed by a processing thread.

(c)   The destruction of processing threads.

These issues interact to some extent.

Trivially (and ignoring exception handling and boundary cases), the processing in a server consists of an connection-accepting loop and a connection processor:

```
ServerSocket server;
for (;;)
{
  Socket socket = server.accept();
  processSession(socket);
  socket.close();
}
```

In the simplest possible server model, everything happens in one thread, like the sequential server of Example 3.1. We will call this Model A. In the commonest server model, a new thread is created per connection, like the concurrent server of Example 3.6. We will call this Model B.

12.2.1 *Elementary queuing theory*

We need some tools to analyse the performance of server models. In terms of elementary queueing theory, a TCP server is a simple queueing network. A queuing network consists of one or more queues and one or more processors as shown in Figure 12.1.

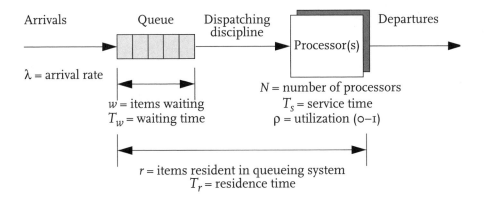

FIGURE 12.1. Simple queueing network[3]

In the case of a TCP server:

(a) *Arrivals* are incoming socket connections.

(b) The *queue* consists at least of the 'listen backlog' queue discussed in section 3.3.3, plus, as we will see later, perhaps an internal queue of accepted connections.

(c) *Processors* are threads.

Figure 12.1 also shows the names used in queueing theory for a number of parameters of interest. Trivially, a number of arithmetic relationships hold be-

---

3. Diagram after William Stallings, *Queueing Analysis*, © William Stallings 2000, via http://WilliamStallings.com/StudentSupport.html. Used by permission.

tween these parameters. *Little's formula* for the number of items r resident in the system (*i.e.* currently queued or being processed) is:

$$r = \lambda T_r \qquad\qquad (\text{EQ 12.1})$$

Similarly, the number w of items waiting in the queue is given by

$$w = \lambda T_w \qquad\qquad (\text{EQ 12.2})$$

The average residence time T_r is given by

$$T_r = T_w + T_s \qquad\qquad (\text{EQ 12.3})$$

The utilization ρ as a number $0 \le \rho < 1$ is given by

$$\rho = \lambda \frac{T_s}{N} \qquad\qquad (\text{EQ 12.4})$$

and therefore the number of items r resident in the system is also given by

$$r = w + N\rho \qquad\qquad (\text{EQ 12.5})$$

Without getting too deep into queueing theory, we must note here that, depending on the statistical distribution of services times T_s, the queue length w can increase without limit as $\rho \to 1$: the worst-case equation for w:

$$w = \rho^2/(1-\rho) \qquad\qquad (\text{EQ 12.6})$$

is dominated by the factor $1/(1-\rho)$ (because $0 \le \rho < 1$), and therefore follows a reverse hyperbola.[4]

This means that the utilization ρ should be kept well below saturation level, certainly less than 0.7, as can be seen in the graph plotted in Figure 12.2.

With that in mind, we are most interested in designing our servers so as to minimize waiting time at clients, or, to look at it from the server's point of view, to maximize the arrival rate. The maximal arrival rate λ_{max} is given by

$$\lambda_{max} = \rho \times N/T_s \qquad\qquad (\text{EQ 12.7})$$

Now, the Model A server corresponds to $N = 1$. Obviously when T_s is non-trivial this model is severely limited in throughput. It only handles one client at a time:

---

4. Assuming the queueing-theoretic 'M/M/1' model, *i.e.* Poisson distribution of arrival times and exponentially-distributed service times, $N = 1$.

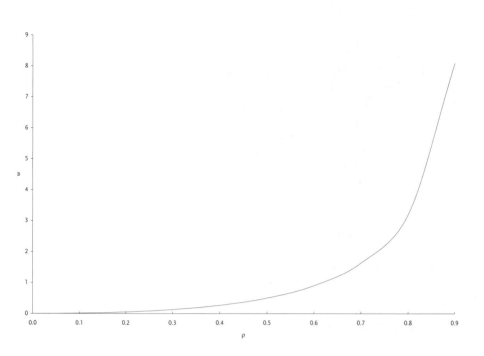

FIGURE 12.2. Queue length versus utilization

other clients which attempt to connect while a connection is in progress are queued up to the limit of the listen backlog, and encounter connection failures beyond that limit. This model is very simple to program, and it is useless for all but the most basic purposes. The only occasions when this model could reasonably be employed would be when either *(i)* the service is so trivial that it involves practically no computation, such as an echo or time service, or *(ii)* service time is small and the nature of the service is such that only one client can be serviced at a time anyway, such as a very simple logging service which merely writes to an unsynchronized file.

We can refine Model A slightly, by separating the task of accepting new connection from the task of handling a connection, by using two queues and two threads. The first queue is the 'listen backlog' as before; the first thread continually accepts new connections and queues them on a second internal queue to a second 'worker' thread; the worker thread continually removes a new connection from this internal queue and handles it. From the point of view of queueing theory this refinement doesn't change Model A at all: since the first queue is fed directly into the second they constitute one large queue. The refined model still forces clients to wait while prior clients are serviced. However, it does solves a specific TCP problem: the problem of clients getting connection failures. Incoming connections are limited not by the 'listen backlog', but by the length of the internal queue, which may be indefinite; in queueing theory this is known as ' lost calls delayed'. This is not in itself a major improvement, but it is conceptually useful to introduce the notion of an internal queue of new connections, of which we will make better use later on.

The Model B server has the number of threads $N = r$, the number of queued items, dynamically for any r: a new thread is created to handle every waiting item (every accepted connection). As soon as $N > 1$, parallelism occurs between connections, and therefore between simultaneous clients, because separate connections are handled in separate threads. This removes the throughput limitation of Model A, and it is the first server model we can take seriously.

To unify the discussion below, we introduce the following interface, representing a task which processes a session:[5]

```java
public interface SessionTask extends Runnable
{
  // inherited from Runnable
  public void run();
  // process a session
  public void processSession(Socket connection);
}
```

This interface extends the Runnable interface, so it exports a run method, and it adds a processSession method, which processes a newly connected Socket.

We now revisit Model B. Java code for this model, including the DynamicSessionTask class to be referred to later, is shown in Example 12.1. (We will deal later with implementing the method processSession of the DynamicSessionTask class.)

```java
class DynamicSessionTask implements SessionTask
{
  Socket connection;

  DynamicSessionTask(Socket connection)
  {
    this.connection = connection;
  }
```

---

5. Extended from ideas in §4.5.1 of Doug Lea, *Concurrent Programming in Java*, 2nd edition, Addison Wesley 2000.

```
public void run()
{
  processSession(connection);
}

// process session, details not shown
public void processSession(Socket connection) {}
}
// driver code: loop handling accepts in new threads
ServerSocket  server; // initialization not shown
for (;;)
{
  try
  {
    Socket connection = server.accept();
    // Start a new DynamicSessionTask
    new Thread
      (new DynamicSessionTask(connection))).start();
  }
  catch (IOException e)
  {
    // ...
  }
}
}
```

EXAMPLE 12.1 Dynamic session task class and driver code

This model is very frequently seen, and indeed is used internally by Java RMI/JRMP.[6] Its principal advantage is the simplicity of its programming. It has two principal disadvantages:

(a) It incurs the overhead of creating a thread for each new arrival: if this is non-trivial with respect to λ it leads once again to the problem of exceeding the listen backlog, and hence to client connection failures. In fact, its maximum arrival rate is limited by the speed with which new threads can be created: $\lambda_{max} = 1/T_c$ where T_c is the time to create a new thread.

(b) The number of threads can increase without limit (if connections are long-lived relative to the arrival rate), ultimately overwhelming the execution environment at the server. If the number of threads is N, the mean share of the CPU available to each is $1/N$, and therefore the mean service time T_s is at best linearly proportional to N, which increases in step with r until we hit a limit.

---

6. so far, up to JDK 1.5.

Realistically, we will hit one or more 'soft' limits first, beyond which performance will degrade. Most probably we will first hit a physical-memory limit, beyond which performance will degrade for each memory increment according to the performance curve of the virtual-memory system, but again affecting all threads, not just the new one.

Sooner or later we will hit a 'hard' limit. If it is a thread-count limit, the new connection gets no service and everybody else proceeds as best they can; if it is something more serious like a virtual memory limit, the whole server process may stop. In this case T_s becomes infinite—for all existing threads as well as the new one which hit the limit. This is a 'graceless degradation', illustrated in the sketch graph of Figure 12.3.

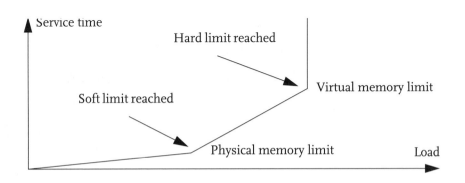

FIGURE 12.3. Service time, new thread per connection

Servers which expect thousands of concurrent clients need more efficiency and more reliability than this model provides. We would probably prefer to limit resource usage at the server and allow client performance to degrade gracefully up to a limit of clients, refusing service ('lost calls') to clients beyond our limit—a graceful degradation with self-protection.

We can solve both these problems by arranging to use an existing thread instead of a new thread. If the thread already exists, the creation overhead per connection is zero; we can avoid overwhelming the execution environment at the server by managing the number of threads which pre- exist; and we can implement some explicit overflow policy when we receive a connection in excess of capacity. The next models to be considered use a pool of pre-existing worker threads, to reduce the process of dispatching a new conversation to simply dispatching the new connection to an existing thread.

12.2.2 Dispatching

A dispatcher despatches each incoming client connection to a service thread. It can do any one or more of the following:

(a) Preallocate service threads

(b) Create service threads dynamically.

To implement a preallocated pool of service threads, we will first need a dispatching mechanism. We will make use of a JDK 1.5 BlockingQueue for Sockets:

```
interface BlockingQueue<Socket>
{
    // add a Socket to the end of the queue.
    boolean  add(Socket s);

    // take a Socket from the front of the queue,
    // blocking while the queue is empty.
    Socket   take();
}
```

A basic MultiSessionTask class, which uses this interface to obtain sessions, is shown in Example 12.2. (We will deal with the processSession method later.)

The code which drives these classes creates a work queue and a number of MultiSessionTask service threads which share the queue; it then adds incoming connections (Sockets) to the queue. The service threads loop, removing connections from the queue and handling the associated session. A simple version of the driver code is shown in Example 12.3 on page 309.

This model, where a fixed number of service threads are created in advance, is suitable at two extremes:

(a) The number of clients is known in advance (*e.g.* an 'intranet' application like a call centre with only a couple of thousand operators).

(b) The number of clients is unknowably large and needs to be controlled, because memory is a critical resource (*e.g.* an FTP server, which typically only permit a few hundred connections at a time).

Its simplicity of programming and minor development time are other attractions.

How many threads should we preallocate? This can be determined by λ, the expected arrival rate of connections per second, and T_s, the expected average duration of a conversation. By transposing Equation 12.4, the number of threads N required to service this rate is given by $N = \lambda \times T_s / \rho$. We should keep $\rho \leq 0.7$, i.e. no more than 70% utilitization of the server, leaving some 'headroom' for peak loads, and keeping queue size in the flat part of the growth curve.

We may not be able to make this calculation. Either the arrival rate λ or the mean service time T_s may be highly variable, unknown, or unknowable. If so, or if we get N wrong by bad estimates of these variables, all the preallocated threads

```
public class MultiSessionTask implements SessionTask
{
  private ServerSocket          ss;
  private BlockingQueue<Socket>  queue;

  MultiSessionTask(ServerSocket ss,
    BlockingQueue<Socket> queue)
  {
    this.ss = ss;
    this.queue = queue;
  }

  public void  run()
  {
    // loop while socket is open or queue non-empty
    while (ss.isOpen() || !queue.isEmpty())
    {
      Socket connection = queue.take();
      processSession(connection);
    }
  }

  // process session, details not shown
  public void  processSession(Socket connection) {}
}
```

EXAMPLE 12.2 MultiSessionTask class

may easily become busy, and new clients must wait after connecting until a worker thread becomes idle.

12.2.3 *Combining preallocated and dynamic service threads*

If we decide we want to overcome this defect, we can combine the dynamic-creation and preallocation models: create *N* service threads in advance *and* create threads dynamically when no idle service threads are available. We can implement it in two ways, depending on whether we want the newly created threads to *(i)* exit immediately or *(ii)* become permanent service threads after they have handled the conversation for which they were created.

We need a waitCount method to return the number of threads currently waiting:

```
int waitCount();
```

```
static final int INITIALWORKERTHREADS = 4;// tune this!
// initializations not shown
ServerSocket server;
BlockingQueue<Socket> queue;
// create and start worker threads
for (int i = 0; i < INITIALWORKERTHREADS; i++)
  new Thread
    (new MultiSessionTask(server, queue)))
    .start();
for (;;)
{
  try
  {
    queue.add(server.accept());
  }
  catch (IOException exc)
  {
    if (!server.isOpen())
    {
      break; // for (;;)
    }
    // ...
  } // catch
} // for (;;)
```

EXAMPLE 12.3 Driver code for preallocated worker threads

Implementing waitCount in MultiSessionTask is simply a matter of increment-
ing an integer before calling the take method and decrementing it on return, as
shown in Example 12.4.

We can combine the driver code of Example 12.1 and Example 12.3, to both preallocate MultiSessionTasks and create DynamicSessionTasks when necessary, as
shown in Example 12.5.

In this model, the existing service threads support a maximum arrival rate
λ_{max} of N/T_s. If T_c is the time to create a thread, the new-thread creation mechanism supports a maximum arrival rate λ_{max} of $1/T_c$. Simplistically assuming we
can just aggregate these together (i.e. as though the two parts of the model are
two parallel but independent queues, which isn't precisely true), the combined
maximum arrival rate would be given by $N/T_s + 1/T_c$.

We would probably implement this combined model with two separate thresh-
olds, *i.e.* allowing N permanent threads and up to N' dynamic threads, so as to
handle temporary peaks by using more resources but releasing them when not
required. Typically N' would be much smaller than N.

This could be implemented by book-keeping the number of extant permanent and dynamic threads, or, much more simply, via the Thread.activeCount method, which re-

```
private static int  waitCount = 0;

public void  run()
{
  // loop while socket is open or queue non-empty
  while (ss.isOpen() || !queue.isEmpty())
  {
    waitCount++;
    Socket  connection = queue.take();
    waitCount--;
    processSession(connection);
  }
}

public static int waitCount()  { return waitCount;}
```

EXAMPLE 12.4 Implementing waitCount

turns an estimate of the total number of threads in the current thread group. Some margin for error must be allowed, remembering that *(i)* this method only returns an estimate, and *(ii)* the driver thread itself counts as a thread in the group. If the server application uses lots of threads for other purposes, the driver thread should be created in a dedicated thread group, so that all threads it creates are in the same group.

Implementing this strategy in Example 12.5 is simple, assuming a maxThreads method which returns a maximum thread-count (which might be constant, variable, or dynamically tuned):

```
if (MultiSessionTask.waitCount() > 0
|| Thread.activeCount() >= maxThreads())
  queue.add(connection);
else
  new Thread
    (new DynamicSessionTask(connection)))
    .start();
```

12.2.4 *Bounded queues*

We may want to limit the length of the internal queue, *i.e.* enforce a maximum number of waiting items w_{max}.

One way of doing this is a modification of the waitCount technique above: when an incoming connection is accepted and there are no idle worker threads, handle the connection in-line, using a DynamicSessionTask directly without starting a new thread:

```
static final int INITIALSERVICETHREADS = 4;// tune this!
// initializations not shown
ServerSocket            server;
BlockingQueue<Socket> queue;

// create and start server threads
for (int i = 0; i < INITIALSERVICETHREADS; i++)
  new Thread(new MultiSessionTask(queue))).start;
for (;;)
{
  try
  {
    Socket connection = server.accept();
    if (MultiSessionTask.waitCount() > 0)
      queue.add(connection);
    else
      new Thread
        (new DynamicSessionTask(connection))).start();
  }
  catch (IOException exc)
  {
    if (!server.isOpen())
    {
      break; // for (;;)
    }
    // …
  } // catch
} // for (;;)
```

EXAMPLE 12.5 Driver code for preallocated and dynamic threads

```
Socket connection = server.accept();
if (MultiSessionTask.waitCount() > 0)
  queue.add(connection);
else
  new DynamicSessionTask(connection).run();
```

Obviously this technique enforces a w_{max} of 1. If we want a higher limit, we could implement a BlockingQueue<Socket>.size method and only enqueue new connections if the queue size is below w_{max}, otherwise process them inline as above.

The in-line technique may appear to temporarily increase N to $N+1$, but this is irrelevant as λ_{max} is also temporarily reduced to zero: no accepts are executed while the connection is being handled in-line. (The 'listen backlog' is still in effect, but once that fills, no further connections succeed until some of the backlog is processed.)

12.2.5 *Dynamic thread exit strategies*

In the discussion so far, all dynamic threads have exited after processing one connection. Is this the only possibility?

No. Dynamic service threads can exit after one connection ('one-shot'), as we have already seen in Example 12.5, but they can also continue life as worker threads, by subsequently processing a work queue like MultiSessionTask, and obey some 'exit strategy', *e.g.*:

(a) Never exit, or

(b) exit when idle in accordance with some dynamic exit strategy.

A DynamicMultiSessionTask class for case (a) is presented in Example 12.6 on page 313. The driver code for this model is simply a variant of Example 12.5, creating DynamicMultiSessionTasks instead of DynamicSessionTasks.

The 'dynamic exit strategy' of case (b) is addressed to the following issue. If we create threads dynamically and they subsequently behave as permanent service threads, their number increases and never declines. (The number increases more and more slowly, because the arrival rate λ_{max} supported by the permanent service threads is N/T_s, which increases linearly with N, and every increase reduces the likelihood that a new thread will be created. In other words N will increase to the number required to service the actual peak arrival rate.)

This means that, after a usage peak, a large number of idle threads still exist, consuming memory resources if nothing else. We could arrange for these dynamic threads to exit in response to some dynamic state of the system, *e.g.* when the total number of service threads exceeds a threshold, or when the system as a whole is idle. The system might be deemed to be idle in a number of ways; for example:

(a) Some maximum number of idle threads is exceeded. This policy might be suitable if the number of clients is unknown or subject to large usage peaks, and it is desired to release resources as quickly as possible. The maximum could be fixed; alternatively, the system could tune it dynamically in accordance with average and peak usage, perhaps using statistical smoothing techniques, which might be suitable where usage is unknown in advance.

(b) A dynamically-created service thread has been idle for some timeout period. This is easy to program, and it has the advantage that threads persist during periods of heavy load and exit during quieter periods, *i.e.* it is self-tuning.

To implement the idle timeout of (b), we use the timed BlockingQueue.poll method:

```
// Return head of queue, or null if 'timeout' expires
Socket poll(int timeout, TimeUnit unit);
```

```
public class DynamicMultiSessionTask
  implements SessionTask
{
  private ServerSocket  ss;
  private BlockingQueue<Socket>  queue;
  private Socket          connection;

  DynamicMultiSessionTask(ServerSocket ss,
    BlockingQueue<Socket> queue,
    Socket connection)
  {
    this.ss = ss;
    this.queue = queue;
    this.connection = connection;
  }

  public void  run()
  {
    // process initial connection
    processConnection(connection);
    // process queue until done
    while (ss.isOpen() || !queue.isEmpty())
    {
      connection = queue.take();
      processConnection(connection);
    }
    // queue terminated
  } // run()

  // process connection, details not shown
  public voidprocessConnection(Socket connection) {}
} // end class
```

EXAMPLE 12.6 DynamicMultiSessionTask class

and modify the DynamicMultiSessionTask class to use this method:

```
connection = queue.poll(timeout, TimeUnit.SECONDS);
```

The timeout might sensibly be a minute or two.

12.2.6 *Dispatching revisited*

So far we have used an explicit queue of accepted sockets for dispatching new connections. Another dispatching technique exists, although there seems to be little awareness of it. Multiple threads may execute ServerSocket.accept simultaneously. The real queueing occurs via Java synchronization inside ServerSocket.accept and, at a lower level, within the underlying TCP implementation (in the *backlog* queue discussed in section 3.3.3).

This technique works without a physical queue: *e.g.* in the preallocated thread technique of Example 12.2, using the driver code of Example 12.3, the entire for(;;) loop is removed, *i.e.* you merely create the required number of MultiSessionTask objects and have them obtain connections via ss.accept() instead of queue.take().

As in section 12.2.4, even though there is no queue, this technique has the same effect of bounding the queue length, and therefore of limiting the arrival rate, because if there are no idle worker threads, none of them are accepting connections.

12.2.7 *Summary tables*

The threading models resulting from different choices of the various parameters presented in the preceding sections are summarised in Table 12.1.

TABLE 12.1 Threading models and parameters [a]

	Number of pre-allocated threads	Create dynamic threads	Exit policy	λ_{max}	Remarks
A	None	No	–	$1/T_s$	Serial servicing of clients; arrival rate limited by length of service; T_s is unaffected by load; clients encounter connection failures if listen backlog is exceeded.
B	None	Yes	1-shot	$1/T_c$	Simple model usually seen. Concurrent connections do not wait for service; arrival rate limited by time to create a new thread; T_s depends on load, *i.e.* T_s varies with r ; clients may encounter connection failures if listen backlog is exceeded.
C	N	No	–	N/T_s	Process es N conversations in parallel; arrival rate independent of T_c; T_s varies with $1/r$; clients wait when $r > N$.
D	N	Yes	1-shot	$N/T_s + 1/T_c$	Incremental improvement over (B): only every N^{th} connection incurs a thread-creation overhead.

TABLE 12.1 Threading models and parameters (continued)[a]

	Number of pre-allocated threads	Create dynamic threads	Exit policy	λ_{max}	Remarks
E	None	Yes	never	As (D), where $N = N_{max}$	Dynamic threads become worker threads after completing their first conversation. Number of threads grows to peak usage and never declines. Behaves like (D) with adaptive N.
					Could vary this by creating dynamic threads only if $N <$ some maximum.
F	None	Yes	dynamic	As (D), where $N = r$	As (E), but thread count declines after peaks.
G	N	Yes	never	As (D), where $N = N_{max}$	As (E), but thread count starts at N instead of zero.
H	N	Yes	dynamic	As (D), where $r < N < N_{max}$	Combines (G) and (F).

a. T_c = mean time to create a thread.

Thread-creation and exit strategies are summarized in Table 12.2.

TABLE 12.2 Exit strategies

Model	Characteristics	Remarks
null	Never exit.	Threads increase indefinitely as required by peak loads.
one-shot	Exit after one conversation.	Threads are always at a minimum; maximises thread-creation overhead.
dynamic	Exit on some dynamic condition, e.g. 'system idle'.	Reclaim threads after peak load. 'System idle' needs to be suitably defined, e.g. the number of idle threads exceeds a static or dynamic threshold, or the thread is idle for some timeout period.

12.2.8 Session handlers

Having now presented a framework for managing threads, we will now separate the concerns of thread-pool management and session-handling form each other. *Thread-pool management* is really an aspect of the internal construction of the server concerned with servicing the network efficiently. *Session-handling* is really an aspect of the application proper, dealing as it does with application protocols and services. We would like to be able to vary these independently. In the framework of this chapter, this means providing implementations of SessionTask implementing various threading models and policies while implementing session-handling separately. To this end we introduce an intermediate session-handler interface:

```
interface SessionHandler
{
  void processSession(Socket connection);
}
```

and a factory interface:

```
interface SessionHandlerFactory
{
  SessionHandler  createHandler();
}
```

The factory provides a single point where connection-handling implementations can be substituted without disturbing the rest of the application. In addition, the factory may implement its own allocation policy: for example, it might return a new handler object per invocation:

```
SessionHandler  createHandler()
{
  return new MySessionHandler();
}
```

or a singleton handler object:

```
private SessionHandler handler = null;
synchronized SessionHandler  createHandler()
{
  if (handler == null)
    handler = new MySessionHandler();
  return handler;
}
```

or a handler object per thread:

```
private ThreadLocal handlers = new ThreadLocal();
SessionHandler  createHandler()
{
```

```
    SessionHandler handler = (SessionHandler)handlers.get();
    if (handler == null)
    {
      handler = new MySessionHandler();
      handlers.set(handler);
    }
    return handler;
}
```

or whatever else is appropriate. Using a factory provides a single point in the code where this policy can be changed.

We can then define the SessionTask.processSession method in the various classes presented earlier to use a separate connection-handler factory, as outlined in Example 12.7 below.

```
public class MultiSessionTask implements SessionTask
{
  private BlockingQueue<Socket>  queue;
  private SessionHandlerFactory  factory;

  // constructor
  MultiSessionTask(BlockingQueue<Socket> queue,
    SessionHandlerFactory factory)
  {
    this.queue = queue;
    this.factory = factory;
  }
  public void  run()
  {
    // ...
  }
  public void  processSession(Socket socket)
  {
    factory.createHandler().processSession(socket);
  }
}
```

EXAMPLE 12.7 Session task class with separate handler factory

12.2.9 Connection models

In transactional application protocols where a 'conversation' consists of a single request and reply, either:

(a) A connection is only used for a single conversation, or

(b)   a connection can be used for multiple conversations.

Case (a), the 'one-shot' case, is enforced in the server by closing the connection after sending the reply. In pseudo-code:

```
public void processSession(Socket socket)
{
  receive(request);
  // process request and construct reply, not shown ...
  send(reply);
  // close connection
  socket.close();// exception handling not shown
}
```

Case (b), the 'multi-shot' case, is used in conjunction with the client-side connection-pooling strategy described in section 12.4.1. It is implemented in the server by writing the main connection handler as a loop. In pseudo-code:

```
void processSession(Socket socket)
{
  while (receive(request)) // i.e. while not end-of-stream
  {
    // process request and construct reply, not shown ...
    send(reply);
  }
  // close connection
  socket.close();// exception handling not shown
}
```

As always in servers, a finite receive timeout should be used, to prevent connections being tied up for excessive periods. Implementing the multi-shot case in the server does not *compel* the client to use the connection for more than one conversation, but it makes it *possible*. It is a necessary but not sufficient condition.

End-of-stream is indicated at the server in different ways depending on what operation is being attempted: a negative result from InputStream.read or ReadableByteChannel.read, or an EOFException from DataInput.readXXX or ObjectInput.readObject.

12.2.10 *Closing*

There are several points at which the server may choose to close a connection:

(a)   On receipt of an end-of-stream when reading the connection.

(b)   If the request or the client is deemed invalid.

(c)   On detection of a read timeout or idle timeout on the connection.

(d)   After writing a reply.

Generally, several of these strategies are employed for safety, rather than just one. For example, implementing just (a) leaves control of the connection completely up to the client. This is most undesirable in a server: you don't want ill-behaved clients tying up server resources indefinitely, so you would generally implement at least cases (a) and (c). Case (d) only applies if conversations are 'one-shot' or if it is desired to be rid of the client after this particular reply for some other reason, possibly related to the semantics of the reply (*e.g.* in response to a logout request).

12.3 CHANNEL I/O SERVERS

We can make quite a few refinements to the models presented above by using channel I/O instead of blocking stream I/O in the server.

12.3.1 *Dispatching with Selectors*

We can use a Selector to tell us when a channel becomes ready. We first encountered selectors in Chapter 4 as part of the channel I/O introduced in JDK 1.4. To use channel I/O on a ServerSocket, we saw in section 5.1.2 that we must create a ServerSocketChannel object, bind it, and use non-blocking mode:

```
static final int  PORT;  // initialization not shown
ServerSocketChannel server = ServerSocketChannel.open();
server.socket().bind(new InetSocketAddress(PORT));
server.configureBlocking(false);
Selector   selector= Selector.open();
SelectionKeykey   = server.register
  (selector, SelectionKey.OP_ACCEPT);
int   nSel = selector.select();
```

If only server socket channels are registered with this selector, an accept operation must be ready if the select method returns non-zero, because OP_ACCEPT is ServerSocketChannel's only valid operation.

The implicit queuing technique of section 12.2.6 can of course be used with a Selector instead of a ServerSocket. The implicit queue forms inside the Selector.select method, or you can think of the readySet iterator constituting the queue. When coding this, remember to use ServerSocketChannel.accept rather than ServerSocket.accept.

Selectors can be used at the connection-accepting level to manage more than one server socket channel in a single thread, *i.e.* to multiplex them, as described in section 12.3.2. They can also be used if it is wished to create dynamic threads only if no workers are idle. Selectors can be used to detect incoming connections without actually accepting them: this leads to a better implementation which never starves worker threads or creates dynamic threads unnecessarily, as shown in Example 12.8 below.

```
ServerSocketChannel server; // initialization as above
Selector            selector = Selector.open();
SelectionKey        key =
  server.register(selector, SelectionKey.OP_ACCEPT);

for (;;)
{
  // clear previous result
  selector.selectedKeys().clear();
  int nSel = selector.select();

  // If channel is ready and no threads are idle,
  // accept a connection in-line
  if (nSel > 0 && MultiSessionTask.waitCount() == 0)
  {
    SocketChannelsocketChannel = server.accept();
    if (socketChannel != null)
    {
      // still no idle thread, because we got a
      // connection: create a dynamic thread
      Socket connection = socketChannel.socket();
      SessionTask        p =
        new DynamicMultiSessionTask(queue,connection);
      new Thread(p).start();
    }
  }
}
```

EXAMPLE 12.8 Dynamic threads and SocketChannelAcceptingQueue

12.3.2 *Multiplexing*

So far we have used one active thread per open connection: *i.e.* we have a 1::1 ratio between threads and connections. In a server which expects thousands of concurrent connections, this means thousands of active threads, each with its own call stack and internal control structures, and its presence on process scheduling queues. When the number of connections is high but the input rate per connection is relatively low, it makes sense to reduce this ratio of 1::1 to a ratio of 1::M, where each thread manages an average of M connections, so that our N service threads can handle a total of $M \times N$ connections. This allows us to reduce N or handle more connections, or both.[7]

If we could implement this and choose our parameters in advance, we might choose N according to our memory or thread-count capacity, and M such that $1/M$ is the average input rate per connection expressed as a fraction of bandwidth, *i.e.* on a scale of 0 to 1.

How can we implement this?

We could control multiple connections from one thread by using short socket timeouts in conjunction with a *polling* technique whereby we scan all our connections for input, as shown in Example 12.9 below.

```
List    connections; // initialization not shown
byte[] buffer;         // initialization not shown

for (;;)
{
  Iterator connectionIterator = connections.iterator();

  while (connectionIterator.hasNext())
  {
    Socket connection = (Socket)connectionIterator.next();
    try
    {
      int count = connection.getInputStream().read(buffer);
      if (count < 0) // EOF
      {
        connection.close();
        it.remove();
      }
      // process incoming data on this connection …
    }
    catch (InterruptedIOException exc)
    {
      continue;// no data on this connection
    }
  } // while
} // for (;;)
```

EXAMPLE 12.9 Pollling for input

This technique is poor. We have no means of deciding which connection to scan for input next, so we must just cycle round them. If the next ready connection is the one before the one we are about to read, it has to wait for timeouts to occur on all the other connections being polled. This worst-case situation is not at all unrealistic: it occurs when only one of the connections is active.

---

7. See also Lea, *op.cit.*, §4.1.5.

We could poll in non-blocking mode. This would at least have the virtue of wasting zero time waiting for timeouts, but the problem then becomes what to do when no input is available on any channel: sleep a few milliseconds? Yield the thread? Just spin furiously round the polling loop? We'd rather do nothing rather than just wasting processor cycles, and we'd rather be told rather than having to keep looking.

We could use Socket.getInputStream().available() to tell us when input is available on a socket, again wasting zero time on timeouts: this is a slight improvement because we only *detect* the input without actually reading it. The question remains of what to do when no input is available on any socket.

The I/O multiplexing feature introduced in JDK 1.4 and described in Chapter 3 and Chapter 4 provides the solution: use Selector.select to tell us both *when* and *which* of a number of registered channels is ready for I/O. In servers where connections are not always busy, or servers on the Internet (*e.g.* Web servers) where maximum concurrency is ultimately more important than responsiveness to individual clients, I/O multiplexing should be used.

Multiplexing can be used at the connection-accepting level, the conversation level, or both. At the *connection-accepting* level, we have already seen the use of parallel non-blocking accepts in conjunction with selectors in section 12.3.1. It is a simple generalization of section 12.3.1 to multiplex this process across multiple server sockets, which is useful if the server is servicing multiple ports, or the same port on multiple addresses: all we need to do to the code of section 12.3.1 is to create the additional ServerSockets and register them with the selector.

At the *conversation* level, multiplexing only makes sense if worker threads are being used, either on their own or in conjunction with dynamic threads. Deciding how to use multiplexing at this level requires a bit more analysis. We need to consider these factors:

(a) Whether to permanently associate a connection with a thread, or allow any thread to process any connection.

(b) If the former, how to assign connections to threads, and how to do so in such a way that the load is shared evenly.

(c) How to actually implement each thread.

12.3.3 *Allocating connections to threads*

There are two strategies for allocating connections to threads: 'do' and 'don't'.

(a) If *(i)* the server is 'stateful', *i.e.* if a connection is associated with client state, or if requests are long or multi-part, and *(ii)* the underlying service is thread-oriented (*e.g.* a database service), it may be convenient to allocate each connection permanently to a specific thread.

This is trivial to implement. If we are using an explicit queue of connections, we only need to enqueue a new connection and it will be picked up by an idle thread. If we are using an implicit queue as in section 12.3.1, again an idle thread will pick up a new connection. Both of these are more or less self-tuning: the idlest threads will tend to pick up the most connections, upon which they will become less idle, when they will tend to pick up fewer connections, until some of their connections terminate and they become idle again.

(You could also organize all this by hand, by book-keeping the level of activity of each thread, maintaining a separate explicit queue to each one, and choosing the queue to dispatch a new connection to on the basis of its statistics. The effect will be exactly the same as letting the system sort itself out with a single dispatch queue, assuming that your statistics are both accurate and well-used: if they aren't, the situation will be worse. It's hard to see why you would bother doing it 'manually'.)

(b) If the server is stateless and requests and service times are short, or the underlying service is not really thread-oriented and can be handled by any thread, it is better to allow any thread to process any connection. This gives better throughput, as your bank and supermarket demonstrate: at the bank, there is generally one queue for multiple tellers; at the supermarket, there is generally one queue per checkout. The bank's system gives better throughput.

In scheme (a), each thread uses its own unique Selector object, with registrations for the ServerSocketChannel and its own SocketChannel connections. In scheme (b), all threads share a single Selector object, with registrations for the ServerSocketChannel and all SocketChannel connections. Implementing this is just a matter of whether the thread is constructed with a Selector argument or whether it constructs its own Selector; otherwise, processing is identical, as shown in the MultiplexingHandler class sketched in Example 12.10 below.

```java
Selector selector;

// Constructor for shared selector handling any connection
MultiplexingHandler(Selector selector)
{
  this.selector = selector;
}

// Constructor handling connections from a single
// ServerSocket only via a private selector
MultiplexingHandler(ServerSocketChannel server)
  throws IOException
{
  this(Selector.open());
  server.register(selector, SelectionKey.OP_ACCEPT);
}
```

```
// NB exception handling not shown …
public void run()
{
  for (;;)
  {
    selector.select();
    Set readyKeys = selector.selectedKeys();
    synchronized (readyKeys)
    {
      Iterator readyKeysIterator = readyKeys.iterator();
      while (readyKeysIterator.hasNext())
      {
        SelectionKey key =
          (SelectionKey)readyKeysIterator.next();
        it.remove();
        if (key.isValid() && key.isAcceptable())
        {
          ServerSocketChannel server =
            (ServerSocketChannel)key.channel();
          SocketChannel channel = server.accept();
          if (channel != null)
          {
            channel.configureBlocking(false);
            channel.register
              (selector, SelectionKey.OP_READ);
          } // if ()
        } // if ()
        // handle isReadable() and isWritable states:
        // see below …
      } if ()
    } // while ()
  } // for ()
} // run()
```

EXAMPLE 12.10 Multiplexing handler

If we want to enforce limits on *both* N and M, we just need to keep track of idle threads *and* the average or actual connections per thread when applying the techniques of section 12.2.3 or section 12.2.4. The simplest way to track M is to book-keep the actual number of currently open connections, which we haven't had occasion to do before now.

If we don't want to control M explicitly, we can just let it grow and let service get slower proportionately, because now $r = w + N \times M \times \rho$ and T_s varies with r.

Assuming the latter, we can get rid of the BlockingQueue<Socket> interface, which was really introduced to show that queueing and accepting techniques are largely independent of threading models. Throughout the rest of this section we will use Selectors explicitly instead of queues, and we will use the parallel-accept technique of section 12.3.1, which is especially appropriate when using multiplexing and selectors. Applying control of *N* and *M* to the ideas presented below is 'left as an exercise for the reader.'

12.3.4 *Multiplexing and I/O*

A thread multiplexing one or more sockets needs to process the OP_READ and OP_WRITE events. Sockets used with a selector must be in non-blocking mode, which means we must use channel I/O and buffers. This suggests that every channel needs to be associated with an input buffer and an output buffer (although in some circumstances the input and output buffers can be the same). The channel must also be associated with a 'readable' action to be triggered when input data arrives, and a 'writable' action to be triggered when output data can be written to the channel.

All these items represent the minimum 'context' of a channel. We saw in section 4.5.6 that context can be associated with channels by using the 'attachment' feature of selection keys. Let's postulate a Handler interface like this:

```
interface  Handler
{
  void handle(SelectionKey key) throws IOException;
}
```

Without yet inquiring too closely into what the handler method might actually do, we can process 'acceptable', 'readable', and 'writable' events for the channel uniformly like this:

```
// ...
selector.select();
Set readyKeys = selector.selectedKeys();
synchronized (readyKeys)
{
  Iterator readyKeysIterator = readyKeys.iterator();
  while (readyKeysIterator.hasNext())
  {
    SelectionKey key =
      (SelectionKey)readyKeysIterator.next();
    it.remove();
    if (!key.isValid())
      continue;
    Handler  handler = (Handler)key.attachment();
    handler.handle(key);
```

```
    }
  }
  // ...
```

What do the handler methods do? There are two kinds:

(a) a request handler, whose basic abstract implementation looks like this:

```java
abstract class  RequestHandler implements Handler
{
  public void handle(SelectionKey key) throws IOException
  {
    if (key.isReadable())
      readable(key);
    if (key.isWritable())
      writable(key);
  }

  abstract void readable(SelectionKey key)
    throws IOException;

  abstract void writable(SelectionKey key)
    throws IOException;
}
```

(b) an accept handler whose implementation looks like this:

```java
class  AcceptHandler implements Handler
{
  public void handle(SelectionKey key) throws IOException
  {
    if (!key.isAcceptable())
      return;
    ServerSocketChannel ssc =
      (ServerSocketChannel)key.channel();
    SocketChannel        sc = channel.accept();
    if (sc == null)
      return;
    RequestHandler rh = new RequestHandler(sc);
    key.selector().register(sc, SelectionKey.OP_READ, rh);
  }
}
```

For an echo server, the request handler can be as simple as Example 12.11 below, using only one buffer:

```java
class EchoRequestHandler extends RequestHandler
{
  ByteBuffer buffer = ByteBuffer.allocate(16384);

  void readable(SelectionKey key) throws IOException
  {
    SocketChannelchannel = (SocketChannel)key.channel();
    int count = channel.read(buffer);
    if (count < 0)
      channel.socket().shutdownInput();
    else
      writable(channel);
  }

  void writable(SelectionKey key) throws IOException
  {
    SocketChannelchannel = (SocketChannel)key.channel();
    // write
    buffer.flip();
    int count = channel.write(buffer);
    buffer.compact();
    // did the write complete?
    if (buffer.position() > 0)
      // No: register for OP_WRITE
      key.interestOps
        (key.interestOps()|SelectionKey.OP_WRITE);
    else
      // Yes: deregister for OP_WRITE
      key.interestOps
        (key.interestOps() & ~SelectionKey.OP_WRITE);
    // close when finished reading & writing
    if (count == 0 && channel.socket().isInputShutdown())
      channel.close();
  }
}
```

EXAMPLE 12.11 Echo server RequestHandler

The readable method above reads as much data as can be read from the channel without blocking and as will fit into the buffer, whichever is smaller. Conversely, the writeable method will write whatever data can be written from the buffer to the channel without blocking, up to the smaller of the data available in the buffer and the space available in the socket send-buffer. In both cases Java updates the buffer state according to how much data was actually transferred. After writing, the buffer is compacted to discard what was written and make room for more. We can't assume that reads and writes strictly alternate, and the code above does not do so: there may be multiple reads in a row, and multiple writes. The internal state-management of the buffers takes care of all the book-keeping for us.

At the end of input we shutdown the input of the socket, mainly as a signal to ourselves later; when we have written everything out and we find we've shut-down the input, we close the channel. This automatically cancels the channel's registration with the selector, which in turn results in the channel key never being returned in the selected-set of the selector, and hence no further calls of the handle method for the associated channel context. It also results in the release of the SelectionKey and the context object, in this case the RequestHandler.

The handle method in a file server would be identical, and the readable and writable methods , using file channel I/O, might look like Example 12.12 below.

```
class FileHandler extends RequestHandler
{
  ByteBuffer inputBuffer = ByteBuffer.allocate(16384);
  FileChannelfileChannel = null;
  long        position = 0;

  // handle() method is inherited from RequestHandler

  void readable(SelectionKey key) throws IOException
  {
    // read a request from the socket.
    SocketChannel channel = (SocketChannel)key.channel();
    try
    {
      int   count = socketChannel.read(inputBuffer);
      if (count < 0)
      {
        // EOF trying to read filename
        socketChannel.close();
        return;
      }
      String request = Charset.forName("UTF-8")
        .decode(inputBuffer).toString();
      String filename; // extract from request, not shown …
      this.fileChannel =
        new FileInputStream(filename).getChannel();
      this.position = 0;
      writable(key);
    }
    catch (IOException exc) { /* … */ }
  }
  void writable(SelectionKey key) throws IOException
  {
    if (fileChannel != null)
```

```
{
  SocketChannel channel = (SocketChannel)key.channel();
  try
  {
    long count = fileChannel.transferTo(position,
                  fc.size() - position,
                  socketChannel);
    if (count < 0)   // EOF
      {
      fileChannel.close();
      fileChannel = null;
      socketChannel.close();
    }
    else
      position += count;
    // Register/deregister for OP_WRITE according as
    // count is/is not shorter than requested.
    if (position < fc.size())
      // register for OP_WRITE, write more next time
      key.interestOps
        (key.interestOps()|SelectionKey.OP_WRITE);
    else
    {
      // deregister for OP_WRITE
      key.interestOps
        (key.interestOps() & ~SelectionKey.OP_WRITE);
      // close file
      fileChannel.close();
      fileChannel = null;
    }
  }
  }
  catch (IOException exc)
  {
    /* ... */
  }
}
```

EXAMPLE 12.12 File server—readable & writable methods

The file-server example uses another approach towards closing the socket: assuming that there is only one filename request per connection, the channel is closed when the output data has been completely transferred; it is also closed as a safety measure if there is no request data at all. It should also be closed if the request is invalid.

12.3.5 *Reading the request*

An echo server only has to echo whatever comes in whenever it appears, but the file-server of Example 12.12 assumes that the entire request was read in one read. This is a most unreasonable assumption. In general we can either:

(a) Use a large enough input buffer to hold any request, and keep accumulating data in it until the request is complete, or

(b) put the channel into blocking mode and use stream I/O to assemble the entire request.

Accumulating data in non-blocking mode requires application-specific logic to examine the buffer after each read to determine whether the request is complete yet. Depending on the application protocol, this may be very easy, e.g. if you are expecting 384 bytes, or 1024 Java doubles, or a byte-count followed by that many bytes:

```
void readable(SelectionKey key) throws IOException
{
  SocketChannel channel = (SocketChannel)key.channel();
  int          count = channel.read(inputBuffer);
  if (inputBuffer.position() == inputBuffer.get(0)+1)
    ;   // request is complete …
}
```

On the other hand it may be difficult, *e.g.* if the request can be an arbitrarily long string like an HTTP request. It may even be impossible, *e.g.* if the request was sent via Java serialization. In such cases, the simplest approach may be to read the request in blocking mode. This requires less application-specific logic, but more generic logic. We must:

(a) Cancel the registration of the channel with the selector,

(b) Put the channel into blocking mode,

(c) Probably set a socket read timeout, and

(d) Obtain an InputStream, DataInput or ObjectInput stream for the channel.

For example:

```
// put channel into blocking mode
key.cancel();
SocketChannel    channel = (SocketChannel)key.channel();
channel.configureBlocking(true);
```

```
// set a read timeout in ms
channel.socket().setSoTimeout(timeout);

// read request via ObjectInputStream
InputStream        in = Channels.newInputStream(channel);
in = new BufferedInputStream(in);
ObjectInputStream objIn = new ObjectInputStream(in);
Object             request = objIn.readObject();
```

12.3.6 Writing the reply

Similarly, we can write the reply in either blocking or non-blocking mode. It is simplest to write it in blocking mode, remembering that socket writes only block while data to be written exceeds the space available in the socket send-buffer. This is also best for the network, as it generates the minimum number of distinct TCP segments and transmits them at the best possible rate; it also avoids waking up the receiver multiple times to receive the bits and pieces of the reply. For example, if the reply is an Object:

```
// write reply in blocking mode
Object reply; // …
SocketChannel    channel = (SocketChannel)key.channel();
Socket           socket = channel.socket();
OutputStream     out = Channels.newOutputStream(channel);
out = new BufferedOutputStream
  (out, socket.getSendBufferSize());
ObjectOutputStream objOut = new ObjectOutputStream(out);
objOut.writeObject(reply);
objOut.flush();
```

The main reason for writing the reply in non-blocking mode is to avoid being stalled by the client when the reply is large. If the client doesn't read his end of the connection fast enough, eventually his socket receive-buffer will fill, which will eventually cause our socket send-buffer to fill, which will cause a blocking write to stall indefinitely. To protect ourselves against this situation we must use non-blocking writes, probably in association with a selector timeout such that if the channel stays unwritable for an excessive length of time we just give up and close the channel. (The blocking-mode socket timeout set with Socket.setSoTimeout doesn't help us here: it only affects reads, not writes.)

To write the reply in non-blocking mode, we must revert the channel to non-blocking mode when we have assembled the complete request as shown in section 12.3.9, construct the reply as an output ByteBuffer, *e.g.* by wrapping the byte array of a ByteArrayOutputStream:

```
ByteArrayOutputStream baos = new ByteArrayOutputStream();
DataOutputStream      dos = new DataOutputStream(baos);
dos.writeXXX(…);// etc
dos.flush();
ByteBuffer outputBuffer =
  ByteBuffer.wrap(baos.toByteArray());
```

or putting it to a direct byte buffer:

```
ByteBuffer outputBuffer =
  ByteBuffer.allocateDirect(baos.size());
outputBuffer.put(baos.toByteArray());
```

and write from the ByteBuffer whenever the channel becomes writable:

```
void writable(SelectionKey key) throws IOException
{
  SocketChannelchannel = (SocketChannel)key.channel();
  outputBuffer.flip();
  int count = channel.write(outputBuffer);
  outputBuffer.compact();

  // close when finished reading & writing
  if (count == 0 && channel.socket().isInputShutdown())
    channel.close();
}
```

If the reply has been completely written to the output buffer before the readable method returns, the outputBuffer.flip and outputBuffer.compact operations are unnecessary; otherwise, operations on the output buffer should be synchronized.

12.3.7 Extended conversations

If the conversation consists of more than a simple request and reply, ultimately it needs to be implemented implicitly or explictly as a state machine whose continuation (next action) can be can be executed by any thread.

12.3.8 Blocking and parallel selection

If we use blocking mode to read the request or reply, we must avoid blocking while synchronized on the selected set of selector keys. This means clearing the original in a different way, and copying the set before processing it:

```
Set readyKeys = null;
synchronized (selector)
{
  selector.selectedKeys().clear(); //replaces it.remove()
  selector.select();
  readyKeys = new HashSet(selector.selectedKeys());
} // drop selector lock

// process local copy of ready keys

Iterator readyKeysIterator = readyKeys.iterator();
while (readyKeysIterator.hasNext())
{
  SelectionKey key =
    (SelectionKey)readyKeysIterator.next();
  // it.remove() not required because of clear() above
  if (!key.isValid())
    continue;
  Handlerhandler = (Handler)key.attachment();
  handler.handle(key);
```

It is unnecessary to synchronize on the copied set because it is local to the thread.

The technique of parallel accepts makes it more likely that the selector will report false results, as discussed in section 4.5.4, as a thread may receive a ready-notification about a channel that another thread is concurrently processing.

12.3.9 *Restoring non-blocking mode and re-registering*

When we are finished with blocking mode, we must restore non-blocking mode and re-register the channel with the selector. To do this, we don't need to cart around any extra state such as the selector and the interest-set, because we can re-use the registration data in the cancelled key, which is guaranteed to remain intact after its cancellation:

```
key.channel().configureBlocking(false);
key.channel().register
  (key.selector(), key.interestOps(), key.attachment());
```

This causes a new registration of the channel with the same selector, using the same interest-set and attachment, and generating a new SelectionKey.

If and when Java supports multiplexing on channels in blocking mode, all this mode-flipping, cancelling, and re-registering will become unnecessary. This enhancement was at one time reportedly planned for JDK 1.5 but it didn't show up.

12.3.10 *Closing*

As discussed in section 12.2.10, a server may choose to close the connection after writing a certain reply. In non-blocking mode, if a reply ByteBuffer is constructed to be written in non-blocking mode, the ChannelContext must be able to signal that the channel can be closed after output of the current output buffer is complete. This is just a boolean state maintained in the ChannelContext.

12.3.11 *Single-threaded services*

Sometimes the underlying service is inherently single-threaded, or at least thread-oriented: for example, a database service or a message-oriented host transaction system. In cases like these it still makes sense to have a number of threads servicing the network—accepting connections and requests—but we need another internal queuing system to communicate with the thread(s) that actually provide the service. To synchronize the activity of these two kinds of threads there is normally some kind of *completion handler*: a callback which is executed when the underlying service is complete: this may do something as simple as setting a boolean 'reply complete' state which permits writing from the reply buffer when the channel is writable.

12.4 CLIENT MODELS

There isn't nearly as much we can do with TCP clients in the area of threads, connections, and multiplexing. Generally clients of a service are single-threaded, and only need special design and coding to handle connection failure and receive timeouts. However there are several techniques which can assist in these areas.

12.4.1 *Connection pooling*

Repeated exchanges with the same server can be made more efficient if the client arranges to re-use the same TCP connection. This strategy amortizes the connection and disconnection overheads over the number of exchanges, so that the second and subsequent exchanges only require a minimum of three new packets each, rather than ten as discussed in section 3.2.3.

It also has a benefit at the server end, by reducing the number of new threads which must be created, leading to a gain in efficiency at the server host. The server must be written so as to handle multiple requests over a single connection as described in section 12.2.9; *i.e.* it must loop reading requests on a connection until it is closed by the client.

Implementing this is simply a matter of returning connections to a free pool instead of closing them, and retrieving a free connection to the correct host from the pool if possible rather than opening a new one. The free pool would therefore be implemented as a java.util.Map mapping *{hostname, port}*.

A connection retrieved from the free pool may of course have been closed at the server end, and should be treated with suspicion, *e.g.* by using a shorter reply timeout, or an application-level 'ping' protocol to test the connection's liveness. Connections in the free pool should expire (by being removed from the free pool and closed) after a short interval rather than being assumed to live forever.

12.4.2 *Request-reply transactions*

Ideally, each request and reply should be sent as one TCP segment: this minimizes network latency and TCP acknowledgment traffic. It can be ensured by using send and receive buffers at least as large as the largest possible request or reply, in conjunction with BufferedInput/OutputStreams or ByteBuffers of similar sizes, as described in section 3.6 and section 3.13. Buffer sizes at the server should be chosen on the same principle.

When using channel I/O and messages consist of multiple parts, *e.g.* the commonly seen header-body-trailer format, 'gathering' channel I/O can be used to write the parts in one action from multiple ByteBuffers, saving the processor and memory overheads of concatenating messages in memory, or the network overheads of writing them in several distinct actions. When the parts of a message are of constant length, or at least of lengths known in advance, 'scattering' channel I/O can be used to read them into multiple ByteBuffers, again saving the overhead of splitting them apart. At the sending end, 'gathering' channel I/O can be used to send the data. This is illustrated in Example 12.13.

```
// Initialization - common to both ends
static final int HEADER_LENGTH  = 16;
static final int BODY_LENGTH    = 480;
static final int TRAILER_LENGTH = 16;
ByteBuffer header   = ByteBuffer.allocate(HEADER_LENGTH);
ByteBuffer body     = ByteBuffer.allocate(BODY_LENGTH);
ByteBuffer trailer  = ByteBuffer.allocate(TRAILER_LENGTH);
ByteBuffer[]
          buffers   = new ByteBuffer[]
                        { header, body, trailer };
// sending end - populate the buffers, not shown
long      count     = channel.write(buffers);
// repeat until all data sent

// receiving end
long      count     = channel.read(buffers);
// repeat until all data read
```

EXAMPLE 12.13 Scatter-gather I/O

The total efficiency for simple request-reply message exchanges can be further improved by conserving connections at the client as described in section 12.4.

Sun's implementation of Java RMI uses this strategy: client-side connections are not closed but returned to a free pool for the given destination, whence they can be removed when a new connection to the same destination is required; connections are expired after they have been idle for 15 seconds (or the number of milliseconds given by sun.rmi.transport.connectionTimeout, if set).

12.4.3 *Multiple interactions*

Where multiple interactions occur with the same server as part of a single overall transaction and their sequencing is unimportant, it can be more efficient to perform them in parallel rather than sequentially. This strategy is seen in Web browsers, where a page which consists of text plus several images is retrieved by several connections reading in parallel. In this way some of the connection overhead is overlapped with real I/O. In a situation like this it may be more natural to use multiplexed channel I/O at the client rather than a number of blocked threads.

12.5 JDK 1.5 EXECUTORS

The java.util.concurrent package introduced in JDK 1.5 contains many built-in solutions to the design issues of this chapter, which was largely written before the advent of JDK 1.5:

(a)   The Executor interface and its derivations, which represent objects with the ability to execute Runnable.run methods in series or parallel with the current thread;

(b)   the ThreadPoolExecutor class and its derivations, which provide thread-pooled implementations of Executors;

(c)   ThreadPoolExecutor.DiscardPolicy settings, which correspond to exit strategies in the foregoing discussion;

(d)   The ThreadFactory interface, which represent objects which can create threads; and

(e)   The Executors class, which provides numerous ThreadFactory implementations corresponding more or less with all the possibilities described in this chapter.

12.6 STAGED EVENT-DRIVEN ARCHITECTURES

Recent work by Matt Welsh at Harvard generalizes the thread-management concepts expounded in this chapter to the entire server. SEDA, or Staged Event-Driven Architecture, defines a suitable framework for building massive servers based on

Java NIO which can handle very large numbers of connections simultaneously. The processing of each request is broken down and redefined as a 'pipeline' of 'stages', with each stage having its own dispatcher and thread pool, such that *every* stage of the processing of a request is dispatched into a dynamic thread pool. All the thread pools are subject to the overall control of a scheduler which can see the stages of the pipeline that need more resources and the stages that can get by with less, so that over time the system can self-tune to ensure there are enough threads where they are needed and not too many where they are not. A SEDA server is also capable of adaptive load-shedding.

The design and construction of such a server is quite a feat, introducing especially all kinds of debugging issues. Matt has defined a Java framework for SEDA servers.[8] The Apache Cocoon project is capable of being another such framework.[9]

---

8. See the SEDA home page at http://www.eecs.harvard.edu/~mdw/proj/seda/

9. See http://cocoon.apache.org/

CHAPTER 13

Fallacies of net-working

DISTRIBUTED PROGRAMMING IS PLAGUED by fallacies and invalid assumptions. A distributed system cannot be designed and programmed merely by unthinkingly carrying over assumptions which are valid in non-distributed programming.

However you can't act on this advice unless you know what the relevant assumptions are! In this Appendix we examine some 'fallacies of networking', and discuss the truth about them.

13.1 EIGHT FALLACIES OF NETWORKING

Essentially everyone, when they first build a distributed application, makes the following eight assumptions. All prove to be false in the long run and all cause big trouble and painful learning experiences.

1. *The network is reliable.*

2. *Latency is zero.*

3. *Bandwidth is infinite.*

4. *The network is secure.*

5. *Topology doesn't change.*

6. *There is one administrator.*

7. *Transport cost is zero.*

8. *The network is homogeneous.*

These are the celebrated 'eight fallacies of networking' of L. Peter Deutsch. Deutsch writes:

I first published my "Eight fallacies of networking" internally while working at Sun Microsystems Labs in 1991–2. (The first 4 were originally described by either Bill or Dick Lyon; I added the other 4.) As far as I know, the only place they are on the Web is at http://java.sun.com/people/jag/Fallacies.html, *thanks to James Gosling of Sun (*http://java.sun.com/people/jag*).*[1]

The following subsections examine these eight fallacies in more detail.

13.1.1 Fallacy: the network is reliable

The network is *unreliable.* Networking software such as TCP gives such a good *appearance* of reliability that it is all too easy to forget that this is merely a well-sustained illusion implemented by an upper layer of the protocol.

At bottom, a computer data network is a mechanism for switching data packets. Packets can collide on the underlying medium, in which case one or both packets are lost. The medium can become saturated, in which case packets are dropped, either deliberately by active components (hosts and routers), or inevitably by the laws of physics. Hosts, routers, and applications can crash, or be brought down and up deliberately. Networking software can fail. Cables can be disconnected, whether by network administrators or backhoes. In some circumstances, *e.g.* saturation, the network is *designed* to fail, in order to protect its own integrity.

13.1.2 Fallacy: latency is zero

Latency, *i.e.* waiting time, is the time taken for a packet to traverse the network between source and destination. Packets cannot move at greater than the speed of light through a wire. Packets traversing hosts and routers are processed at speeds limited by the available computing power, and are subject to queuing at those places. Packets which have been dropped are subject to re-transmission. Latency in certain networking technologies such as phone modems and xDSL can be amazingly high. For all these reasons, it cannot be assumed that transmissions arrive instantaneously.

Latency is sometimes measured as the *round-trip time,* i.e. the total time for a data packet to be sent and an acknowledging packet to be received.

---

1. (See his professional home page at http://www.aladdin.com/users/ghost/). Deutsch is also associated with the saying 'to iterate is human: to recurse, divine'—itself a rather divine pronouncement—although he doesn't remember whether it was original or borrowed [personal correspondence, July 2002].

13.1.3 Fallacy: bandwidth is infinite

Bandwidth, the number of bits (or bytes) that can be transmitted per second, is finite, and sometimes surprisingly small. Bandwidth is shared among all users of the network. The total bandwidth of an end-to-end connection is the bandwidth of the slowest network segment in the path. Data cannot be transmitted into a network faster than its bandwidth: this implies queuing at transmitters and therefore leads to additional latency—see section 13.1.2. The design of any non-trivial networked application must model current transmission volumes and future growth against network bandwidth and latency to obtain expected response times, and verify these against required response times.

13.1.4 Fallacy: the network is secure

Networks are inherently insecure. Data packets can be 'sniffed' by anyone with physical access to the network, using readily available hardware or software. Networks can be made more secure in various ways, *e.g.* physical isolation, applying cryptology, and so on.

13.1.5 Fallacy: topology doesn't change

You cannot assume that the route between two end-points of a communication will not change, either over long periods or even during the period of the communication itself. In the short term, the network may change routes automatically several times during a connection: TCP/IP was specifically designed to allow dynamic routing, in order to provide fail-safe multi-path operation and to allow automatic detection of optimum paths. In the long term, if your application is any good, it must survive several major network configurations.

13.1.6 Fallacy: there is one administrator

There may be zero or more network administrators. There may be more of them than you can ever discover. They may be responsible to zero or more different organizations, both internal and external. The greater their number, the more unlikely it is that you can obtain a uniform response from them. One or more of the administrators or organizations may be indifferent or actively hostile to your purposes. You cannot assume without proof that installation or operation of your application will be straightforward *or even possible* if it requires cooperation from network administrators.

13.1.7 Fallacy: transport cost is zero

The transport cost between two computers, even when you own both of them and all the cabling and components in between, is not zero: consider the cost of electrical power, service contracts, amortization, and depreciation. If the network is heavily used you may also have to consider opportunity costs. The transport cost within an organizational LAN may not be zero, as it may be subjected to an internal usage charge. The transport cost in a network involving a third party is most unlikely to be zero and may be rather high. Third-party costs are likely but not certain to consist of a fixed rental component plus a variable usage component per megabyte of data received or transmitted or both. The design of any non-trivial networked application should include a costing model for network components and data transmission.

13.1.8 Fallacy: the network is homogeneous

The network path between any two end-points may consist of RAM, a LAN segment; an XDSL segment; a TI line; a gigabyte segment; a 56Kbps modem; and another LAN. As remarked in section 13.1.3, the total bandwidth of this path is 56Kbps, the bandwidth of its slowest segment. You may not know about the existence of the slowest link. The slowest link may appear after the deployment of your software, or it may *dis*appear. As we said above, if your application is any good it will survive several network configurations.

13.2 FURTHER FALLACIES

Here are some 'further fallacies of networking' of my own—I was going to say 'my own invention' but what I really mean is 'my own, painful, discovery'.

13.2.1 Fallacy: network I/O is like disk I/O

The network I/O API in most operating systems and class libraries is usually very like, or indeed identical to, the disk I/O API.[2] The similarity ends there. The network is not at all like a disk. It is a mixture of hardware and software whose combined probability of failure is many orders of magnitude larger than that of a disk device. Its behaviour is far less predicable than that of a disk device. In particular, its timing is *in principle* highly unpredictable, even within wide limits, once application components are included.

By contrast, disk I/O is highly reliable and predictable. The mean time between failure for disks is measured in years, not seconds, and the maximum time for an I/O transfer is bounded by seek time and transfer rate, so it is customary for an entire disk I/O request to be serviced before the API returns. Implementing network APIs to work the same way would not be reasonable, and using those APIs as though they were disk APIs is not reasonable either.

---

2. This is certainly true in Java: the java.io.* classes use the same API for files and Sockets, and equally so do the java.nio.channels.* classes.

In contrast, you don't always get all the data you asked for when reading from a network. This is probably the single most common network programming error, and it is seen daily in programming forums and newsgroups all over the Internet. Depending on the networking API, its current mode of operation, and the network protocol being used, you may get any of:

(a)   Nothing

(b)   One or more bytes

(c)   The current contents of the receive buffer

(d)   The next data packet received

(e)   The requested data length modulo 512, 534, 4096, 8192, 32768, 53248, 65536, or some other familiar or strange number

(f)   An end-of-file indication

(g)   An error or exception

(h)   Everything you asked for.

This is a lot of possibilities: you must program defensively so as to cope correctly with all of them. Case (b) is the most usual in TCP, and case (h) is just as exceptional as all the others.

These remarks also apply to *writing* to the network. In some APIs you can't assume that the write method wrote all the data: you have to check a return value which tells you how much was written, and react accordingly. Depending on the API, its current mode of operation, and the underlying protocol, this result may be any of the above except the end-of-file indication, reading 'send' for 'receive' and so forth throughout.

These remarks also apply to setting the sizes of socket send and receive buffers. You can't assume that you got exactly the size you specified. You may have been given more: you may have been given less. Getting more is normally unimportant; getting less can be significant, *e.g.* if you know the maximum transaction size and you're trying to ensure that transactions are sent in a single TCP segment.

13.2.2 Fallacy: you are synchronized with your peer

In general, the only synchronization that occurs between distributed components of a networked application is the synchronization you provide in your application protocol. You can only assume that the other end has received your data if you build explicit acknowledgements into your application protocol.

For example, when a network write API returns, the data written hasn't necessarily been received by the target application, or by the target computer. The data may not even have left the source computer: the write operation may only buffer data for later transmission.

Similarly, closing a TCP socket only queues a close message for transmission after all pending data. When the close API returns, the close message hasn't necessarily even left the source computer. You can't assume that the other end has received the close. You *certainly* can't assume that the other end has executed a close API of its own: these are not interlocked. In fact, by the previous paragraph, you can't even assume that the other end has finished reading data yet.

13.2.3 Fallacy: all failures can be detected

One of the peculiarities of TCP/IP as against earlier protocols like SNA and IPX is that a network path can fail in ways which cannot be detected by one or both ends.

As we saw in section 13.2.2, socket writes are asynchronous, so an application which writes data to a connection which subsequently breaks cannot possibly be informed about the failure until it executes another network operation. Recovering synchronization in this case is once again the responsibility of the application protocol.

Similarly, it is possible for an end-point or the network to fail in such a way as to cause an application blocked in a socket read to stall forever. A non-trivial application should never block on a network read without setting a finite read timeout interval, and it must have a strategy for dealing with timeouts.

13.2.4 Fallacy: resources are infinitely available

Network resources such as buffers and ports are finite. You will run out. Don't pre-allocate them statically if you can have the system allocate them dynamically, and don't just assume that you got what you asked for: see section 13.2.1.

The network cannot contain an infinite amount of data. I have recently debugged an application protocol which was stalling. Its design implicitly assumed that an arbitrary (*i.e.* infinite) amount of data could be written by both ends before either end executed a read. It's not that the application designer actually thought all this data could fit somewhere: he didn't think about the issue at all, because he didn't realize he was designing a network protocol.

13.2.5 Fallacy: applications can wait forever for a remote service

No: there is almost always a time beyond which it is pointless to continue waiting. Patience is not and should not be infinite, in networking as in life. The design of any non-trivial application requires careful attention to expected service times, reasonable timeout periods, and behaviour when timeouts occur.

13.2.6 Fallacy: remote services are rendered in a timely manner

No, they aren't. Networking implies packet switching, which implies queuing, which implies waiting. When loads get very heavy, waiting times increase enormously—see Figure 12.2. Also, remote services are by definition remote, and often the only way you can observe them is via the network, often only via the very application protocol you are trying to exercise, so it can be difficult to discover their status under heavy load—which, of course, is the only time you want to discover its status!

13.2.7 Fallacy: there is a single point of failure

No, there isn't. A distributed system usually doesn't have a single point of failure. It is not a single system: it doesn't crash all at once. It often *cannot* be stopped all at once even if desired. A distributed system is not like multiple threads running in a single process, where a failure may stop the whole process, or the process as a whole can deliberately exit, or be externally terminated relatively easily. It's not like multiple processes running in a single processor either, where a failure may stop the whole processor, or the processor can be brought down more or less easily. The elements of a distributed system are very loosely coupled indeed, and a failure in one of them is unlikely to bring down the whole system: indeed, the network as a whole is *designed* to survive isolated failures.

13.2.8 Fallacy: there is a single resource allocator

No, there isn't. Each host allocates its own resources. One component of a distributed system may get everything it asked for; another component may get enough of what it wants to at least function partially, or in a degraded mode of operation; and another component may be unable to function at all.

13.2.9 Fallacy: there is a single time

Not in a distributed system there isn't. There are multiple clocks running, certainly with minor if not major disagreements between them, and possibly at slightly different rates. The existence of network time servers and distributed time protocols alleviates but does not eliminate this problem. System clocks may be set to the wrong time, accidentally or deliberately, and for reasons legitimate or otherwise. There are such things as timezones: if your system has enough geographical spread some of its nodes will be in different time zones, and of course this is the *default* case over the Internet.

13.3 IN CONCLUSION

Network programming is lots of fun, and very interesting indeed, but it is not the same as the sequential programming usually taught in Computer Science 101. Don't try to force it into this mould.

Part VI

Appendices

T C P port states

The current state of a TCP port can be displayed with the *netstat -a[n]* command. This very useful command observes the existence and state of TCP and UDP ports, and can be used to watch the behaviour of clients and servers from the outside.

The various states of a TCP port are defined in RFC 793. Table A.I shows the name, RFC 793 definition, and Java meaning of each port state. The port states are listed in the order in which they normally occur over the lifetime of a port.

TABLE A.I TCP port states

Name	RFC 793 definition	Meaning in Java
LISTEN	*Represents waiting for a connection request from any remote TCP and port.*	Corresponds to a bound ServerSocket.[a]
SYN-SENT	*Represents waiting for a matching connection request after having sent a connection request.*	Corresponds to a client Socket which has implicitly or explicitly executed Socket.connect but whose isConnected state is still false. If the matching connection request is received from the server, the socket's isConnected state becomes true and the port state changes to ESTABLISHED; otherwise the client's connection request eventually fails.

TABLE A.1 TCP port states (continued)

Name	RFC 793 definition	Meaning in Java
SYN-RECEIVED	*Represents waiting for a confirming connection request acknowledgment after having both received and sent a connection request.*	Corresponds to an incoming connection being constructed on a ServerSocket's backlog queue. Once the desired acknowledgement has been received from the client, a corresponding server-side Socket can be constructed and returned by a future ServerSocket.accept.[b]
ESTABLISHED	*Represents an open connection, data received can be delivered to the user. The normal state for the data transfer phase of the connection.*	Corresponds to a connected Socket in a client or server. In this state, the Socket's isConnected and isOpen states are true, and its isOutputShutdown state is false.
FIN-WAIT-1	*Represents waiting for a connection termination request from the remote TCP, or an acknowledgment of the connection termination request previously sent.*	Corresponds to a Socket which has been closed[c] by the local application, but the close has not been acknowledged by the remote TCP.[b]
FIN-WAIT-2	*Represents waiting for a connection termination request from the remote TCP.*	Corresponds to a Socket which has been closed[c] by the local application; the close has been acknowledged by the remote TCP; but the remote application has not yet issued a close. This state persists as long as the remote application chooses to keep its end of the socket open.
CLOSE-WAIT	*Represents waiting for a connection termination request from the local user.*	Corresponds to a Socket which has been closed[c] by the remote application but not by the local application. This state corresponds to FIN-WAIT-1 or FIN-WAIT-2 at the other end; it persists as long as the local application chooses to keep the socket open.
CLOSING	*Represents waiting for a connection termination request acknowledgment from the remote TCP.*	Corresponds to a Socket which has been closed[c] by both the local application and the remote application (simultaneous close) but the local close has not yet acknowledged by the remote TCP.[b]

TABLE A.1 TCP port states (continued)

Name	RFC 793 definition	Meaning in Java
LAST-ACK	*Represents waiting for an acknowledgment of the connection termination request previously sent to the remote TCP (which includes an acknowledgment of its connection termination request).*	Corresponds to a Socket which has been closed[c] by both the local application and the remote application (simultaneous close); the remote close has been acknowledged by the local TCP, but the local close has not yet acknowledged by the remote TCP.[b]
TIME-WAIT	*Represents waiting for enough time to pass to be sure the remote TCP received the acknowledgment of its connection termination request.*	Corresponds to a Socket which has been closed[c] by both the local and remote applications and all acknowledgements exchanged; the port persists for a few minutes at both ends so that any further delayed packets for the connection can expire.
CLOSED	*Represents no connection state at all.*	This state is *imaginary*. It corresponds to the port being non-existent, and so is never displayed. It is used as the starting and ending point of state diagrams and state machines.

a. In Microsoft Windows versions before Windows Server 2003, for every ESTABLISHED client port the *netstat* command incorrectly reports an additional non-existent LISTEN port with the same port number. See http://support.microsoft.com/default.aspx?scid=kb;en-us;331078.

b. This state is transient and short-lived, depending mainly on network delay.

c. In TCP port states, and throughout this table, 'closed' means that *either* Socket.close or Socket.shutdownOutput has been called: i.e. the Socket's isClosed or isOutputShutdown state is true. If a socket which has been shutdown for output is kept open for long enough after the shutdown and after the other end closes its end of the connection, the corresponding local port will eventually reach the CLOSED state and disappear from the *netstat -a* output, even though the local socket is still open.

    Platform dependencies

A research report into implementations of T C P / I P has appeared which enumerates very precisely some of the variations between FreeBSD, Windows XP, and Linux. The report shows that it is possible to derive a formal specification for the actual behaviour of T C P / I P in higher-order logic (HOL),[1] and it contains such a specification covering T C P / I P on these three platforms only, and apparently without examining the behaviour at the peer when certain conditions arise within a platform, some of which have already been described in the present book and are summarized in Table B.1 below. Even within these constraints, the researchers found 'around 260' differences between these platforms.

This is rather a startling number of platform dependencies. Fortunately most of them don't affect network programming in Java, either because they concern internals or because they are API issues that either don't arise by design in Java[2] or have been engineered away in the JDK implementation.

Table B.1 summarises the platform differences that can be encountered by a Java program using the Java classes described in this book.[3]

1. Bishop *et al*, *Rigorous specification and conformance testing techniques for network protocols, as applied to* T C P, U D P, *and Sockets,* University of Cambridge Computer Laboratory & NICTA, Canberra, 2005, http://www.cl.cam.ac.uk/uers/pes20/Netsem/index.html

2. The most interesting API issue is that in FreeBSD you can shutdown datagram sockets and listening sockets, with consequences which are entirely plausible in each case. Another curiosity exposed by this paper is that, in both BSD Sockets and WINSOCK, you can call *listen()* again on a listening socket to alter the backlog value: this is not reflected in the Java API.

3. All numbers quoted in this table are either from the paper cited above or the present book *passim*, in which case the ultimate source is W.R. Stevens, either *TCP/IP Illustrated* or *Unix Network Programming*. All numbers for Linux in this table apply to version 2.4.20.8.

TABLE B.I Platform dependencies affecting Java TCP/IP

Class.method	Issue	Comments
DatagramSocket .send	Maximum size of a datagram: 65507 in the UDP protocol RFC; bounded by the socket send buffer size	Linux: 9216 bytes.[a]
ServerSocket .bind	Length of default backlog queue; adjustment to application-supplied value	Originally 5; seems to be at least 50 on most current platforms; varies between workstation and server versions of Windows.
Socket .close and SocketChannel .close after calling Socket .setSoLinger	If timeout is set and expires, whether unsent data is still sent or the connection is reset	Unix-based platforms leave unsent data queued for transmission; Windows resets the connection.
		On Linux, if a positive linger timeout is set, SocketChannel.close blocks even if the channel is non-blocking.
Socket .connect	Behaviour if the target backlog queue is full	Unix-based platforms ignore the connect request, so the client times out and retries within connect.
		Windows: issues a reset, so Windows clients therefore also retry within connect on receiving a reset. This is not the intent of the RFC.
Socket .getReceiveBufferSize Socket .getSendBufferSize	Default size of socket buffers	Originally 2k.
		Up to 56k on various Unix-based platforms:
		FreeBSD: send=32k, receive=56k. Linux: send=16k, receive=43689 bytes (!). Solaris 52k.
		Windows: 8k.[a]

TABLE B.1 Platform dependencies affecting Java TCP/IP (continued)

Class.method	Issue	Comments
Socket .setKeepalive	Whether supported by the platform; keep-alive interval	Can be detected by checking Socket.getKeepalive after calling setKeepalive.
		Keep-alive interval is normally 2 hours globally and if changeable requires privilege to change.
Socket .setReceiveBufferSize Socket .setSendBufferSize	Adjustment to application-supplied values	Will be adjusted to fit the platform's maxima and minima (see below), and may be rounded up or down to suit the platform's buffer-size granularity as well.
Socket .setReceiveBufferSize Socket .setSendBufferSize	Maximum size of socket buffers	FreeBSD: depends on various kernel constants. Linux: 131070 bytes.[a] Windows: 131070 bytes.[a]
Socket .setReceiveBufferSize Socket .setSendBufferSize	Minimum size of socket buffers	FreeBSD: 1 byte. Linux: send=2048, receive=256 bytes. Windows: zero (!).
Socket .setSoLinger	Maximum linger timeout value, nominally $2^{31} - 1$ seconds in Java specification	Some platforms limit it to $(2^{15} - 1)/100 = 32.767$ seconds, by using an internal 16-bit signed quantity representing hundredths of a second.
Socket .shutdownInput	Whether SelectionKey.OP_READ is selected for such a socket	FreeBSD: yes Linux: yes Windows: no.[b]

TABLE B.I Platform dependencies affecting Java T C P / I P (continued)

Class.method	Issue	Comments
Socket .shutdownInput at receiver	Behaviour as seen by remote sender	Most Unix-based platforms accept and ignore the data, so the sender's writes all succeed.
all write, writeXXX methods at sender		Windows sends an RST, so the sender incurs a SocketException 'connection reset by peer'
		Linux accepts and buffers the data but cannot transmit it to the local application, so the sender eventually gets blocked in write, or is returned zero from non-blocking writes.
Socket .shutdownOutput	Whether SelectionKey.OP_WRITE is selected for such a socket	FreeBSD: no Linux: no Windows: yes.[b]

a. This is too small for modern Ethernets or high-latency links such as DSL or ADSL. Socket buffers should be at least equal to the bandwidth-delay product for the intervening network: at least 16k on a 10Mb LAN, more like 63k on 100Mb LANs or links with high latency, or a multiple of 64k when window-scaling can be used.

b. Note the inconsistency of all platforms as between their behaviour for shutdownInput/OP_READ and shutdownOutput/OP_WRITE.

APPENDIX C

References

Baker, F., RFC 1812, *Requirements for IP Version 4 Routers,* June 1995.

Bishop *et al., Rigorous specification and conformance testing techniques for network protocols, as applied to TCP, UDP, and Sockets,* University of Cambridge Computer Laboratory & NICTA, Canberra, 2005.

Braden, R., RFC 1122, *Requirements for Internet Hosts—Communication Layers,* October 1989.

Bug Parade, http://developer.java.sun.com/developer/bugParade

Chan, Lee, & Kramer, *The Java Class Libraries,* 2nd Edition, Addison Wesley 1998.

Comer, D.E., and Lin, J.C., *TCP Buffering and Performance over an ATM Network,* Technical Report CSD-TR 94-026, Purdue University, West Lafayette, Indiana, ftp://gwen.cs.purdue.edu/pub/lin/TCP.atm.ps.Z.

Dierks & Allen, RFC 2246, *The TLS Protocol, Version 1.0,* January 1999.

Finlayson, R., RFC 2771, *An Abstract API for Multicast Address Allocation,* February 2000.

Frier, Karlton, & Kocher, *The SSL 3.0 Protocol,* Netscape Communications Corp., Nov 18, 1996.

Gamma *et al., Design Patterns: Elements of Reusable Object-Oriented Software,* Addison-Wesley, 1995.

Gunther, N. *The Practical Performance Analyst,* McGraw-Hill, 1998.

Handley, M., *et al.,* RFC 2887, *The Reliable Multicast Design Space for Bulk Data Transfer,* August 2000.

Hanna *et al.,* RFC 2730, MADCAP—*Multicast address dynamic client allocation protocol,* December 1999.

Hardjono and Dondeti, *Multicast and Group Security,* Artech House, 2003

Hickman & Kipp, *The SSL Protocol,* Netscape Communications Corp., Feb 9, 1995.

Hinden *et al.,* RFC 2732 *Format for Literal IPv6 Addresses in URL's,* December 1999.

Hinden, R. & Deering, S., R F C 2373, *IP Version 6 Addressing Architecture*, July 1998.

IEEE, *Posix 1003.1 Standard for Information Technology Portable Operating System Interface, Base Definitions, Issue 6, December 2001.*

java-security mailing list.

Kabat *et al.*, R F C 2853, *Generic Security Service API Version 2: Java Bindings*, June 2000.

Lea, Doug, *Concurrent Programming in Java*, 2nd edition, Addison Wesley 2000.

Lea, Doug, *Scalable I/O in Java*, lecture slides,
    http://gee.cs.oswego.edu/dl/cpjslides/nio.pdf.

Linn, J., R F C 2743, *Generic Security Service Application Program Interface Version 2, Update 1*, January 2000.

Martine, R. *Basic Traffic Analysis*, Prentice-Hall, 1993.

Meyer, D., R F C 2365, *Administratively Scoped IP Multicast*, July 1998.

Papadopolous, C., & Parulkar, G.M., *Experimental Evaluation of SunOS PC and TCP/IP protocol implementation*, IEEE/ACM Transactions on Networking, Vol. I, no. 2, 1993.

Piscitello, D.M. & Chapin, A.L., *Open systems networking: OSI & TCP/IP*, Addison-Wesley, 1993.

Pitt, E.J. & McNiff, K., *java.rmi: The Remote Method Invocation Guide*, Addison-Wesley, 2001.

Postel, J., R F C 768, *User Datagram Protocol*, August 1980.

Postel, J., R F C 791, *Internet Protocol*, September 1981.

Postel, J., R F C 793, *Transmission Control Protocol*, September 1981.

Rescorla, Eric, S S L *and* T L S, Addison Wesley, 2001.

Reynolds & Postel, R F C 1700, *Assigned Numbers*, October 1994.

Schmidt *et al.*, *Pattern-Oriented Software Architecture, Vol 2: Patterns for Concurrent and Networked Objects*, Wiley, 2000.

Schneier & Wagner, *Analysis of the SSL 3.0 Protocol*, Second USENIX Workshop on Electronic Commerce Proceedings, Usenix Press, 1996.

Schneier, *Applied Crytogragraphy*, Wiley, 1996.

Schneier, *Secrets and Lies*, Wiley, 2000.

Senie, D., R F C 2644, *Changing the Default for Directed Broadcasts in Routers.*

Singh, Simon, *The Code Book*, Fourth Estate Ltd, 1999.

S S L Talk List F A Q, available at http://www.faqs.org/faqs/computer-security/ssl-talk-faq/.

Stallings, W., *Queueing Analysis*, 2000, lecture notes, via
    http://WilliamStallings.com/StudentSupport.html.

Stevens, W.R., *TCP/IP Illustrated Volume I*, Addison-Wesley, 1994.

Stevens, W.R., *Unix Network Programming*, 2nd edition, Prentice Hall P T R, 1998.

Tanenbaum, *Computer Networks*, 3rd edition, Prentice Hall, 1996.

Tanner, M., *Practical Queueing Analysis*, McGraw-Hill, 1995.

Van Jacobson, *Congestion Avoidance and Control*, Computer Communications Review, vol. 18. no. 4, pp. 314–329, Proceedings of the ACM SIGCOMM '88 Workshop, August, 1988.

Java Cross-Index

This is a complete cross-index of Java packages, classes, and members mentioned in the text. First-level entries are present for classes and members, as follows:

A class entry has subentries for its package, its direct descendants (*extended by* or *implemented by*), and its *members*. The entry also cross-references each use of the class by this or other indexed classes, wherever *passed to*, *returned by*, or *thrown by* a method.

Java packages are not indexed.

A member (method or field) entry has subentries for the class(es) in which such a method or field is declared.

General Index